HELL

and Other Destinations

PIERS PAUL READ

HELL

and Other Destinations

A Novelist's Reflections
on This World and the Next

First published in 2006 by
Darton, Longman and Todd Ltd
1 Spencer Court
140–142 Wandsworth High Street
London SW18 4JJ

ISBN 0–232–52651–6

A catalogue record for this book is available from the British Library.

Unless otherwise stated, the Scripture quotations in this publication
are taken from The Jerusalem Bible © 1966, 1967 and 1968
by Darton, Longman & Todd Ltd and Doubleday & Company, Inc.

Designed by Sandie Boccacci
Phototypeset in 11/12.5pt New Baskerville by
Intype Libra Ltd
Printed and bound in Great Britain by
The Cromwell Press, Trowbridge, Wiltshire

'The fear of the Lord is the beginning of wisdom'

Psalm 111:10

CONTENTS

HISTORY

SEX AND MARRIAGE

WRITERS

SAINTS

Introduction

IN THE DIARIES THAT I KEPT intermittently throughout the 1960s and 1970s, there are many entries about Catholic faith and morals but no mention of the Second Vatican Council. Given the strong reaction of other Catholic writers to the Council which I describe in some of the essays which follow, my own lack of interest is difficult to explain. Evelyn Waugh and Alice Thomas Ellis were dismayed and disheartened; David Lodge, John Cornwell and, to some extent, Graham Greene were enthusiastic and were caught up in 'the spirit of Vatican II'.

I fell into neither camp at the time. First of all, though I went to Catholic schools, I did not come from a Catholic family with roots in the Catholic community. My father was an agnostic and the atmosphere in our home was cultured rather than devout. Secondly, well before the publication of *Gaudium et Spes*, I had adopted a quasi-Marxist analysis of how Catholics should engage in the world. I had left Ampleforth prematurely, not because I rejected the Catholic faith but because I thought its 'public school' ethos owed more to Matthew Arnold than St Benedict. The only effective way to help the poor, as commanded by Christ, was to expropriate the expropriators and redistribute their wealth.

When I went up to Cambridge in 1959 I found that there were like-minded Catholics who contributed to a magazine called *Slant*. I saw something of the radical Dominican Fr Lawrence Bright OP but also became fond of the wholly traditional university chaplain Monsignor Alfred Gilbey. I played no active part in the life of the chaplaincy and after graduating went to live abroad.

On my return to England, it was difficult not to notice certain changes that took place in the practice of my religion. Suddenly one Sunday Mass was said in English rather than Latin – something that seemed sensible enough to me because I was bad at Latin and, though I had parroted the responses as a server at Ampleforth, I had never understood what they meant. Equally unexpected but also welcome, I found that members of the congregation would turn to me at the 'kiss of peace' and, with a beatific smile, shake me warmly by the hand.

When I became engaged to marry a non-Catholic in 1968, my bride-to-be received instruction from a monk at Ampleforth called Dom Cuthbert Rabnett as required by canon law. I thought it odd that he kept reminding her that, being baptised in the Church of England, she was a Christian since she professed to be an atheist, and he almost enticed her to object on the grounds of *conscience* to the promise she was required to make that our children should be brought up as Catholics. Since the question seemed as yet remote – she was only eighteen at the time – she was happy to sign anything to hurry things along: the new thinking by the good Benedictine fell on stony ground.

After our marriage in Strasbourg, we lived for a year in New York; then in London, Yorkshire and Nice. I never missed Mass on a Sunday, and took our children with me from an early age, but I was not sufficiently established in a parish to play an active part, even had I been so inclined. It was only around 1980 that we finally settled in a house in Notting Hill in London that was to remain our home for the next twenty-five years.

Coincidentally, it was at this time that a young priest, Fr Oliver McTernan, was moved from a church in Islington to the parish of St Francis of Assisi, Notting Hill, around the corner from where we now lived. The previous priest had been considered a fusty relic of pre-Conciliar times and it was Oliver's brief to bring about an *aggiornamento* to his flock. Imbued with 'the spirit of Vatican II', he set about this task with great zeal. The little church in Pottery Lane designed by the Victorian architect John Francis Bentley was 'reordered': the plaster statues were removed and some of the artefacts designed by Bentley sold at auction. Oliver believed that the parish community should be more than a sum of its congregations. Each Sunday we were chastised for meeting only at Mass: and for a time the worshippers, who included around twenty different nationalities and as many social classes, were herded into the parish centre after Mass to make stilted conversation over coffee and soft drinks.

Oliver also organised an ecumenical discussion group which used to meet for tea on Sunday afternoons. It included the Anglican vicar of St John's, a Methodist minister and a few Catholic parishioners with university degrees. It was in the course of these discussions and subsequent ecumenical gatherings that I came to realise just how different Oliver's view of the Catholic faith was from mine. He rejected the ruling of Pope Leo XIII that Anglican orders were invalid: at an ecumenical gathering with his two Protestant counterparts he said how much he regretted that they could not concelebrate the Mass. He told me that the Declaration on Sexual Ethics by the Sacred Congregation of the Faith, published in 1975, which confirmed the Church's traditional teaching that homosexual acts were sinful, was the result of political intrigue in the Vatican. God loved us, Oliver insisted: that was all we knew and all we needed to know.

Fr Oliver was a kind and charismatic man – an inspired pastor who did more than most to befriend the sick and lonely living in high-rise council flats towards Shepherd's Bush. At the kiss of peace, towards the end of Mass, he would shake hands with every member of the congregation on the grounds that for many it was the only human contact they experienced during the week. The warmth of his personality, his idealism and his zeal for 'the spirit of Vatican II' were all inspiring: out came the cheque books of the merchant bankers living in the grand houses in the plummier parts of the parish. Fr Oliver flew to Russia to make friends with the Orthodox priests under Communist rule, and to deprived regions of Brazil, returning to tell his congregation that all of us living in the First World were damned.

These were the views I had held at Cambridge but as I had grown older I had grown wiser: a year spent in West Berlin studying the People's Democracy on the other side of the Wall had tempered my enthusiasm for a socialistic solution to the problem of the poor. A trip to El Salvador on the tenth anniversary of the assassination of Archbishop Romero had persuaded me that Liberation Theology was a distortion of Catholic teaching. In an article for *The Tablet* included in this collection I suggested that the way to raise standards of living in Third World countries was to encourage investment in their economies and trade with the developed nations.

In the past, Catholics disapproved of shopping around to find a sympathetic parish priest and for a number of years I continued to attend Mass at St Francis of Assisi despite my differences with Fr Oliver on points of doctrine and ecclesiology. He baptised our youngest child. However, when it came to the older children, there was an increasing discrepancy between what he preached from the pulpit and what I tried to impart to them at home. Not only Oliver, but the catechists he recruited had the same radical views. When, along with other parents, I took my second son along for instruction prior to receiving his First Communion, we were told by a bossy nun that we were not to infect our children with our old pre-Conciliar beliefs because since the Council all had changed. My son subsequently spent several weeks studying the story of Zacchaeus who climbed the palm tree to get a glimpse of Jesus and agreed to give half his money to the poor. He was told next to nothing about the Last Supper or the True Presence of Christ in the Eucharist.

Enough was enough: I defected to the parish of Our Lady of Victories over the hill in Kensington where the priests were more orthodox. I remained a friend of Fr Oliver's: every now and then, we would bump into one another in the street and, wholly at cross-purposes, bemoan the state of the Church. He remained an inspired pastor who drew like-minded Catholics to St Francis from all over London. 'There is no one I would rather convert to the Catholic faith,' I used to say to my friends, 'than Fr Oliver McTernan.' Around the year 2000, after twenty years or so in the parish, Oliver took a course in crisis management at Harvard University, after which he left the priesthood and, based with his wife in Normandy, engaged in non-governmental conciliation in troubled parts of the world.

At around the time I came to live in Notting Hill and made the acquaintance of Fr Oliver McTernan, I was invited by a Catholic writer and journalist, Robert Nowell, to contribute to a collection of essays to be called *Why I am Still a Catholic.* I was puzzled by the use of the word 'still' – it seemed to imply that there were good reasons for leaving the Church. Would my fellow contributors be traditionalists like Evelyn Waugh, sorely tested by the post-Conciliar changes?

In 1982 the collection was published by Collins and I was astonished by what I read. Some of the contributors, it seemed to me, were not 'still' Catholics at all. Robert Nowell, the editor, did not believe that Jesus had performed miracles: 'I am prepared to accept that there is a coherent natural explanation underlying all the apparently miraculous events recorded in the gospels, even perhaps the resurrection.' He also claimed that 'being a Catholic did not necessarily mean, for example, having to accept the virgin birth as a physical reality.' Mary Craig also seemed to have doubts about the reality of the Resurrection – the empty tomb was 'not the crux of the matter': she had not been to confession for fifteen years. To Bernard Bergonzi, 'being a Catholic now is like being a Jew, in belonging to a people and a tradition rather than upholding a particular set of clearly defined doctrines.' To James P. Mackey, a theologian who was once a priest, 'The essence of Christianity lies in orthopraxis rather than orthodoxy' and the way in which the decrees of Vatican II only envisaged the future union of Christians as 'the return of all separated brethren to Rome' was a 'sobering' fact.

Most puzzling of all, to me at the time, was why Clifford Longley, a convert from atheism, still considered himself a Catholic. He thought the dogma of the Assumption 'unlikely' and the doctrine of papal infallibility, too, 'an unlikely thing'.

I share none of the Roman Catholic Church's attitudes

on contraception, divorce, abortion, the religious education of my children and so on.

I do not any longer look towards the Roman Catholic Church or any other as a supernatural society, and cannot in all honesty put my name to whatever might be officially described as 'the teaching of the Catholic Church'. I do not accept its jurisdiction over my private life; would not dream of going anywhere near the confessional; go to Mass very little; and do not worry about it.

What became clear to me, in the course of the 1980s, was that the views of Fr Oliver McTernan and the contributors to *Why I am Still a Catholic* were not those of maverick radicals but were widely shared by others within the English Church. Their alternative Magisterium was to be found in the columns of *The Tablet*, edited by John Wilkins, in Catholic agencies such as CAFOD, the CIIR (Catholic Institute for International Relations) and, most disturbingly, in Catechetical programmes in Catholic schools all with the apparently tacit approval of the Catholic Bishops of England and Wales.

In 1991, I published a pamphlet entitled *Quo Vadis? The Subversion of the Catholic Church* attacking the corrosive ideas of some modern theologians, and the apparent acquiescence of the English and Welsh bishops in the promotion of unorthodox teaching. I criticised in particular the 'modular programme of Religious Education for Catholic Secondary Schools', *Weaving the Web*, for its feminist, indifferentist and Liberationist agenda with Jesus portrayed as 'a kind of Che Guevara of the ancient world' and the Roman Catholic Church as just one member of the 'different families among the large Christian community which is called the church'. I asked whether our bishops, in permitting such distortions, were being obedient to their duty as defined in *Lumen Gentium* to 'ward off whatever errors threaten their flock'. I sent a copy of the pamphlet to every English and Welsh bishop and the papal nuncio: the nuncio acknowledged its receipt with a friendly letter. None of the bishops replied.

I might at this point have accepted that I was the one who

was out of step; that together with a small coterie of fellow traditionalists I should humbly accept my place in the dust-bin of history. Yet, though we were indisputably out of step with most of our fellow Catholics in Britain, were our beliefs at variance with those of the universal Church? Pope Paul VI, towards the end of his pontificate, had grown alarmed at what was being done in the name of Vatican II, complaining that 'the smoke of Satan had entered the Church': after 1978, the new Polish Pope, John Paul II, and the man he chose as Prefect for the Sacred Congregation for the Faith, Cardinal Joseph Ratzinger, both vigorously reasserted the teachings of the Church's mainstream Magisterium. A new *Catechism of the Catholic Church*, published in 1994, confirmed all those beliefs which had supposedly been dropped by Vatican II.

This background will put in context many of the pieces in this collection. The first essay on Hell is the most recent and has not been published before. It was originally written as a talk to be given at the Jesuit house at Farm Street and I should like to thank Anthony Meredith SJ for reading a first draft and correcting some of my historical and theological errors. In the event, it was decided that the subject did not conform to the criteria established for the series and, at the suggestion of Brendan Walsh, the editorial director of Darton, Longman and Todd, it is published here together with articles, essays and book reviews written over the past twenty-five years. I am most grateful to Brendan for making the selection from my cuttings and typescripts.

After reading my essay on Hell, Father Meredith raised the pertinent question: who was the reader I had in mind? The answer is not straightforward. 'Hell' is addressed to Catholics, and some of the pieces in the collection were written for Catholic journals such as *The Catholic Herald* or *The Tablet;* others for secular newspapers and magazines – *The Spectator, The Independent, The Guardian, The Sunday Times.* A non-Catholic reader may find Catholic controversies parochial and a Catholic reader may be annoyed at being told things he or she already knows. Nonetheless, I would hope that most of the essays would appeal to anyone interested in the dilemma of a Christian in the modern world.

There are a number of repetitions – I seem to have been haunted by Ezekiel 3:16–21 – and, at a time when Christians are encouraged to 'accentuate the positive', many may seem negative in tone. Early on in my career as a freelance journalist, I was pigeonholed by editors and literary editors as a 'traditionalist' Catholic and was therefore sent books to review, or asked to write articles, on topics that would provoke in me a critical response. Some also provoked a critical response in my readers, particularly the two reprinted here in the section on Liberation Theology. The article in *The Tablet*, 'Rich Man, Poor Man', infuriated Graham Greene: he wrote an angry letter to the editor and, as I describe in 'The Quest for Graham Greene', the exchange damaged our friendship. The longer piece on El Salvador written for *The Independent Magazine*, 'Catechists and Commissars', dismayed the deputy editor of the magazine: he insisted on inserting a rebuttal within the article itself by a Jesuit. The article was denounced from the pulpit at Farm Street and at a party shortly after its publication I was accosted by Harold Pinter: 'Piers, you know *fuck all* about El Salvador!'

Pinter's wrath did not last. More damaging, perhaps – though we now enter into the realm of authorial paranoia – was the effect on my career as a novelist in the secular world by appearing to be on the wrong side of these religious controversies: I treat this problem in 'The Catholic Novelist in a Secular Society'. What is indisputable is that within my lifetime some of the commonly accepted criteria for judging moral behaviour, particularly sexual behaviour, were reversed so that homosexual acts, for example, which in my childhood were criminal offences, came to be regarded as beyond reproach. It was those who *did* reproach who came to be subject to stigma.

As a result of this increasingly intolerant climate of opinion, a number of my Catholic friends working in the media kept their heads down on controversial questions; or made it plain that they disagreed with the Church's traditional teaching. In defending it, I did not think that I was being courageous. Rather, I liked to think that I was placing myself firmly on the winning side. 'For if anyone declares himself for me in the presence of men, I will declare myself for him in the presence of my Father in heaven. But the one who disowns me in the presence of men, I will disown in the presence of my Father in heaven' (Matthew 10:32–3).

The essays in this collection do not amount to an exposition of my Catholic faith. Because of their polemical nature, there is little mention of what I value most highly – for example, the sacrament of Reconciliation that has saved my sanity and the Eucharist which, to use the words of Pope John Paul II in *Ecclesia de Eucharistia,* has inspired 'a sense of profound amazement' in me since I was a child. There is little mention of the *love* of God yet, more than most in this suffering world, I have had reason to be grateful to God – not just for those earthly joys described by St Augustine in his *Confessions* – the brilliance of earthly light, the sweet melody of harmony and song, the fragrance of flowers, perfumes, and spices; manna and honey and 'limbs such as the body delights to embrace'; nor for peace, health, prosperity, fulfilling work and the joy that comes from a happy family life; but above all for the gift of an immortal soul and the promise of the beatific vision in the world to come.

FAITH

I

Hell

1. INTRODUCTION

Aｌｔｈｏｕｇｈ ｔｈｅ ｌａｉｔｙ ｉｎ ｔｈｅ Catholic Church has been
encouraged since Vatican II to play a greater part in the life
of the Church, it may seem presumptuous for an author
who has studied neither theology nor ecclesiology to write a
critique of the Church's current eschatological thinking.
Even that word 'eschatology' which would trip effort-
lessly off the tongue of a graduate of Heythrop College I
use only after checking in the dictionary to make sure that
I know what it means. What knowledge I have of the
Catholic faith comes from the religious instruction I
received from the Benedictine monks at Ampleforth in the
1950s, supplemented by haphazard reading in later life.

My religious instruction began at Gilling, the Ampleforth
Prep school, which I attended from the age of eight to
twelve. It followed the Penny Catechism with its numbered
questions and answers. To encourage us to remember the
answers, we were set a 'stick test': too many wrong answers
led to a beating. It was important to get them right not just
to avoid being thwacked on the hands by a ferule in this
world but to escape a more terrible punishment in the next.
'What are the four last things to be ever remembered?'
asked Question 332. 'The four last things to be ever remembered are Death, Judgement, Hell, and Heaven.' What was
Hell? Eternal punishment. What would lead to eternal punishment? Dying unrepentant in a state of mortal sin. What
sins were mortal? Murder, adultery – and choosing not to go
to Mass on a Sunday.

The essay which follows asks why these 'four last things

ever to be remembered' appear to have been forgotten in today's Catholic Church. Why in particular are we so rarely warned that we run a real risk of spending eternity in torment? If the Benedictines at Ampleforth believed what they taught us in the 1950s, why was damnation dropped from Catholic preaching in the last few decades of the twentieth century when a monk from Ampleforth, Basil Hume, was Archbishop of Westminster? There has never been, to my knowledge, any clear and unambiguous statement from Archbishop's House, or from the Bishops' Conference of England and Wales, that the Church has changed its mind on the question of Hell; yet one searches in vain for any mention of Satan or his domain in the press releases from the Bishops' Conference, in Catholic journals such as *The Tablet*, in programmes prepared for the teaching of the Catholic faith to Catholic children in Catholic schools such as *Weaving the Web*, or in booklets published to guide the small groups formed to foster spiritual renewal in the Diocese of Westminster, *At Your Word, Lord*.

Indeed, it would seem to a dispassionate observer that there is no longer any real belief among contemporary Catholics in the last item of the Nicean Creed, 'life everlasting'. There are calls to conversion and repentance, but no suggestion, explicit or implicit, of what may befall those who are not converted or fail to repent; much talk of salvation but no definition of what it is from which we are to be saved; no warning that while the gospel may be good news for some, it is decidedly bad news for others.

Yet, as Blaise Pascal wrote in the seventeenth century,

> The immortality of the soul is a matter of such importance to us; it affects us so deeply that we must have lost our wits completely not to care what it is all about. All our actions and our thoughts must follow such different courses depending on whether there are eternal rewards to hope for or not, that it is impossible to take a single step with sense and judgement unless it is determined by our conception of our final end.[1]

While Pascal's contemporary, René Descartes, made the philosophical observation 'I think therefore I am', Pascal would have us say: 'I believe therefore I am *forever*'. The last item of the Apostles' Creed, life everlasting, is by no means the least because, as Ronald Knox pointed out, 'once a man or woman has attained the age of reason he is bound for one of two ultimate destinies, fixed and eternal – hell or heaven; and this is true even of those myriads of souls which have never had the opportunity or never had full opportunity, to hear the Christian message preached.'[2]

Knox also warned his readers, in the late 1920s, that 'the prevalent irreligion of the age does exercise a continual unconscious pressure upon the pulpit; it makes preachers hesitate to affirm doctrines whose affirmation would be unpopular. And a doctrine which has ceased to be affirmed is doomed, like a disused organ, to atrophy.' As early as 1915 George Bernard Shaw wrote in the Preface to his play *Androcles and the Lion* that 'belief in . . . hell is fast vanishing. All the leaders of thoughts have lost it; and even for the rank and file it has fled to those parts of Ireland and Scotland which are still in the XVII century.' 'Even there,' he added, 'it is tacitly reserved for the other fellow.'[3]

To insist that some of us may be damned inevitably makes a Christian apologist unpopular: it is something horrible to contemplate and therefore best pushed to the back of the mind or even out of the mind altogether. A belief in damnation is deemed unsophisticated and 'fundamentalist' – viz. not something that could be taken seriously by a contemporary Christian outside Ireland and Scotland, as Shaw said, or – we might now add – the Bible Belt in the United States. Each man is entitled to his opinion and one is as good as another. To suggest that one set of beliefs or mode of behaviour is better than another is deemed 'judgemental'; and while it is right to warn that smoking will cause the death of the body, it is intolerable to point to sins that might lead to the death of the soul.

2. HELL IN THE BIBLE

The Synoptic Gospels

Are such attitudes justified? Can we dismiss the Hell of the Christian Gospels as a primitive notion that has no meaning

in the modern world? Was Jesus merely recycling the
assumptions that prevailed in the ancient world? The idea
of some kind of posthumous *reglement des contes* is found
both inside and outside the Judeo-Christian tradition prior
to the time of Christ. Even among the ancient Greeks, the
demands of justice suggested rewards or punishment after
death with Plato the earliest author to state categorically
that the fate of the extremely wicked is eternal punishment[4] –
although it should be noted that this punishment, in Plato's
Gorgias, has a corrective function.

In the earliest books of the Old Testament, by contrast,
there is no consistent idea of what awaits us after death. The
word 'Sheol' is used to describe some kind of vast collective
sepulchre and only with the prophet Ezekiel is a section of
Sheol assigned to the wicked – a response to Job's complaint
that all the dead are treated equally.[5] A new word,
'Gehenna', came to be used for the part of Sheol where the
wicked were punished for their sins – a word derived from
'Ge-Hinnom, the valley of Hinnom', a ravine outside
Jerusalem believed to have been the site of human sacrifice,
and used as a tip for the bodies of executed criminals, and
therefore 'associated with burning, shame, and wickedness'.
The prophet Daniel, closer to the time of Christ, tells us
that 'many of those who sleep in the dust of the earth shall
awake, some to everlasting life, and some to shame and
everlasting contempt.'[6]

However, only a few passages in the Old Testament suggest a belief in punishment after death (Psalm 49; Ezekiel
32:18–28; Daniel 12; Isaiah 66:24; Jeremiah 7; and others).[7]
It cannot therefore be said that Jesus' teaching about an
afterlife came simply from the intellectual conditioning of
his upbringing. Indeed, at the time of Jesus, opinion among
the Jews was divided between the Sadducees who denied
that there was life after death and the Pharisees who
believed not only in life after death, but also that the souls
of the just would be rewarded while those of the wicked
punished for all eternity.

Thus, while it was, as it were, open to Jesus to reject
the notion of an afterlife, we find that both he and John the
Baptist subscribed to the Pharisees' belief. Preaching in

the wilderness, John warns that 'any tree which fails to produce good fruit will be cut down and thrown on the fire' and that 'the one who follows me . . . will clear his threshing-floor and gather his wheat into the barn; but the chaff he will burn in a fire that will never go out.'[8]

Jesus confirms the existence of an afterlife: in answer to a question put by some Pharisees, he tells us that there are no married couples in Heaven where the human condition will be like that of an angel. He also describes, in the most unambiguous terms in some of the Gospels, and by means of vivid parables, the fate that awaits sinners who die unrepentant. After describing how a farmer, when an enemy has sown weeds among his corn, sifts this 'darnel' from the wheat following the harvest and burns it, Jesus spells out its meaning to his disciples:

> 'The sower of the good seed is the Son of Man. The field is the world; the good seed is the subjects of the kingdom; the darnel, the subjects of the evil one; the enemy who sowed them, the devil; the harvest is the end of the world; the reapers are the angels. Well then, just as the darnel is gathered up and burned in the fire, so it will be at the end of time. The Son of Man will send his angels and they will gather out of his kingdom all things that provoke offences and all who do evil. And throw them into the blazing furnace, where there will be weeping and grinding of teeth.'[9]

A little later, the image is of a dragnet which brings in a haul of fish after which 'the fishermen . . . sitting down . . . collect the good ones into a basket and throw away those that are no use. This is how it will be at the end of time: the angels will appear and separate the wicked from the just to throw them into the blazing furnace where there will be weeping and grinding of teeth.'[10]

Other images are of the unforgiving steward who is handed over by his master 'to the torturers till he should pay all his debt';[11] the wedding guest who fails to dress up for the occasion and is bound hand and foot and thrown out into the dark 'where there will be weeping and grinding of teeth' – with the postscript that 'many are called, but few are chosen;'[12] the foolish bridesmaids who, having failed to fill their lamps, miss the arrival of the bridegroom and so are shut out of the wedding; the man who fails to exploit his single talent and is, like the dressed-down wedding guest, thrown 'out into the dark, where there will be weeping and grinding of teeth';[13] and, pertinent to our own time as to that of Christ, the punishment of those who have shown themselves indifferent to the plight of the poor and needy.

> '"Go away from me, with your curse upon you, to the eternal fire prepared for the devil and his angels. For I was hungry and you never gave me food; I was thirsty and you never gave me anything to drink. I was a stranger and you never made me welcome, naked and you never clothed me, sick and in prison and you never visited me . . . I tell you solemnly, in so far as you neglected to do this to one of the least of these, you neglected to do it to me". And they will go away to eternal punishment, and the virtuous to eternal life.'[14]

A man who blasphemes against another 'will answer for it in hell fire'[15] and, of chilling pertinence to what Pope John Paul II called our 'aphrodisiac civilisation', is the advice Jesus gives us in St Matthew's Gospel:

> 'You have learnt how it was said: *You must not commit adultery.* But I say to you: if a man looks at a woman lustfully, he has already committed adultery with her in his heart. If your right eye should cause you to sin, tear it out and throw it away; for it will do you less harm to lose one part of you than to have your whole body thrown into hell. And if your right hand should cause you to sin, cut it off and throw it away; for it will do you less harm to lose one part of you than to have your whole body go to hell.'[16]

In St Luke's Gospel, emphasis is placed by Jesus on social injustice, particularly the hard-hearted indifference of the rich to the suffering of the poor. 'But alas for you who are rich: you are having your consolation now. Alas for you who have your fill now: you shall go hungry. Alas for you who laugh now: you shall mourn and weep.'[17] In chapter 16,

Jesus tells the story of the rich man 'who used to dress in purple and fine linen and feast magnificently every day' and the beggar, Lazarus, who had sat starving at his gate. After their death, Lazarus lies happy in the bosom of Abraham while the rich man, Dives, is tormented in Hades. Dives begs Abraham to take pity on him and send Lazarus to 'dip the tip of his finger in water and cool my tongue, because I am in agony in these flames'; but Abraham tells him to remember

> 'that during your life good things came your way, just as bad things came the way of Lazarus. Now he is being comforted here while you are in agony. But that is not all: between us and you a great gulf has been fixed, to stop anyone, if he wanted to, crossing from our side to yours, and to stop any crossing from your side to ours.'

The rich man then begs Abraham to send Lazarus to warn his five brothers of the fate that awaits them. Abraham says that they should listen to Moses and the prophets. 'Ah no, father Abraham, but if someone comes to them from the dead, they will repent.' No, Abraham tells him, 'If they will not listen either to Moses or to the prophets, they will not be convinced even if someone should rise from the dead'.[18]

It is in the Gospel of St Matthew that we find the largest number of clear and unambiguous warnings of the terrible fate that awaits unrepentant sinners but they are to be found in the other three. St Mark records the advice of Jesus that it is better to take out your eye or lop off a limb that might lead you to sin than go intact into hell 'where *their worm does not die nor their fire go out*'.[19] At the tail end of Mark's Gospel, which scholars believe may not have been written by Mark himself, salvation and damnation are linked not just to wrong-doing but to belief. 'He who believes and is baptised will be saved; he who does not believe will be condemned.'[20] Whether or not belief is a matter of human choice, or an arbitrary gift from God, was a question that would preoccupy many in the centuries which followed. Most sobering for today's optimists was Jesus' warning that we should 'enter by the narrow gate' which 'only a few find', 'since the road that leads to perdition is wide and spacious, and many take it.'[21] Or, as he succinctly puts it later in St Matthew's Gospel, 'many are called, but few are chosen.'[22]

St John and St Paul

When we come to the Gospel of St John, there is the same final damnation of unrepentant sinners but God's punishment seems to be no more than 'a denial of eternal life'.[23] Damnation means extinction: the soul dies with the body. The same less terrible definition of Hell can be found in the epistles of St Paul which were written prior to the Gospels. In general, St Paul tended to emphasise the positive in Christ's teaching but 'the theme of judgement according to one's deeds is nevertheless clear'.[24] In his Epistle to the Romans, Paul warns of God's anger incurred by 'all the impiety and depravity of men who keep truth imprisoned in their wickedness' and warns those who stubbornly refuse to repent that God will 'repay each one as his works deserve'. For those who take depravity as their guide 'there will be anger and fury. Pain and suffering will come to every human being who employs himself in evil . . . , renown, honour and peace will come to everyone who does good . . .'[25]

St Paul is more clement towards the rich than St Luke, not damning them simply for being rich but reminding them that 'they are not to look down on other people', nor 'set their hopes on money, which is untrustworthy', to 'be rich in good works' and 'generous and willing to share'.[26] Clearly, he believed that he himself would be rewarded after his death; that, though he was not yet perfect, he was 'still running, trying . . . racing for the finish, for the prize to which God calls us upwards to receive in Christ Jesus.'[27] But, as St Augustine and, following St Augustine, Luther, Calvin and the Dutch bishop Jansenius were to conclude, St Paul believed that he would be saved not by good works but by his faith in Christ.

Until now, we have seen only in the postscript to St Mark's Gospel the suggestion that unbelief is itself a sin that merits eternal damnation. But in St John's Gospel, too, we read that there will be 'eternal life for those who believe but judgment, wrath, death for those who do not'.[28] There is in fact a narrowing in St John's Gospel of the criteria for salvation. 'Unless a man is born through water and the Spirit,' Jesus tells Nicodemus, 'he cannot enter the kingdom of God'.[29] Thus baptism becomes a prerequisite to salvation, but also the authentic Eucharist. 'I am the living bread which has come down from heaven. Anyone who eats this bread will live forever . . . I tell you most solemnly, if you do not eat the flesh of the Son of Man and drink his blood, you will not have life in you.'[30]

'Nobody, we may be sure, who considered it with a really unbiased mind,' states the 1951 edition of *The Catholic Dictionary*, 'would doubt Christ's teaching on Hell.'

> The fact is, men persuade themselves that the doctrine is untrue and inhuman, and therefore that Christ, being eternal truth, could not have taught it. Their exegesis scarcely finds acceptance either with Christians prepared to accept the doctrine or with non-Christians who come with purely historical interest to the study of the Gospels.[31]

3. HELL IN THE HISTORY OF THE CHURCH

St Augustine of Hippo

If we now move on to the Doctors of the Church, we find that St Augustine, Bishop of Hippo (354–430), was much preoccupied with the consequences of sin. 'The God of the African Christians was very much the awe-inspiring Judge,' we are told by his biographer, Peter Brown. 'A streak of this primitive terror was strong in Augustine; even when he seemed to be very far from his roots . . . in Milan, he was haunted by "fears of death and Judgement"'.[32] It was not just the *actual* sins of wicked men of the kind that Jesus castigates in the Gospels that Augustine believed would result in eternal damnation, but the *original* sin of Adam and Eve whose consequences could only be averted by the waters of baptism. Neither innocence nor virtue sufficed for salvation.

'There were pagans,' he wrote to Evodius, Bishop of Uzalis,

> who . . . have lived praiseworthy lives by their own lights. Except for the fact that they did not serve God, but erred in worshipping the vanities that were the established religion of their time . . . they can be justly held up as models of all the other virtues – of frugality, self-denial, chastity, sobriety, courageous in the face of death for their country's sake, keeping their sworn word to their fellow-citizens and even to their enemies. All these things are . . . in a sense, worthless and unprofitable; but as signs of a certain character, they please us so much that we would want those in whom they exist to be freed from the pains of Hell: but of course, it may well be that the verdict of human feelings is one thing, and the justice of the Creator, quite another.[33]

For Christians in the twenty-first century, it is precisely this divide between 'the verdict of human feelings' and 'the justice of the Creator' that is hard to accept. As Lezek Kolakowski puts it in his book on Pascal's religion,

> To contemporary minds nourished on the tradition of the Enlightenment, the Augustinian doctrine appears . . . bizarre . . . How indeed can we believe in a just and benevolent God who rewards and punishes his children according to his incalculable caprice, like a tyrant rather than a loving father? And how can he cast his children into the infernal abyss while knowing that their wrongdoings are performed under compulsion and that they cannot help what they do and what they are?[34]

Equally obnoxious to the contemporary mind is Augustine's teaching that 'knowledge of the punishment of the damned constitutes part of heavenly bliss'[35] – particularly since he included among the damned unbaptised babies. Paradoxically at the time, Augustine may have seemed more lenient in his outlook than the theological adversaries against whom many of his polemics were directed – the Donatists and Pelagians. 'I do not blame you,' he told his imperfect congregation, 'I do not criticize you, even if this life is what you love . . . You can love this life all you want, as long as you know what to choose.' He rejected the perfectionism of both the Donatists and the Pelagians: 'the victory of Augustine over Pelagius', writes Peter Brown, 'was also a victory for the average good Catholic layman of the Later Empire, over an austere, reforming ideal.'[36]

What some today consider the Catholic Church's 'obsession' with sexual sin is often traced back to St Augustine, not just because of his vivid description of his own struggles with unchastity in his *Confessions*, but also his view that the 'unspeakable sin' through which Adam brought down the whole human race was something to do with sex and is transmitted through the sexual act.

> When they had disobeyed God by eating the forbidden fruit, they had been 'ashamed'; they had covered their genitals with fig-leaves. That was enough for Augustine: 'Ecce unde. That's the place! That's the place from which the first sin is passed on'. This shame at the uncontrollable stirring of the genitals was the fitting punishment of the crime of disobedience.[37]

To counteract the teaching of Pelagius that men could be saved through their own resources, Augustine emphasised the necessity of God's grace – a teaching that was to preoccupy theologians in the centuries which followed and become the bedrock of the Protestant Reformation. The debate was always about what was required to be saved from Hell, never about Hell itself: however, there were those among the early Church fathers who, though they did not doubt the existence of Hell, took from Plato the idea that the torments of Hell were not eternal, but a smelting that allowed for final salvation. Thus Origen is censured by Augustine in *The City of God* for suggesting that all might eventually be saved, and St Gregory of Nyssa for extending God's mercy ultimately to Satan himself; and these 'universalist' teachings were formally condemned at the Council of Constantinople in the year 543. 'If anyone says or holds that the punishment of devils and wicked men is temporary and will eventually cease, that is to say, that devils or the ungodly will be completely restored to their original state: let him be anathema.'[38]

The Middle Ages

St Augustine lived in a community of celibate clergy but believed that, under his guidance, the frail lay Christians of his diocese might be saved. There were others, however, who decided that perilous temptations could only be resisted by a total withdrawal from the world. Belonging to a generation prior to St Augustine, and living at the other end of the Mediterranean, there was St Antony (251–356) who first became a hermit in the desert of Egypt, then gathered other hermits into a community – the prototype of the monastic community that became so widespread in the Middle Ages. St Benedict of Nursia (480–547), two hundred years later, established the prototype for western monasticism at Monte Casino. The movement he started was constantly renewed by men and women who withdrew from the world to follow his Rule. Bernard of Clairvaux (1090–1153), believing that salvation was difficult outside a monastic community, not only persuaded many of his friends among the Burgundian nobility to take vows of poverty, chastity and obedience and live in community behind closed walls, but also the young women they might have married. The community of Cistercian nuns at Juilly was headed by his sister Humbeline who had left her husband to take the veil.

It was not just the sins of violence and concupiscence that would lead to damnation, but also beliefs that conflicted with the teaching of the Church. St Dominic (1170–1221) founded his Order of Preachers to combat the errors of the Cathars which he believed would condemn those who held them to the eternal torments of Hell. The fire that burned unrepentant heretics gave a foretaste of what was to come.

The Dominican theologian St Thomas Aquinas (1225–74) considered such wrong-thinking fatal in both a material and spiritual sense. Catholics might disagree, he wrote in his *Summa Theologiae*, on matters of no consequence to the faith or not yet decided by the church; but when such matters are decided by the authority of the universal church (vested principally in the Pope) anyone who stubbornly resists the decision must be adjudged a heretic. About heretics there are two things to say. Their sin deserves banishment not only from the church by excommunication but also from the world by death.[39]

Though St Thomas does not dwell on the risks of eternal torment, he is in no doubt but that it is the fate that awaits sinners: 'All sins that turn us away from God by destroying the love of charity are intrinsically liable to an eternal penalty.'[40] Such sins he terms 'fatal' or 'mortal' as opposed to 'venial' or 'excusable' sins which do not lead to a rupture in our relationship with God. 'A non-fatal sin like frivolous chatter can become fatal if we add to it disorder, fatal by nature, directing it toward illicit sex, for instance.'

By and large, St Thomas Aquinas was less preoccupied with sexual sin than was St Augustine: to him, offences against God such as blasphemy were more serious, and those which destroy the reason which distinguishes man from beast. 'Drunkenness is only non-fatal because of ignorance and weakness, but ignorance can't excuse frequent drunkenness; the drunk is now choosing to drink too much and returning his sin to its true fatal nature.'[41]

We find the same ostensibly bleak view of life on earth in *The Imitation of Christ*, a short work of religious devotion written a hundred years or so after Aquinas's *Summa Theologiae*. The author, the German monk Thomas à Kempis, is neither a saint nor a doctor of the Church, but his work influenced Christians as disparate as St Thomas More, St Ignatius Loyola, St Francis Xavier, General Gordon, John Wesley and Dr Johnson. 'After the Bible itself, no other work can compare with its profound wisdom, clarity of thought, and converting power':[42] it was found by the bedside of Pope John Paul I after his death.

For à Kempis, there was a causal relationship between self-denial and the provision of grace. 'My son,' says Christ in the second half of the book, 'carefully observe the impulses of nature and grace, for these are opposed one to another, and work in so subtle a manner that even a spiritual, holy and enlightened man can hardly distinguish them.' Spiritual comfort 'surpasses all worldly delights and bodily pleasures. All worldly pleasures are either vain or unseemly; spiritual joys alone are pleasant and honourable . . .'[43] He showed a deep mistrust of human affections: 'The love of creatures is deceptive and unstable . . . Whoever clings to any creature will fall with its falling; but he who holds to Jesus will stand firm for ever.' The man who seeks salvation must embrace suffering: 'Be assured of this, that you must live a dying life. And the more completely a man dies to self, the more he begins to live to God.'

The Imitation of Christ holds out the promise that virtue in this life will bring its own reward – an inner serenity and an invulnerability to life's vicissitudes – but it also tells us, following St Luke, that sin will be punished in the next world with torments specifically tailored to a man's besetting sins.

> In whatever things a man sins, in those will he be the more severely punished. Then will the slothful be spurred by fiery goads, and the gluttonous tormented by dire hunger and thirst. Then will the luxurious and pleasure-loving be plunged into burning pitch and stinking sulphur, while the envious will howl their grief like wild dogs.[44]

The Reformation and Counter-Reformation

It is not within the compass of this essay to explore at any length the attitude to Hell of the Protestant Reformers. It is enough to say that damnation was a real fear for Martin Luther and we find, say, in the text of J.S. Bach's Cantata 20 an expression of the vivid belief in Hell among German Protestants at this time.[45] Jean Calvin, believed – as did Luther – that men were 'justified' – i.e. saved – by faith in Christ, not by 'good works'. Calvin went further than Luther, however, in teaching that man, 'utterly devoid of goodness', cannot be saved through the exercise of his own free will but only in response to God's grace. Why God should choose some – 'the elect' – as the recipients of this bounty and consign others to Hell was a mystery beyond human comprehension.

From 1564, Calvin – a native of Picardy – was both the spiritual and temporal ruler of the city-state of Geneva. Anyone who deviated from his teaching was either forced into exile or, like the Spaniard Michael Servetus, burned at the stake. Roman Catholics were included among the damned and the Roman Catholic Bishop of Geneva, St Francis of Sales (1567–1622), was obliged to reside over the border at Annecy in Savoy. The eldest son of a Savoyard nobleman, St Francis had become a priest despite his father's opposition after 'doubts about his own hope of salvation'.[46] Gentle, learned, 'enlisting the Classical learning of the Renaissance in the service of the Christian mind', St Francis devoted his life to preaching, spiritual direction and pastoral work within his diocese.

St Francis's best-known work, *An Introduction to the Devout Life*, was based on his counsel to one of his penitents, Madame de Charmoisy. It is far gentler than Thomas à Kempis's *Imitation of Christ* – directed not to monks and nuns but to lay men and women – particularly women – showing them how they could be holy in their particular walk of life. However, he was acutely aware of the danger of damnation. 'Look up to heaven, and do not forget it for earth. Look down to hell, and do not cast yourself into it for the sake of fleeting things.'

For St Francis, some pleasures were innocent. 'To get out into the open air,' he wrote,

> to be entertained by happy, friendly conversation, play the lute or some other musical instrument, sing to a musical accompaniment, and go hunting are all such innocent forms of recreation that to use them properly all that is needed is common prudence that gives due order, time, place, and measure of all things.[47]

He thought games such as tennis, chess and backgammon were 'by nature good and licit forms of recreation' but he was wary of dancing.

> Balls and dances are forms of recreation that are in themselves morally indifferent but because of the way in which they are conducted lean very much towards evil and are consequently full of risk and danger. Generally held at night in partial or complete darkness, it is easy for many dark and vicious things to take place in them since the situation is itself so favourable to evil.

St Francis advised Philothea, the composite young woman to whom he addressed his *Introduction to the Devout Life*, to remember, after an evening's dancing, that 'while you were at the ball many souls were burning in the flames of hell for sins committed at dances or occasioned by their dancing'.[48]

Unlike the more severe moralists of the Middle Ages such as St Peter Damien (1007–72), who regarded marriage as 'a doubtful cover for sin', St Francis taught that marriage was honourable and 'a great sacrament' and that sexual intercourse for married couples was 'holy, virtuous and praiseworthy in itself'. Nevertheless, he enjoined chastity within marriage, and warned against conjugal licentiousness which 'effectively kills the soul by mortal sin, as when the order appointed for the procreation of children is violated and perverted.'

> In the latter instance, accordingly as one departs more or less from the appointed order, the sins are abominable in greater or less degrees but they are always mortal. Procreation of children is the first and principal end of marriage. Hence no one can ever lawfully depart from the due order that this end requires.[49]

St Francis reminded the married couples among his readers how in her vision of Hell:

> St Catherine of Siena saw many souls grievously tormented for having violated the sanctity of marriage. This resulted, she said, not from the enormity of the sin, for murders and blasphemies are even more enormous, but 'because those who commit it do not make it a matter of conscience', and hence continue in it for a long time.[50]

Blaise Pascal

In his *Introduction to the Devout Life*, St Francis addresses himself to Catholics who wish to renew their spiritual life. He does not discuss whether or not Muslims or Protestant heretics would be damned or saved. Nor does he consider the fate of those who reject Christian beliefs altogether – a species almost unknown in the Middle Ages but increasingly to be found in intellectual circles in France in the seventeenth century. Was unbelief itself a sin? And what of those who only practise the Catholic religion to conform to convention, and repent not because they are sorry for their sins but simply because they are afraid of damnation?

To the Calvinists of Geneva such questions posed no problem: God had predestined some to be saved and others to be damned. However, for serious minded Catholics in France such as Blaise Pascal, the answer was not so simple. Clearly, Catholics who commit 'mortal' sins deserve Hell as St Francis of Sales suggests: but what of those who, after conscientious enquiry, decide that there is no God and no life after death? They are impervious to his admonitions because they believe that there is only one life, however short, and only earthly pleasures, however fleeting.

Now, for the first time since the age of St Augustine, the choice is no longer limited to rival religions such as Judaism or Islam, or to different forms of Christian belief (Pelagianism, Lutheranism, Calvinism): instead, just as St Augustine was obliged to counter or absorb different forms of paganism such as neo-Platonism, Pascal must deal with the scepticism that he sensed in Montaigne, was to become explicit in David Hume and flourish in the philosophers of the Enlightenment. In the realm of politics, the religious rivalries that had led to the Thirty Years War had given way, under Cardinal Richelieu, to the pragmatic *raison d'état* – Catholic France aiding the Protestant enemies of the Catholic Habsburgs; so, in the realm of ideas, the fissure was not just between Catholic orthodoxy and Protestant heresy, but also between Christian belief and a philosophic rejection of the claims of all religions.

This makes Pascal's preoccupations particularly relevant

to the present day when the Christian's chief adversary is the atheist or agnostic whose values predominate in the secular world. Pascal's *pessimism* might not strike a chord with contemporary readers: those enjoying the fruits of prosperity and good health in the developed world would not accept 'that there is no true and solid satisfaction to be had in this world, that all our pleasures are only vanity, that our misfortunes are infinite'; but, however much we attempt to conceal it, no one can dispute 'that death, which dogs us at every moment, must in the space of a few years inevitably bring us face to face with the dreadful necessity of being either eternally annihilated or eternally unhappy . . .'[51]

It is also undeniable that many of us today show that lack of curiosity about what happens to us after our death that Pascal found so baffling.

> I can feel only compassion for those who are sincerely distressed by their doubt, who regard it as the greatest of misfortunes, and who, by sparing no pains to escape from it, make the search one of their main and most serious occupations.
>
> But I take a very different view of those who live their lives without giving a thought to the final end of life, and who solely because they do not discover within themselves the light necessary to convince them of it, neglect to seek elsewhere, and to decide after mature reflection whether belief is one of those ideas that people accept out of mere credulity, or one of those which though obscure in themselves nevertheless possess a solid and unshakable foundation.[52]

Two further observations have a contemporary ring. Pascal remarked on the way people distract themselves from thinking about death with what he called *divertissements*: 'Nothing is more intolerable to man than a state of complete repose, without desires, without work, without amusements, without occupation';[53] and he recognised the limitations of the disciplines of philosophy and mathematics ('its profundity is useless') which today are held in such high regard – this judgement being all the more convincing because Pascal was one of the most brilliant physicists and mathematicians of his time. Pascal does not deduce that there must be a God, and subsequently that Jesus of Nazareth was this God incarnate; but rather apprehends, through the distinct faculty of faith and through the reading of the Gospels, that Jesus was who he claimed to be – the Word of God. 'It is not only impossible, but useless to know God without the intermediary of Jesus Christ.'[54]

Pascal's aim in his writing was not just to prove to sceptics that the Catholic religion was true, but also to expose the compromise and corruption that he saw in the Church itself, and for which he blamed the Jesuits. 'The post-Tridentine reforms,' writes Leszek Kolakowski in his book on Pascal's religious beliefs,

> may have worked relatively efficiently among the secular and regular clergy, but they could not affect the mentality and the habits of the upper classes, and the royal court was what it was. The Augustinian moral stringency and inflexibility were simply not for ballrooms or comedy-goers. One could not tell the upper classes that curiosity is a dreadful sin, that theatre is a diabolic contrivance, that flirting with one's neighbour's wife is irrevocably a straight path to eternal fire, and that we ought to give our belongings, apart from bare necessities, to the poor.[55]

Pascal wrote his polemical *Provincial Letters* in defence of the Jansenists whose views on predestination were close to Calvin's; and against the Jesuits whose laxity in the confessional he satirised to great effect. 'Men are in these days so corrupt,' says his imaginary Jesuit,

> that, being unable to raise them to our standard, we are obliged to lower the standard to them. But for this, they would forsake us; they would even do worse – they would abandon themselves . . . The main rule of our Society, in order to promote the interests of Religion, is to repel none that none may be discouraged or despair.

A modern reader might side with Pascal in some of the cases raised in the *Provincial Letters* – for example, Jesuit confessors excused duelling; but on others he would sympathise with the Jesuits – for example, their judgement that for a girl to choose her own husband against her parents' will is no sin. He will also set against the laxism of some Jesuits the heroism of others who risked and often lost their lives to preach the gospel to the indigenous populations of India, China and North America – all because they were convinced that it was the best, and perhaps only way to ensure the salvation of their souls. There was, after all, one thing upon which Jesuit and Jansenist were agreed: the danger that after their death many men and women might go to Hell.

4. HELL TODAY

From the Thirty Years War to World War II

The treaty of Westphalia in 1646 marked the recognition by Catholics and Protestants alike that neither Reformation nor Counter-Reformation would be achieved by force of arms. The formula *cuius regio, eius religio* established that political and religious lines of demarcation would now be the same. Having caused so much suffering in the course of the Thirty Years War, religious zeal itself went out of fashion and opened the way for the scepticism that triumphed philosophically in the French Enlightenment, and politically in the French Revolution. From the high point in the Middle Ages when Popes such as Gregory VII (1073–85) had claimed both temporal and spiritual jurisdiction over the entire world, the Church had been reduced to a state of dependency, first on European monarchs, then on Republican institutions and the post-Republican despot, Napoleon Bonaparte.

The Catholic Church's approach to Liberalism, which was not the Liberalism of Gladstone but anti-clerical and Free Masonic movements in the traditionally Catholic countries of Latin Europe and South America, was adversarial; Pope Pius IX published his *Syllabus of Errors* in 1864 condemning Liberalism and, it might be noted, the proposition, 'We should at least have good hopes for the eternal salvation of those who are in no way in the true Church of Christ.' The Liberal faith in both science and democracy was spurned with the promulgation of the Dogma of Papal Infallibility in 1870. To use a hackneyed but serviceable image, the Catholic Church became a fortress in which the deposit of faith was protected from compromise and contamination behind walls of doctrinal intransigence and tribal exclusivity.

The teaching of the Council of Trent on the eternal torment that awaited those who died unrepentant in mortal sin remained intact and, indeed, was shared by other Christian denominations. John Henry Newman, who converted from Anglicanism to Roman Catholicism, and famously defended the rights of conscience against the more extreme ultramontane claims for the authority of the Pope, brought with him a lively fear of eternal damnation. Geoffrey Faber, in *Oxford Apostles*, described how 'the device of fear' had been the essential element in Newman's Anglican sermons.

> Again and again in his sermons it seems as if he had to force himself to speak of God's love and mercy. The assurance of these is less real to him than the fear of condemnation and wrath. The fact of sin, its heinousness, its inconceivably ghastly consequences in the world to come – it is when he speaks of such topics as these that he speaks most obviously from the heart and with most effect. 'Who is there,' he asked his congregations in 1832, 'but would be sobered by an actual sight of the flames of hell-fire and the souls therein hopelessly enclosed?'[56]

In 1913, some eighty years after Newman preached this sermon, such a sight of souls burning in Hell formed part of the visions of four peasant girls at Fatima in Portugal. In her *Memoirs*, one of these visionaries, Lucia, described how

> we saw, as it were, a vast sea of fire. Plunged in this fire, we saw the demons and the souls [of the damned]. The latter were like transparent burning embers, all blackened or burnished bronze, having human forms. They were floating about in that conflagration, now raised into the air by the flames which issued from within themselves, together with great clouds of smoke. Now

they fell back on every side like sparks in huge fires, without weight or equilibrium, amid shrieks and groans of pain and despair, which horrified us and made us tremble with fright . . .

Catholics are not obliged to believe in the apparitions of the Virgin Mary at Fatima but they were deemed genuine by Pope John Paul II. He had a particular devotion to Our Lady of Fatima and believed that it was thanks to her intercession that the bullet fired by the Turkish assassin, Ali Agca, did not kill him: extracted from his body, the Pope sent it to be set in the crown of the statue of the Virgin at the shrine.

In more recent apparitions in other parts of Europe, the Virgin Mary has confirmed to the visionaries that there are souls in Hell. 'Today', she told Mirjana Dragicevic at Medjugorje in Bosnia-Herzegovina, 'most people go to purgatory, the next greatest number go to Hell, and only a few go to Heaven.' 'Souls who go to Hell have ceased thinking favourably of God – have cursed Him, more and more. So they've already become part of Hell, and choose not to be delivered from it.' Being a Catholic was no guarantee of salvation. 'Many cardinals, many bishops, and many priests are on the road to perdition,' the Virgin told the visionaries at Garabandal in northern Spain in the 1960s, 'and are taking many souls with them.'

The authenticity of these apparitions by the Mother of God is not part of the teaching of the Catholic Church, and there are many devout Catholics who treat them with a measure of scepticism. What is beyond dispute, however, is that the prediction by Our Lady of Fatima in 1913 that a terrible fate awaited an unrepentant humanity turned out to be true. Over the next few decades, in the trenches of eastern France, in the Bolshevik gulags, on the plains of Armenia, in the cities of China, in Hiroshima and above all in the Nazi death camps, humankind created a vivid image of Hell for all to see.

Vatican II

Was it, perhaps, the experience of such atrocity in this world that led Christians to lose interest in what awaited them in the next? Was there, indeed, a worry among Christians that their very preoccupation with a spiritual world to come had distracted them from the temporal battle between good and evil during World War II? Certainly the decline in Catholics' anxiety about damnation came in the decade which followed the Second Vatican Council (1963–65). Because Vatican II was a *pastoral* and not a *dogmatic* Council, no radical changes were made to the Church's Magisterium: as a Protestant observer, Dr Edward Norman, noted, 'its reformulations of faith were, in the event, surprisingly unitary and conservative'.[57] However, there was a change of emphasis from individual virtue and sin and that individual's consequent condition after death to a collective salvation through the permeation of the world with Christian values. Particularly in the Pastoral Constitution on the Church in the Modern World, *Gaudium et Spes*, we see the world no longer as the principality of the Devil, and mortal life no longer a 'vale of tears'. The dire effects of Original Sin could now be mitigated by an effective drive for social justice. 'Ours is a new age of history' with an enormous potential for both good and bad: a 'generation of new men, the moulders of a new humanity' would transform the world.[58]

This was not just a far cry from the pessimism of a Bernard of Clairvaux or Blaise Pascal; it also gave a different meaning to the word 'world', changing it from something pejorative as in 'worldly' or 'the world, the flesh and the devil' into something essentially good. The eternity of the individual's afterlife seemed now to be subsumed into the destiny of the human race: Catholics, like Communists, now believed in 'progress' in this world and seemed to lose interest in what might await us in the next.

There was nothing in the decrees of the Council to suggest that the Church had changed its mind about an afterlife, but they were perhaps implicit in some of the ideas that were, or were said to be, embedded in its decrees. *The sovereignty of the individual conscience* (a teaching that, it is sometimes forgotten, predates Vatican II[59]) appeared to permit Catholics to pick and choose from the Church's Magisterium; and, in many cases, disregard the Magisterium altogether in favour of their own private judgement on what was right and wrong. *Conciliarism* suggested a democracy of 'the People of God' and, since there can be no democracy without debate and no debate without diversity of opinion, it followed that a Catholic might hold hitherto unorthodox opinions and yet still consider himself in good standing with the Church.

Then there was *Liberationism.* A 'hunger and thirst for justice' in this world – the 'preferential option for the poor' – led many conscientious Catholics to seek to build Heaven on earth. Like Marx, the Liberationists saw the promise of recompense or punishment in an afterlife as 'the opium' that had led the oppressed to accept their fate. A focus on justice in this world, and a complete neglect of the very idea of a world to come, is found in the textbooks approved for catechesis in Catholic schools such as *Weaving the Web.*

The *Ecumenical movement* also had its effect on Catholic attitudes towards Hell. To further the cause of Christian unity, it was thought proper for Catholic priests and bishops to emphasise what the Christian religions had in common and play down the differences. It was not unusual to find Catholic priests who regarded not just Anglican orders as valid but Methodist orders as well and this, as the historian Eamon Duffy has observed, led to 'the dissolution of inherited Catholic certainties'. Roman Catholicism was no longer the *spes unica* – its Eucharist no longer the only true Body and Blood of Christ; its Absolution in the sacrament of Reconciliation no longer the only sure way to avoid damnation. Catholics were told that all that had changed as a result of Vatican II.

> The surest way of damning and dismissing any idea, institution or emphasis in those years was to say that it was 'pre-Conciliar', as if the Council had invented the Gospel, and as if the test of Christian authenticity was radical discontinuity with the Christian past. Of course, much that was then discarded was indeed worthless or

tacky, and much that posed as 'traditional' was in fact
the product of the quite recent past. It is now possible
to see, however, just how wholesale and indiscriminate
this communal repudiation of the past was, and in a
Church which claims to set a high theological value on
tradition and continuity, this is a mystery which needs
explanation.[60]

The Catechism of the Catholic Church

Such was the confusion caused by this 'wholesale and in-
discriminate' repudiation of traditional beliefs that Pope
John Paul II commissioned a new Vatican II catechism
which would replace that of the Council of Trent. This was
published in 1994 as the *Catechism of the Catholic Church*.
Progressive Catholics were dismayed and traditional
Catholics reassured to find in it a reaffirmation of the
Church's pre-Conciliar beliefs – in angels and devils, in
Heaven and Hell. 'The teaching of the Church affirms the
existence of hell and its eternity. Immediately after death
the souls of those who die in a state of mortal sin descend
into hell, where they suffer the punishments of hell,
"eternal fire".'[61] The *Catechism* talks of mortal sin and venial
sins. It states that 'the Sunday Eucharist is the foundation
and confirmation of all Christian practice. For this reason
the faithful are obliged to participate in the Eucharist on
days of obligation . . . Those who deliberately fail in this
obligation commit a grave sin.'

The *Catechism of the Catholic Church* was intended to put an
end to the arguments that had gone on since the end of
Vatican II about what Catholics now believed. However, as
the Cambridge academic John Casey wrote in the *Sunday
Telegraph* on 29 May 1994, there was a sense of detachment
in the manner in which some traditional teachings were
presented.

The new catechism leaves you with the curious impression that modern Catholics may give 'real' assent to different things that moved their forebears. The angels and
devils, miracles, our First Parents – they are all there in

this splendidly orthodox document. There is no trim-
ming of the supernatural element in Christianity . . .

Yet the supernatural seems to have less imaginative
reality in this catechism than it does in Trent . . . Take
the catechism's teaching about the next life. It is the
same in all essentials as what you find in the Catechism
of the Council of Trent – which was written to combat
the 'errors' of Protestants. Everyone who believes in the
resurrection of the body must be quite curious about
what it would be like. Trent confidently satisfied this
curiosity: 'The bodies of the risen Saints will be beyond
the reach of suffering . . . Neither the piercing severity
of cold, nor the glowing intensity of heat, nor the
impetuosity of waters can hurt them . . . they shall shine
like the sun.' There is nothing so pithy or vivid in the
new version. Nor has Hell quite retained its terrors. It
is there all right, but we are not invited to dwell on its
tortures as we are in Trent.[62]

Rather, wrote Casey, 'you feel that the elaborate discussions of sexual and family morality and social justice are
closest to the hearts of the authors . . . these are the equiva-
lents of the bitter disputes in the 16th century about grace,
free will and predestination.' Missing Mass on a Sunday, sexual relations outside marriage, the use of artificial means of
contraception were all still serious sins; and the *Catechism*
repeated the Church's traditional teaching that those who
died in a state of serious sin would be damned; but there
was no sense of urgency – no impression, from the tone in
which it was written, that its authors were worried that the
Catholic girl on the pill who only went to Mass at Christmas
and Easter, and came up to take Communion straight from
the bed of her boyfriend, was in grave danger of eternal
torment in Hell.

Has the Church changed its mind?

The suspicion therefore arises in the mind of the Catholic
layman that somewhere, buried deep in the impenetrable
mass of modern theological writing – in the heavy tomes of

an Yves-Marie Congar or a Karl Rahner – is a complex exegesis that proves that Jesus did not mean what he said. Is it possible that the Church has changed its mind about Hell? Is it possible that it has changed its mind but cannot say so because to disown a belief that conforms so explicitly to the sayings of Jesus in the Gospels, and through its universal acceptance has the qualities of infallibility, would be to undermine the authority of the Church's Magisterium?

The idea that all men will ultimately be saved – universalism – is not new. It was, as we have seen, put forward by some of the early Church fathers such as St Clement of Alexandria, St Gregory of Nyssa, and above all Origen – only to be condemned by a local Church Council held in Constantinople in 543. It remained quiescent until the middle of the twentieth century when it reappeared in a 'conjectural essay' by the French philosopher Jacques Maritain; and later the weighty German Jesuit theologian Karl Rahner suggested that the words ascribed to Jesus in the Gospels on the subject of damnation and eternal torment were admonitory rather than prescriptive like the threats that parents sometimes make to their children but never intend to carry out. Rahner held that it was possible to believe, and therefore to hope, that all might be saved.

The most significant figure in the camp of the universalists, however, was a theologian held in high esteem by Pope John Paul II, Hans Urs von Balthasar. In a book entitled *Dare We Hope That All Men be Saved?* he suggests that we may hope – even that we *should* hope – that all will be saved. He refers to the writing of Edith Stein, the Carmelite nun killed in Auschwitz – and recently canonised as St Teresa Benedicta of the Cross – who postulated that God's love is so overwhelming that it finds a way to overcome the resistance of even the most obdurate sinner.

The American Jesuit theologian Avery Cardinal Dulles, in a lecture delivered at Fordham University on 20 November 2002,[63] suggests an influence of Balthasar's view on Pope John Paul II. In his own book, *Crossing the Threshold of Hope*, the pontiff wrote that it was unlikely that God's infinite justice could allow terrible crimes to go unpunished, and so final punishment 'would seem to be necessary to reestablish the moral equilibrium in the complex history of humanity': but, in a General Audience talk of 28 July 1999, he appeared to have shifted his position. '"Eternal damnation remains a possibility, but we are not granted without special divine revelation, the knowledge of *whether* or *which* human beings are effectively involved in it". This seemed to suggest that we are entitled to believe that there are none and therefore that the Pope has changed his mind.'

As Cardinal Dulles reported in his lecture, Balthasar's theory came under attack from other theologians: one wrote that it 'removes all effectiveness from the warnings issued by Jesus, repeatedly expressed in the Gospels'; another that his theory was 'tantamount to a rejection of the doctrine of hell and a denial of man's free will'; a third that von Balthasar was a covert relativist who 'smuggles into the heart of the Catholic a serious doubt about the truth of the Catholic faith'. The controversy continued in the pages of the American journal of religious opinion, *First Things.*

Cardinal Dulles' own conclusion is that there *has* been a shift in Catholic theology on the question of Hell. The Church no longer teaches that 'outside the Church there is no salvation' except in the sense that the Church is the community of the living and the dead so that anyone saved is by definition within the Church. He also thinks it right that Catholic apologists no longer dwell on the torments of Hell, fostering an image of God 'as an unloving and cruel tyrant'.

However, he writes that 'today a kind of thoughtless optimism is the more prevalent error. Quite apart from what theologians teach, popular piety has become saccharine. Unable to grasp the rationale for eternal punishment, many Christians take it for granted that everyone, or practically everyone, must be saved.' Dulles believes that people should be told that they ought to fear God who, as Jesus taught, 'can punish soul and body together in hell'.

Who goes to Hell?

One of the chief obstacles in accepting the reality of Hell is the difficulty in knowing who might go there. Certainly, no one would want to usurp the role of Christ as the Judge of the Living and the Dead; we judge not that we be not judged: but for the doctrine to be coherent, there must be some idea of what sins merit damnation.

The criteria for 'mortal' sin put forward by the old catechism now seem unsatisfactory. These were:

1. The thing that is thought of or said or done must be something very serious . . .
2. You must know quite well that it is a serious sin at the time of committing it, and that if you do it, and die with that sin on your soul, you will go to Hell.
3. You must do it deliberately – that is, you must be free to do it or not as you like. Therefore a grievous matter, full knowledge, and full consent are necessary to make a sin mortal.

This seems to suggest that only bad Catholics who die unrepentant go to Hell. The parable of the Prodigal Son, or of the Labourers in the Vineyard, are consoling for those of us who never seem to surmount our failings but they mean that those who have led blameless lives must be prepared, after death, to find Myra Hindley lying in the bosom of Abraham.

More problematic is the man or woman – the majority of the human race – who does *not* believe in God, let alone that Christ was the Son of God, and therefore has no reason to accept the teaching of the Catholic Church. He either makes his own morality or adopts an alternative morality based upon some secular ideology. He does not share the Catholic's view of what is sinful and therefore does not fulfil the criteria for a mortal sin. This means, arguing *ad absurdum*, that the Catholic who dies unrepentant after deliberately choosing to miss Mass on a Sunday will be damned while a sincere National Socialist such as Klaus Schilling who performed medical experiments on the inmates of concentration camps would end up in paradise.[64]

History shows us over and over again that our sense of right and wrong can be distorted by false reasoning as well as self-interest. It is also a common human failing to make excuses for oneself while projecting evil onto alien cultures, different periods of history or impersonal political systems ('structural sin'); and at the same time making further excuses for the besetting sins of one's own culture and times. Today we are horrified by the idea of slavery but St Peter Claver, the Jesuit who in the seventeenth century devoted his life to the care of slaves in the Americas, never spoke against the institution as such.

Yet it has always been taught by the Church that some deeds are 'intrinsically evil', the term used to describe the use of artificial means of contraception by Pope Paul VI in his Encyclical *Humanae Vitae.* Is it possible that some thoughts and deeds poison the soul whether or not they offend our conscience as St Catherine of Siena suggests in her vision of married couples suffering in Hell? Is it possible that the doctor who performs an abortion or the scientist who experiments on a live embryo does something as 'evil' in the eyes of God as Klaus Schilling, the medical researcher at Dachau? And that all those who are implicated in such sins – the woman who asks for an abortion, the legislator who permits experiments on embryos – are also culpable? And, if it is better to pluck out one's eye than look lustfully on a woman, what of the voyeurism of the modern movie-goer or the exhibitionism of the Hollywood actress; or the complicity of those who enjoy the sexual amorality portrayed in TV series such as *Frasier, Friends* or *Sex and the City?*

Two developments, I would suggest, have distorted the consciences of many Catholics today and so put them at risk in the world to come. The first is *humanism;* the second *anthropomorphism.*

Few now are able to conceive of a sin that does not in some way injure another human being. Presenting the Christian ethic in a humanistic light may make it more intelligible and attractive to the modern sceptic but it distorts the teaching of the gospel. All the commandments may be contained in 'You must love your neighbour as yourself', as Jesus says in Mark 12:29–30 – but *before* the commandment to love your neighbour comes '"the first of all the commandments" . . . "you must love the Lord your God with all your heart, with all your soul, with all your mind and with all your strength"'. The first three of the Ten Commandments are about our relations with God, not our fellow man.

But who is God? What is he like? What does he expect of us? I suspect that, just as humanism has infected Christian ethics, so *anthropomorphism* is found in the idea we have formed of God which leads to that 'thoughtless optimism' and saccharine piety described by Cardinal Dulles. Our God may not be a Golden Calf but he often resembles a Disneyesque Father Christmas. Revelation describes some of God's qualities: he is loving, he is merciful, he is just and he has made us in his image and likeness. We accept from Thomas Aquinas that reason is the divine faculty that distinguishes man from beast and we therefore deduce that he is a reasonable fellow. We feel we can know him as we might know our natural father, and equate his sense of right and wrong with our own. Thus, while it might seem reasonable for God to mete out some severe punishment to genocidal murderers and Islamic terrorists, it seems unlikely that he would take a stern view of sex before marriage or using the pill or having an abortion; and utterly disproportionate to condemn anyone – perhaps even mass murderers – to *eternal* torment.

Is this confidence in God's indulgence justified? The present Catholic chaplain to Cambridge University, Fr Alban McCoy, points out in his *An Intelligent Person's Guide to Catholicism*,[65] that it is a mistake to think that God

> can be understood and judged and spoken of in the same way as any object within our experience . . . this is to fall into anthropomorphism. The notion of evaluating what God does or is, is unintelligible. God does what he does and is what he is. Against what set of expectations would we measure the source of all expectations? God transcends any reason for acting, other

than himself. What he is *is* his reason for acting as he does. And this is precisely what we cannot know.[66]

For this reason the optimism of today's lax Catholic, not just about his own ultimate destiny but also that of his non-Catholic friends, may be misplaced. 'Is it for you to question me about my children and to dictate to me what my hands should do?' (Isaiah 45:11). We already recognise that there are aspects of Christian revelation that are incomprehensible, among them the central mystery of the Christian religion – why could mankind only be redeemed through the atrocious suffering of the Son of God? It is therefore unreasonable and inconsistent for us to feel so confident, after such clear warnings from Christ himself, and subsequently from the Church's Magisterium, that no one will go to Hell. To paraphrase Pascal's most famous dictum: God may have his reasons which our reason cannot comprehend.

Does this mean that many of us are at greater risk of damnation than we might suppose? Many priests, I suspect, are reluctant to suggest this – browbeaten by the vocal Catholics, some prominent in the media, who claim that they were traumatised in their youth by the fear of Hell. The sins they now disavow are invariably sins against the Church's sexual mores:[67] and few priests now dare to claim, as did St Francis of Sales, that it is chastity that is 'the lily of virtues and makes men almost equal to the angels'.[68]

However, to minimise or disregard altogether the danger of damnation is surely a grave matter for the Catholic priest and layman alike. 'If I say to a wicked man, You are to die,' says the Lord in Ezekiel 3:18, 'and you do not warn him; if you do not speak and warn him to renounce his evil ways, and so live, then he shall die for his sin; but I will hold you responsible for his death.' 'When St Augustine read from the prophet Ezekiel,' wrote his biographer Peter Brown, 'that "A watchman is absolved if he gives the cry of danger", he would have rent his clothes in front of his congregation.'[69]

Conclusion

There is a danger, it seems to me, that the shift among Catholics from a preoccupation with eternity to an engagement in the world has now gone so far that it effaces the very idea of an afterlife and so distorts the teaching of the gospel and endangers the coherence of the Christian religion. I would also suggest that neglect of the Four Last Things is one of the causes for the relative decline of the fortunes of the Catholic Church in the developed world.

In Britain, as in other European nations, there is now a critical scarcity of priests and seminarians and few conversions to the Catholic faith. Many nominal Catholics have ceased to practise their religion: it is estimated that between 1990 and 2005, half a million Catholics in Britain stopped going to Mass. The 'decade of evangelisation' that began with such optimism in 1990 failed in its purpose, and contrasts with extraordinary growth and confidence of the Roman Catholic community in England in other periods, most recently in the 1950s when it was, as Eamon Duffy put it, 'on the crest of a wave of self-confidence and success'.[70] And, though a comparable decline is found in other mainstream Christian denominations such as the Free Churches and the Church of England, some smaller denominations such as the Evangelical, Pentecostal and Orthodox Churches, which do not hesitate to talk of damnation, have grown in size.

This is not to condemn Vatican II. It is indisputable that Christians should be the leaven in the dough and the light of the world; that they should be judged by the fruits of their good works; and that Christians should work for the unity of their churches. There is no doubt, too, that virtue is its own reward: sanctity brings serenity and a measure of invulnerability from the vicissitudes of life in this world.

But the message proclaimed by the gospel is not principally one of social betterment, or an effective therapy for the individual: there are other groups that offer psychological balms and work for the common good. Any attempt at evangelisation will fail if it ignores man's anxiety about what awaits him after his death. The contemporary Catholic should recognise that, not just among the impoverished and oppressed in the Third World, but in the developed nations of the First World too, there are men and women who are so lowered by poverty, illness, anxiety or depression that they see little reason to thank God for a life that will in all probability end in agony and degradation. Life, as we pray in the *Salve Regina*, is 'a vale of tears'. 'There is no true and solid satisfaction to be had in this world,' wrote Pascal. 'The mass of men lead lives of quiet desperation,' wrote Thoreau in *Walden*. 'Life is hard and then you die,' says the hero of William Nicholson's novel *The Society of Others*.

Not only does the neglect of the Church's teaching on Hell remove any meaning from the word 'salvation' and make nonsense of our prayer in the Mass, 'save us from final damnation', it also removes the most conclusive argument for loving God – the promise of the heavenly banquet that awaits the just. The modern Catholic must rediscover the truth at the heart of his Faith – that there *is* an afterlife, a world to come, a Heaven and a Hell; and that, in the words of the Fathers of Vatican II, 'it is through Christ's Catholic church alone, which is the universal help towards salvation, that the fullness of salvation can be obtained'.[71]

NOTES

1. Blaise Pascal, *Pensées*, translated by Martin Turnell (Harvill Press, 1962), p. 103.
2. Ronald Knox, *The Belief of Catholics* (Sheed & Ward, 1927), p. 205.
3. Bernard Shaw, *Androcles and the Lion*. Preface on the Prospects of Christianity, p. ciii.
4. See *The Formation of Hell* by Alan E. Bernstein (UCL Press, 1993), p. 61.
5. *ibid.*, p. 165.
6. Daniel 12:2 (RSV).
7. Bernstein, *The Formation of Hell*, p. 200.
8. Matthew 3:11–12.
9. Matthew 13:38–43.
10. Matthew 13:48–50.
11. Matthew 18:34.
12. Matthew 22:11–14.
13. Matthew 25:30.
14. Matthew 25:41–6.
15. Matthew 5:22.

16. Matthew 5:27–30.

17. Luke 6:24–5.

18. Luke 16:19–21.

19. Mark 9:48.

20. Mark 16:16.

21. Matthew 7:13.

22. Matthew 22:14.

23. Bernstein, *The Formation of Hell*, p. 225.

24. *ibid.*, p. 207.

25. Romans 1:18; 2:6, 8–11.

26. 1 Timothy 6:17–18.

27. Philippians 3:12, 14.

28. Bernstein, *The Formation of Hell*, p. 225.

29. John 3:5.

30. John 6:51–3.

31. *The Catholic Dictionary* (Routledge & Kegan Paul, 1951), p. 390.

32. Peter Brown, *Augustine of Hippo* (Faber, 1967), p. 196.

33. Quoted in *ibid.*, p. 307.

34. Leszek Kolakowski, *God Owes Us Nothing. A Brief Remark on Pascal's Religion and on the Spirit of Jansenism* (The University of Chicago Press, 1995), p. 33.

35. Brown, *Augustine of Hippo*, p. 331.

36. *ibid.*, p. 348.

37. *ibid.*, p. 388.

38. See *The Church Teaches. Documents of the Church in English Translation* (p. 345).

39. *Summa Theologiae, A Concise Translation*, edited by Timothy McDermott (Eyre and Spottiswoode, 1989), p. 342.

40. *ibid.*, p. 272.

41. *ibid.*, p. 275.

42. *Thomas à Kempis: The Imitation of Christ*, translated and with an Introduction by Leo Sherley-Price (Penguin, 1952), p. 11.

43. *ibid.*, p. 81.

44. *ibid.*, p. 61.

45. The words of the cantata come from a hymn by Johann Rist (1606–67):

> Eternity, you make me anxious,
> Endless, endless is too long!
> Ah, for sure, this is no sport.
> Flames which are forever burning
> Are all fires past comparing;
> It alarms and shakes my heart
> When I consider the pain
> And my thoughts lead to hell.

46. *The Saints. A Concise Biographical Dictionary*, edited by John Coulson, with an Introduction by C.C. Martindale sj (Guild Press, 1957), p. 304.

47. *Introduction to the Devout Life,* p. 208.
48. *ibid.,* p. 211.
49. *ibid.,* p. 228.
50. *ibid.,* p. 158.
51. Pascal, *Pensées.*
52. *ibid.,* p. 103.
53. *ibid.,* p. 149.
54. *ibid.,* p. 382.
55. Kolakowski, *God Owes Us Nothing,* p. 57.
56. Geoffrey Faber, *Oxford Apostles* (1974), p. 171.
57. Quoted in *Modern Catholicism. Vatican II and After,* edited by Adrian Hastings (SPCK, 1991), p. 349.
58. *Gaudium et Spes,* 30.
59. See Karl Adam, *The Spirit of Catholicism* (1924). 'The Catholic in his moral life has only one subjective law, and that is his conscience. So that if a divine ordinance be not plain and evident to his conscience, or if he be in a state of invincible error, then the Catholic is not bound by the objective law', p. 195.
60. Eamon Duffy, 'The Catholic Church on the Eve of the Millennium', talk given on Wednesday 27 October 1999 to the International Conference on Benedictine Education. Published on the Internet.
61. *Catechism of the Catholic Church,* para. 1035, p. 236.
62. *The Sunday Telegraph,* 29 May 1994.
63. Adapted and published in *First Things,* May 2003.
64. Klaus Schilling, a bacteriologist, was executed for performing experiments on human beings at Dachau: he was a highly cultivated man with a particular feeling for the paintings of Giorgione.
65. Continuum, 2001. 'The topics covered,' writes Fr McCoy, 'reflect the kinds of questions which . . . intelligent and informed enquirers . . . most frequently ask about Catholicism at the present time'. He does not treat the question of Hell.
66. Alban McCoy, *An Intelligent Person's Guide to Catholicism* (Continuum, 2005).
67. A parish priest assured the daughter of a neighbour that sleeping with her boyfriend was no sin because 'Jesus had said nothing about it'. A homosexual acquaintance told me that he had been assured by two confessors that having sex with his male lover was no sin.
68. *The Saints. A Concise Biographical Dictionary.*
69. Brown, *Augustine of Hippo,* p. 207.
70. Duffy, 'The Catholic Church on the Eve of the Millennium'.
71. Vatican II, *Redintegratio,* Decree on Ecumenism, para. 3, p. 456.

2

Upon this Rock

First published in *Why I am Still a Catholic*,
edited by Robert Nowell (Collins, 1982)

IN TWENTY YEARS OF ADULT life I have never for a
moment doubted either the teachings or the disciplines of
the Catholic Church.

The historical reasons for my Catholicism are these. In
1933 my mother, Margaret Ludwig, then a professional
musician and lecturer in music at Edinburgh University, was
converted to the Roman Catholic faith. Some months after
she had been received into the Church she fell in love with
my father, Herbert Read, who was professor of fine art at the
same university. He was married with a ten-year-old son.

They ran off to London, and after my father's divorce
were married in a registry office. My mother bore four children of whom I was the third. Her respect for my father's
intelligence was reverential – she had German blood in her
veins – but never for a moment was she inclined to adopt his
agnosticism. Her faith was stronger than his reason, and
almost as if to propitiate the God whom she had offended
by her adulterous liaison, she brought us all up in the religion which denied her its sacraments and condemned her
to Hell-fire.

I myself was baptised at the church of St Teresa in
Beaconsfield when exactly nine months old. I was taught
the rudiments of religion by my mother, and at the age
of eight was sent to be educated by Benedictine monks.

Faith preceded reason in my mind and has preserved its precedence ever since.

This faith developed not because of my upbringing but despite it. I disliked Gilling and Ampleforth, where I went to school, for what still seem to be quite proper reasons. Family life should be the basis of a Christian upbringing, and boarding schools undermine it. Moreover the public school values which the monks were so eager to instil into their pupils were less Christian than pagan Greek. There were among the monks both good and intelligent men, but they were all tainted by that pervasive snobbery which is so frequently found among English Catholics. At fifteen I schemed to leave Ampleforth, and might have left the Church as well had it not been for a secular priest, Michael Hollings, who came to Ampleforth to give a retreat and told me to distinguish between the school and the religion.

I also rebelled in adolescence against most of the values of my fervent, strong-willed mother and should by rights have gone over to the agnostic humanism of my father, whom I not only loved but admired. 'How can anyone,' he wrote, 'with a knowledge of the comparative history of religions retain an exclusive belief in the tenets of any particular sect?' He had that knowledge, and gently mocked the monks I had come to despise, but never for a moment was I tempted to adopt his scepticism and abandon my Catholic beliefs. The very remoteness and serenity of his paternal love made it easier to conceive of God the Father.

Even at sixteen, when I left school, my faith was neither naïve nor blind. It had given me such a taste for philosophical enquiry that when I went up to Cambridge I applied to read moral sciences rather than history to refine and deepen my beliefs.

The faculty of moral sciences at the end of the 1950s was in the hands of the most austere and pedantic of linguistic philosophers. They were agnostic not just about the existence of God but about the existence of the table upon which they laid their notes. For some months I persevered in the course of studies they offered, hoping that we might progress from the proofs of the table's existence to something more substantial. We did not. I suspected, though without the confidence to be sure, that the attempt to make mathematics out of language was futile and the corollary – that if this cannot be done then nothing can be known – bogus. After a couple of months we were still unable to prove to ourselves that the table was not a hallucination, so I abandoned moral sciences for history and pursued my philosophical curiosity alone.

My faith seemed to present me with two things – the first the phenomenon of faith itself, an autonomous method of knowing just as sure as the evidence of my senses or the inference of my reason. Christ the Son of God was a real person with whom I conversed in prayer and joined through the Eucharist.

The second was the more extensive Judaeo-Christian hypothesis concerning God and man. In brief this held that everything is created by a perpetual being whose salient characteristic is love. If he did not love then nothing would exist but he is, as it were, lonely and needs other beings to receive and return his love.

Love by its nature must be voluntarily given so these beings must be demi-gods who are free to reject him. Like the prince who disguises himself as a pauper to find a girl who will love him for himself, God hides his omnipotence from those he has created. Free will is necessary to make them worthy companions.

First Lucifer and then Adam, under the influence of Lucifer, choose to do wrong. The archetypal man is flawed: the whole race is damned. Whatever the precise nature of the original sin, 'the human race is implicated in some terrible, aboriginal calamity' (Newman) which reduces us to the status of beasts.

God's love, however, persists and looks for a way to exculpate the sinner. What can propitiate God? Who can win him round? Nothing but an aspect of himself – his own love embodied in a son who to reinstate his father's affection must take on human form and be sacrificed like a ram.

There must be some merit in man – some glimmer of faith, some sign that at least one among the many has faith enough to rise above his animal nature and do for God what

God must do for man. In obedience to God, Abraham pre-
pares to sacrifice his son. That is enough. His progeny, the
Jews, are chosen to preserve faith in a single God throughout the pagan prehistory of man until a sinless woman – an
immaculate Mary – becomes the acceptable repository for
God made flesh.

Christ is born; preaches; gives ample evidence of his
supernatural powers and a clear, unambiguous account of
what men and women must do to shed their fallen natures
and become, once again, the demi-gods of God's original
creation. Before rising to Heaven Christ founds a Church.
He appoints leaders with authority to teach, judge and
enact the everyday miracle of turning bread into his body
and wine into his blood. To one of these leaders – the weak,
impulsive but faithful Peter – he delegates his own authority. When Peter is crucified this authority is passed on to a
successor, and so on until the Pope of the present day.

How can one prove or disprove such a hypothesis? The
supernatural like the aesthetic is not susceptible to scientific
tests; indeed any incontrovertible proof would contradict
the demands of free will. The only test is to measure it
against one's own experience of life. 'For a religion to be
true,' wrote Pascal, 'it must have understood our nature. It
must have grasped its littleness and its greatness; and the
reason for both.' For a novelist in particular it would be
impossible to sustain a view of man which contradicted what
he observed in himself or his fellow human beings.

In studying the human personality in this respect one is
faced with the phenomenon of conscience. Just as an aesthetic sensibility tells us that there is beauty, so a moral sensibility makes us aware of good – not a relative, subjective or
conditioned good but an absolute good for all men at all
times. 'As we have our initial knowledge of the universe
through sense,' wrote Newman, 'so do we in the first
instance begin to learn about its Lord and God from
conscience.'

If we infer that this sense of right and wrong, implanted
in human chromosomes by something superhuman, points
to the existence of a Creator; if we surmise like Newman

'that there is a God who cares about what we do, then it is reasonable to suppose that he will try to communicate with us further'. It is also reasonable to suppose that he will communicate with man in a way man can understand – viz. through language. 'I, Yahweh, speak with directness – I express myself with clarity.'

Now because I have always believed in Christ my knowledge of the sacred texts of other religions – the Upanishads, the Koran, the Book of Mormon – does not equal my familiarity with the Bible: but I have read enough to contradict with some confidence my own father's contention about different religions. The combination of the Old Testament and the New Testament makes the Bible unique. The historicity of Christ together with his character, the subtlety of his teachings and the audacity of his claims are not equalled in the writing of any other religion. If the Gospels were works of fiction then, as Rousseau said, 'l'inventeur en serait plus étonnant que les héros'.

Knowing from the experience of a moral sensibility that there is a God, and believing from a reading of the Gospels that Jesus Christ is the Son of that God, it is nonetheless possible to reject the particular claims of the Roman Catholic Church. There are, indeed, some contemporary Catholics who appear to regard it as of little importance whether a Christian is a Catholic or not.

It is hard to see how this can be so. If Christ made promises to St Peter and St Peter's successors, and endowed them with certain supernatural powers, it would suggest that Christ thought them necessary or at least useful for salvation. Without authority from above, it is hard to know what is true. The human mind is always self-interested and fickle, and it is only to be expected that those Christian Churches which are separated from Rome are seen to be built on shifting sand.

The ecumenical spirit requires that we should be civil to members of other Christian denominations, but our desire for unity must not lead us to accept the lowest common denominator of Christian faith. We cannot proceed upon a pretence that Catholic teachings can be abandoned to accommodate the Protestant conscience. It is difficult, anyway, to identify the Protestant conscience since Protestants appear now to be heretics from habit rather than from conviction. It is hard to find one who believes in predestination, or will say which of Luther's ninety-five theses can be applied to the contemporary Catholic Church. It is hard, too, to find an Anglican to explain how the spirit of God worked through the political compromises in the reign of Elizabeth I; or why a Church governed by a Head of State should seem any less blasphemous and absurd to us now than it did to Thomas More in the sixteenth century.

The only faith other than Catholicism which has ever attracted me was Marxism. As a young man it seemed to me to pursue the concept of charity with an efficacy and vigour which was not evident among Christian societies.

A brief study of history made me realise that, because their paradise must be on this earth, the Marxists pursued it with such savage impatience that most post-revolutionary societies at best resembled Purgatory and at worst Hell.

I also came to realise that Marxism – for all its profession of atheism – depended entirely upon the ethics of Judaism and Christianity and as such was but the last in a series of Christian heresies. Its fundamental premise is that all men are inherently equal and should be treated with justice when in all measurable ways they are patently unequal, and instinctively are as savage as animals in the wild.

The only reason for going against the evidence of one's senses is the word of Christ that we are all equal before God and should treat others as well as we treat ourselves. This Communists mean to do, and in certain places and certain times they have undoubtedly improved the material and cultural condition of men; but their materialistic atheism leads them to poison the soul as they fill the stomach and deprives them of any moral constraints. The end justifies the means and the end is put in a mythic future. To a Christian, as to Camus, the means and the end should be one, for 'what does it profit a man if he gains the whole world and suffers the loss of his soul?'

A more prosaic, rationalist atheism – sometimes called 'humanism' – has never seemed to me to merit serious consideration. 'There are two forms of excess,' says Pascal, 'to exclude reason and to admit nothing but reason.' Rationalists admit nothing but reason yet will not accept what reason itself should tell them – that if there was a being who created man, he would be as incomprehensible to man as man is to an ant. The Christian only suggests that we know something about God because God has chosen to reveal himself. A rationalist may lack faith, but he cannot reasonably deny that a God, if he exists, can provide such a method of knowing.

Pascal invented the computer and dismissed it as a mere bagatelle in comparison to the mysteries of religion. The Victorians developed the steam engine and it went to their head. Faith like superstition seemed an insult to human intelligence and the scientific spirit of the age. Yet few of them had the courage of Nietzsche to throw out Christian ethics with Christian belief. While proudly asserting their moral self-sufficiency, they lived off the capital of Christianity. Despite modern adherents like A. J. Ayer, this positive atheism of a Marx or a Bertrand Russell now seems somewhat old-fashioned and is rarely to be found.

What has replaced it is a vast agnosticism – not the honest doubt of those who have searched but have not found, but the spiritual indifference of those described by Newman as 'too well inclined to sit at home, instead of stirring themselves to inquire whether a revelation has been given.'

This indifference is perhaps the most unreasonable position of all, 'since it is clear beyond doubt that this life only lasts for a moment, that the state of death is eternal whatever its nature, and therefore that all our actions and thoughts must follow very different paths according to the nature of this eternity' (Pascal).

It is clear, too, that even an agnostic must lead his life according to some system of values – if only for his self-esteem. Most are content to conform to the ethical consensus as reflected in the law of the land; but this has now retreated from its Christian foundations to a kind of benign welfarism which is philosophically absurd. Political pressures lie behind the making of laws in Parliament which are as unlikely to arrive at moral truths as aesthetic ones.

It would be difficult to point to any one moral philosopher whose principles inspire the civic conscience. There is some Marx, some Mill, some Burke and some Bentham. Perhaps the most plausible description of the way people decide what is right and wrong can be found in Adam Smith's *The Theory of Moral Sentiments*. To him morality is based upon sympathy: it is wrong to do to others what one would not want done to oneself.

At first sight such a basis seems reasonable enough – close indeed to the injunction of Christ – but there soon arise victims who are sufficiently different from our legislators, their electors and those who help form their opinions to fall outside the scope of their empathy. Thus the citizen *in utero* may own property – may indeed inherit the Crown itself – but has no right to life. It seems now that the deformed child is expendable while the senile and the insane wait in line. The capital of Christianity is spent.

This brings me back to the phenomenon of conscience and the affront to my moral sensibility of certain acts of others – whether or not they offend the law. It is possible, of course, to suggest that a Catholic only feels revulsion at such legal acts as sodomy and abortion because he has been conditioned by the teachings of his religion; but even an atheist who is indifferent to 'sins' such as these should see the dangers inherent in a system where morality is based solely upon adult sympathy. Where there is no sympathy (or empathy), morality does not apply. There were Germans who thought Jews inhuman, and Bolsheviks who thought the bourgeois were without human rights. Once man makes his own morality anything is possible because man is capable of anything.

I have often observed in testing the Catholic hypothesis that those who live quite contentedly without a faith in God are instinctively decent people. My father was such a man. His faith in humanism was based upon his own righteousness and he would not concede that this righteousness in its turn came from his Christian upbringing.

Towards the end of his life, however, he lost confidence in the blithe agnosticism he had expressed when younger and looked increasingly not to God but to those philosophers who had believed in God. 'All my life,' he wrote in an essay called 'The Cult of Sincerity', 'I have found more sustenance in the work of those who bear witness to the reality of a living God than in the work of those who deny God – at least the witness of the deniers, Stirner, Marx, Nietzsche, Freud, Shaw, Russell has been outbalanced by the witness of those who affirm God's existence – George Herbert, Pascal, Traherne, Spinoza, Kierkegaard, Hopkins, Simone Weil. In that state of suspense, "waiting on God", I still live and shall probably die.

'Maybe I have not suffered enough, or been sufficiently conscious of the suffering of others, to need the kind of consolation that a saint such as Simone Weil found in God. Behind every "sincere" belief I detect a special kind of experience which has not come to me.'

In the last years of his life my father suffered very much indeed and perhaps this suffering, at the eleventh hour, led him to God. I myself have never had such 'a special kind of experience' – no dramatic moment of conversion or re-conversion to a faith in God – but I was conscious from quite early in my life of a capacity for evil which by confirming the diabolical made it easier to accept the divine. Novelists, by the nature of their profession, reveal more about themselves than most men; and the facility with which perverse and depraved characters have come to life in my imagination has demonstrated to me my own potential for evil. I am always conscious of the conflict between good and evil within myself; and in the last analysis I believe in God and in the grace of God because I am not what I might be.

Faith today is made easier by the condition of the Catholic Church. How much harder it must have been for Thomas More to remain loyal to Rome in the era of Pope Alexander VI!

Now, for the first time since Constantine, the Church has

disentangled itself from the tentacles of state. No Julien Sorel would today put on the priest's cassock as a cloak for worldly advancement. There is less corruption and more purity of purpose now among the Catholic clergy than at almost any other period in the Church's history.

The very freedom of the Church to pursue its original mission has led to some changes in my life-time. None, I would suggest, are in essentials. The vernacular Mass, communion in both kinds, priests without dog-collars – these are all trivial adjustments when compared to the momentous truths of the religion itself.

There has been a shift of emphasis from prayer and contemplation to good works – a reflection in some areas of the world of the competition for men's souls between Catholics and Communists. There is a less pedantic, legalistic attitude towards sin – more emphasis upon loving than fearing the Lord. Thus the moral behaviour of Catholics may seem less different now to that of those around them. On the other hand those who remain in the Church do not do so for the sake of social conformity but from genuine conviction. With the exception of Ireland and Poland where faith and nationalism mingle together, there are no Catholic countries any more. Nor is there a Catholic culture. There is only Catholic belief.

The contrast between Catholic teaching and the growing moral chaos in the world at large gives a heroic status to the Church's mission and shows the strength of the rock upon which it is built. The only danger is that confidence in the promise of Christ never to abandon his Church leads one to dismiss the threat from the enemies of the Church. Communism may be discredited in its holy cities of Moscow and Peking, but it remains an appealing ideology to the young and the poor. Islam, too, with its simplistic monotheism and the promise of paradise at a bargain price makes headway in many parts of the world; but neither are perhaps as dangerous as the antagonists within.

For convenience one might describe these as antagonists to the left and antagonists to the right. To the right are the fanatics for the Latin Mass – those who reject all the reforms of the Second Vatican Council because they are aesthetically unpleasing.

The Church, certainly, should be proud of its history and tradition; but it is the Word of God and its meaning which is important – not the sound of it when spoken or sung. To me it is clear that the greater comprehension of the Mass, and the greater participation of the congregation which results, justify the vernacular Mass a hundred times over. I would rather hear and understand the Gospel in poor prose spoken with an Irish accent than listen to elegant, archaic and incomprehensible plainchant.

The antagonists to the left are perhaps more insidious because they call themselves 'reformers' and 'progressives', both terms which carry an inherent approbation. They are Protestants in inspiration and like the historic Protestants are commonly found in England, Holland, Germany, Switzerland and North America. They make much of the English concept of 'common sense' and, lacking the imagination to believe in the magical and extraordinary, explain away the supernatural in the Catholic faith with ingenious formulas of obfuscation.

Thus papal infallibility, the real presence of Christ in the Eucharist, the virgin birth, even the resurrection itself are gently laid aside as the improbable exaggerations of a more superstitious age. Like Pascal, 'How I hate all this nonsense, not believing in the Eucharist and that sort of thing. If Christ is God, where is the difficulty?'

Most of their objections seem to stem from the weakness of their faith and their attack is concentrated on the Church's teaching on sexual morality. Many of the issues such as communion for the remarried, the celibacy of the clergy and above all birth control are implicitly a revolt against the Church's traditional mistrust of eros, and their agitation is amplified by their non-Catholic compatriots because more than anything else the Church's strictures on sex defy the indulgent ethic of the age.

It is certainly undeniable that the Church mistrusts the sexual drive in men and women. Apart from the Song of Solomon there is little in either Testament to sanctify or even condone the erotic element in the human personality.

Jesus, Mary and Joseph were all celibate and the Church has always prized virginity. The very use of the word 'purity' for the sex-free soul denigrates the act of copulation.

There have been times when this anti-eroticism of the Church has depressed me. Erotic liaisons combined with tender feelings are not just the staple of the novelist's art: they also seem one of the chief joys of God's creation.

It is therefore with some sorrow that I have come to accept that the Church is right and that novelists are wrong. Art portrays the pleasures of this life, not the next. The whole drift of revealed truth suggests a divine distaste for the erotic. It even seems likely that the aboriginal calamity of original sin was sexual in kind, for why else should Adam and Eve have covered their bodies with fig-leaves? Copulation is undoubtedly man's most animal act. Even as he eats or defecates his mind can be elsewhere, but in copulation body and soul are concentrated in his loins. Orgasm is the surrogate ecstasy peddled by the Devil – an easy pastiche of that mystical state achieved by the most holy saints and ascetics.

This truth about God is hard to accept. We tend to forget that we are made in his image and likeness, not God in ours, and consequently convince ourselves that something so powerful and pleasant must accord with his will. Alas, it is not so, and it would be presumptuous to criticise our Creator for the way things have turned out. 'Is it for you to question me about my children,' asks Yahweh in Isaiah, 'and to dictate to me what my hands should do?' Only in marriage, when sexual intercourse between husband and wife may lead to the propagation of more souls, does God smile on copulation.

The Protestant spirit of the reformers rejects this view which so patently can be gleaned from a reading of Scripture. The idea of predestination still inspires them. If the elect make sterile love with a good conscience, then it cannot be a sin. So also if they leave their wives or husbands and marry other men and women.

I myself have no doubt whatsoever that the Church is right in its teaching on sexual morality – even in its teaching on contraception; and if for twenty years I have not practised what is preached it is from the weakness of the flesh, not the commitment of the spirit. I also console my conscience – and perhaps delude it too – that sterile copulation cannot be such a grave sin if it nurtures the bond between a husband and wife, a father and mother.

This view of God's distaste for sex convinces me too that we should retain if we can a celibate clergy. The celibacy of the priests astonishes the unbeliever and attests to their supernatural vocation. The reasons advanced by the reformers for the marriage of priests are always practical – like pushing memoranda from middle-management in a multinational corporation. Priests, it appears, are leaving the Church to marry, and would-be priests are balking at a life without a wife. Yet even on a practical level the Church would need three times as many priests if they were married, because as any paterfamilias can testify family life makes considerable demands and would not only distract the clergy from their mission but tie them into a particular social class.

It is easy to call for heroism in others while showing little oneself. If I was ever to doubt the Catholic faith it would only be because God's gratuitous gift of faith, together with grace gleaned through the sacraments, has not made me a better man. Like the rich man in the Gospel, I may hope to keep the commandments, but the prospect of selling all I have and giving to the poor fills me with dismay. The grace of God saves me from the extremes of evil: the weakness of the flesh prevents me from doing much good. My gaze is towards Heaven but my feet are firmly stuck on the ground.

3

The Book of God

A review of *The Book of God* by Gabriel
Josipovici (Yale University Press), first published in *The Spectator*, 7 January 1989

For some time i have been curious to know what a perceptive and agnostic critic would make of the Bible when
reading it for the first time. It is not something which could
have been done before the present generation because
everyone was once raised on the stories from Scripture. Now
many graduate from schools and universities knowing nothing whatsoever about the sacred texts of the Jewish and
Christian religions.

The Book of God, although subtitled 'a Response to the
Bible', is not quite what I had in mind because the author,
Gabriel Josipovici, was read the Bible as a child. In all other
respects, however, it exceeds the hopes I had of a book of
this kind. It is erudite yet lucid, impassioned yet impartial,
and filled with insights gained from Josipovici's familiarity
with European literature – with Dante, Proust or Joyce.

Yet while Josipovici is clearly enthralled by the Bible, and
has been affected by his immersion in its texts, he professes
neither a Jewish, Christian, atheist nor agnostic faith. Thus
he comes as close to detachment as is probably possible in
his attempt to decide what kind of book it is.

As a professor of English his first question is naturally
whether the Bible can be considered as literature. 'Should we
think of it,' he asks, 'as ancient Hebrew literature plus some
rather later literature from the Eastern Mediterranean?

Should we, that is, think of it as we would of a book which brought together all that survives of ancient Greek or Mediaeval English literature?' The answer is no. The Bible is much more than that. Even in the first century AD (Josipovici uses the irritating ACE – After the Christian Era?) Josephus reminded his Roman readers that 'it is an instinct with every Jew from the day of his birth to regard [the scriptures] as the decrees of God, to abide by them and, if need be, cheerfully to die for them . . . What Greek would endure as much for the same cause?'

Yet if the Bible is not literature, what is it? Josipovici sets off to find out, equipped not just with his perception as a critic or experience as a novelist, but also with a knowledge of Greek and Hebrew which he acquired for the express purpose of writing this book. He has also read all the Jewish and Christian commentaries as well as the younger scholars like Sternberg and Rosenberg and contemporary literary critics who have tackled the Bible like Frank Kermode. He decides that most of them cannot see the wood for the trees. An example he gives in a full chapter is of 'the man in the field' whom Joseph meets when looking for his brothers in the desert. Some commentators think that he is there to suggest danger; others that he is the angel Gabriel. Thomas Mann, in *Joseph and his Brethren,* makes the man into a diabolical Hermes, 'a Gnostic, or Manichaean figure, an idealist who turns appalled from the flesh because it is corrupt'.

Yet is it not possible, Josipovici suggests, that the man's purpose is simply to tell Joseph where he could find his brothers? And is this not how the Bible should be read – not as a work of art, nor a history 'but a memory which is alive' of God's dialogue with man. But the 'God in this book does not have features which can be described, or a biography which can be recounted, as do the gods in ancient Near Eastern myths, and in Homer and Virgil. He appears to be pure potential realised in activity . . . his potential is only realised . . . in the unfolding narrative.'

Nor is he even the 'I am who am' revealed to Moses for, as Josipovici points out, this translation of St Jerome's *ego sum qui sum* suggests distinctions in Greek philosophy between essence and existence alien to Hebrew thinking. It would seem, if I understand Josipovici correctly, that 'I am what I do' would be closer to the truth, and the Bible is principally God's self-revelation through the stories of what he has done and what he will do.

The very majesty of God is therefore demonstrated through 'the complexity of life, of emotions and desires beyond the range of the intellect and of language, squeezed together so tight that they cannot be separated out, which is what we find in the Hebrew Bible, and which makes it impossible to reduce its narratives to either an ethical or a mystical meaning.'

Of course this creates a problem for Josipovici when he comes to the books of the Christian New Testament which are written specifically to give an ethical and mystical meaning to the prophecies of the Old Testament. He takes exception in particular to the Epistle to the Hebrews which is didactic in the extreme. He gives us 'the great and justly famous roll-call' of the Old Testament heroes of the faith in chapter 11 – Abel, Enoch, Noah, Abraham, Sara, Isaac, Jacob, Joseph, Moses and so on – but then asks: 'Is this all there is to say about these people?' Do we not feel that there is more to them than their faith in Jahweh? Does not this insistence upon a pattern in the books of the Old Testament in fact diminish them and deprive them of that extraordinary *human* richness which is largely absent from the Gospels?

In a sense one is obliged to agree. After the stories about Joseph, Saul and David, which by this stage in his book Josipovici has covered with great elegance and illumination, the characters around Jesus lack that element of uninterpretable paradox and confusion which makes the Old Testament unique. Mary, Joseph and the other apostles are mere acolytes of the central figure of Jesus: Peter shows a little more life, but it is only in the character of Jesus himself that 'we experience what it means to be a human being in this world of ours'.

Josipovici is excellent in showing the effectiveness of the dead-pan style of the four canonical evangelists when compared to the fairy-tale style of the apocryphal evangelists. They 'force us to enter into the world of the narrative . . .

not because of any excess of detail but by forcing apparent contradictions upon us and yet giving us the confidence that this and no other way was how it was.' Thus Jesus appears 'as a force, a whirlwind which drives all before it and compels all who cross his path to reconsider their lives from the root up. He has access, not so much to a secret of wisdom as to a source of power. This power is inseparable from his physical presence and his mode of speech . . .' In other words, *le style est l'homme même* – his authority resides in the mode of telling. 'We read, or listen, because we have come to trust the teller.'

The paradox here is that if we do trust the Jesus who speaks to us through the Gospels, then we must accept the pattern he imposes upon the books of the Old Testament and this, as we have seen, Josipovici is unwilling to do. One can understand why. His chapters on David and Joseph are so illuminating and beautifully written – so full of poetry and paradox, like the texts they are considering – that it seems impossible to accept an interpretation which can be distilled into the trite dogmas of a penny catechism. Yet perhaps, from a Christian perspective, it is Josipovici's very love of words which is his undoing. So enthralled is he by the flesh made word in the Old Testament, that he is unable to accept the word made flesh in the New. 'The true deity of the Jews,' wrote Miguel de Unamuno in *The Agony of Christianity*, 'is not Jahweh, but the Jewish people itself.' The true deity of Josipovici, one suspects, is neither Jahweh nor Christ but the Bible.

4

Jesus as a Character in Fiction

First published in *The Guardian* on
23 December 1995

THERE ARE IN THE WORLD around a billion people who believe that Jesus Christ was the Son of God. Their knowledge of Jesus comes from the Gospels but never before has the link between their faith and these ancient texts been so confusing.

On the one hand, there are the fundamentalists who believe that everything described in the Bible must be literally true; on the other, there is an ever-growing band of specialists and exegetes who place the veracity of Scripture in doubt. Scholars such as E.P. Saunders, Robin Lane-Fox, Geza Vermes and Hyam Maccoby, best-selling authors like A.N. Wilson, and Conservative politicians like Enoch Powell, have produced studies which suggest that the 'historical' Jesus was not what we have hitherto imagined. Even the Pontifical Biblical Commission in Rome encourages an investigation and analysis of sacred texts that in former ages would have been thought profane.

This has led some Christians to lose their faith. Unwilling on the one hand to accept the crude literalism of the fundamentalists, and unable to understand the complex controversies of the professional exegetes on the other, the baffled believer comes to accept that there is a scholarly consensus that Jesus was not the man, let alone the God, that he or she had hitherto thought he was.

Such a conclusion underestimates the susceptibility of

even the most erudite scholars to intellectual fads and fash-
ions, or the axes that some of them have to grind. There is
no generally accepted source for information about Jesus
outside the letters and narratives found in the New
Testament. He is mentioned by Tacitus in the context of
troublesome early Christians; there are some references of
questionable authenticity in Josephus's histories; and any
number of fanciful speculations can be advanced based on
fragments of the Dead Sea Scrolls; but by and large we can
only know Jesus through the words of the Evangelists who
believed him to be the Son of God.

But if their tendentiousness makes the Gospels worthless
as history, and if a strictly scientific investigation reduces
Jesus to a figure about whom little or nothing can be
known, what kind of man emerges if we read the Gospels as
if they were fiction? What if we approach the character of
Jesus of Nazareth as we would Casaubon in *Middlemarch* or
Pierre in *War and Peace?*

The best translation for this exercise is the 1966 edition
of the Jerusalem Bible published by Darton, Longman and
Todd. The Authorised Version confuses the picture by the
beauty of its archaic prose; while state-of-the-art translations
alienate many readers with their neutered language and
dreary style. I would also start with the Gospel of St Luke,
imagining oneself to be the Theophilus for whom it was
written.

Luke sets off at a fast pace, and tells a good story with
some charming vignettes. The young Jesus is portrayed as
somewhat surly: at the age of twelve after a visit to
Jerusalem, he stays behind 'without his parents knowing it',
obliging them to return after a day's journey to find him
talking to doctors in the Temple. When his mother gently
rebukes him, 'My child, why have you done this to us? See
how worried your father and I have been, looking for you',
he answers abruptly, almost rudely, in tones familiar to any
parent of an adolescent son: 'Why were you looking for me?
Did you not know that I must be busy with my Father's
affairs?'

Jesus treats his mother equally dismissively when she
comes looking for him with his 'brothers', and is somewhat

abrupt when at the wedding at Cana (as described by St John) Mary points out that their hosts have run out of wine. 'Woman, why turn to me? My hour has not come.' Yet he rises above his own objection and turns jars of water into wine; and later demonstrates his solicitude for Mary when from the cross he consigns her to the care of his 'beloved' disciple, John.

By and large, women were fond of Jesus and Jesus appears to have been fond of them, for example Martha and Mary, Mary Magdalene, and Joanna, the wife of Herod's steward Chuza. He was more lenient towards women's weaknesses than he was towards those of men, permitting the 'woman who had a bad name' to wash his feet in her tears and saving the woman accused of adultery from the death by stoning prescribed by the law, while warning that a man who so much as 'looks at a woman lustfully . . . has already committed adultery with her in his heart', and should therefore tear out his eye and throw it away 'because it will do you less harm to lose one part of you than to have your whole body thrown into hell' (Matthew 5:21–2).

Despite St Paul's assurance that 'he was a man like us' and the speculation in *The Last Temptation of Christ*, there is no suggestion in any of the Gospels that Jesus himself was subject to sexual temptations, not even when he was tested by Satan in the wilderness. Was he ugly or handsome? There is no description of his physical appearance. Had he a sense of humour? Again, there is little to suggest it though humour travels badly over both space and time. He was frequently stern but also kind: most of his miracles suggest a compassion for the distressed and the diseased, although some were to solve temporary catering problems (Cana, the feeding of the five thousand), and others to astonish his disciples (walking on the water, catching fish).

Josephus refers to Jesus as superhuman because 'he worked such wonderful and amazing miracles' but it is not this role as a miracle-worker that makes him challenging as a character in fiction. Rather, as Gabriel Josipovici points out in *The Book of God*, it is his extraordinary air of authority. He seems utterly sure of the ideas he puts forward even though they are met with incredulity by his contemporaries quite as much as they are by sceptics today. Little by little, he gets across that he is not a mere prophet but the Son of God. When he says it too clearly, some in the audience try to stone him. When he goes on to say that his flesh is real food and his blood real drink, and that only those who eat this flesh and drink this blood will live for ever, 'many of his followers said, "This is intolerable language. How could anyone accept it?"'

How indeed. Yet as G.K. Chesterton recognised, it is precisely this insistence that he was God that makes Jesus unique both in history and fiction.

> Normally speaking, the greater a man is, the less likely he is to make the very greatest claim. Outside the unique case we are considering, the only man who ever does make that kind of claim is a very small man; a secretive or self-centred monomaniac. Nobody can imagine Aristotle claiming to be the father of gods and men, come down from the sky, though we might imagine some insane Roman Emperor like Caligula claiming it for him, or more probably for himself.

Jesus, however, 'was exactly what a man with a delusion never is: he was wise.'

Here we reach the point where an approach to Jesus as a character in fiction reaches its limits. For what author or, in this particular case, what team of colluding authors, could invent a character so contradictory and yet so convincing? One who was wise and yet deluded. One who could calm the winds and seas, and yet permitted himself to be scourged and crucified. If the Gospels were fiction, said Jean-Jacques Rousseau, then the authors would be more extraordinary than their hero. The only hypothesis that satisfactorily explains this paradox is that the substance of the story told by the Evangelists is true.

5

A Reasonable Man

A review of *St Thomas Aquinas. Summa
Theologiae. A Concise Translation. Edited by
Timothy McDermott (Eyre and Spottiswoode)

MODERN TIMES FOR THE MODERN man begin either with
the Enlightenment or, at the earliest, with the Renaissance.
The Middle Ages appear both too distant and too different
to have any bearing on our present lives. Yet, as Timothy
McDermott points out in his preface to his concise translation of the *Summa Theologiae*, we continue to admire the
great Gothic cathedrals and take for granted the universities
which were mediaeval foundations.

The *Summa* is the intellectual equivalent of York Minster –
a huge and magnificent statement of Christian belief
unequalled in the centuries which followed. Its architect,
Aquinas, was the son of an Italian count who though des-
tined to become a Benedictine monk chose instead to join
the recently established order of preaching friars, the
Dominicans. He studied under St Albert the Great in
Cologne and later taught in Paris, Rome and Naples.

It was a time of intellectual confusion when Christian
faith was grappling with the rediscovered philosophy of
ancient Greece – particularly that of Aristotle which had
filtered into Western Europe in Arabic translations and
through the influence of the Muslim philosopher Averroes.

Some theologians such as Siger of Brabant took the view
that philosophy and theology were two distinct disciplines
that could not be brought together. It was the achievement

of Aquinas to integrate the two – not proving, philosophically, what were matters of faith but demonstrating by reason 'that what faith teaches us is not impossible'.

If his *Summa* has seemed inaccessible to all but theologians and seminarians in the past, it is partly because it was appropriated as the rule book of the Roman Catholic Church at the counter-Reformation (it was placed beside the Bible on the altar at Trent); and partly because its style and structure make it difficult for the modern reader. The original work follows the pattern of mediaeval debate – questions divided into objections, each of which is answered by a response.

What Timothy McDermott has done with great skill is rearrange the whole work into a continuous text with sentences, paragraphs, chapters and parts of a kind familiar to the contemporary reader; and guide us through the work with intelligent, unobtrusive introductory comments to each of the different sections. He has also cut certain passages such as those discussing details of Old Testament ritual and law. Where possible he has rendered philosophical terms in modern turns of phrase.

It is for a trained Thomist to say how faithful this concise translation is to the original: to the general reader and amateur theologian it is undoubtedly a magnificent achievement – opening, as it were, the doors to the cathedral so that we can see both its magnificent proportions and intriguing detail for the first time.

The result is that St Thomas now sounds like an English don. Since such a don might well have been moulded via Mods and Greats by the same Latin and Greek writers as St Thomas, this is perhaps hardly surprising. It is reassuring, all the same, to see Christian faith expounded as the culmination of common sense. It is also fascinating to see the roots of so many of the teachings of the Catholic Church – the catechism, as it were, writ large.

What are we to make of them now when so much of his theology (such as the distinction between mortal and venial sins) has been virtually abandoned? By and large the lucid style and tone of common sense carry one along. Every now and then one stumbles upon an incongruous conclusion

drawn from a faulty premise – for example that a woman is
only conceived when a moist south wind prevents the conception of a man. There are also times when his argument
leads inexorably to conclusions unpalatable to the modern
mind – for example that blasphemy and unbelief are graver
sins than murder. It is the same with his assumption that
heretics should be delivered by the Church to the secular
courts 'to be removed from the world by death'.

By and large, however, the reasonable tone reflects the
thinking of a reasonable man. When it comes to sex, for
example, he shows none of the obsessive abhorrence of St
Augustine or St Jerome, or even the fastidious distaste of a
more recent saint like St Francis de Sales. As with everything
else, it should only be subject to reason. It is reassuring too,
for Catholic novelists, that pleasure taken in thinking about
sexual sin, 'if it is useful for preaching or discussing morals
or some such purpose . . . is no sin at all'.

If any misgiving remain it is that perhaps there is something about the *Summa* that is a little too mechanical; that St
Thomas under the influence of Aristotle placed too much
faith in reason and makes God seem less of an artist and
more of a mathematician.

St Paul had less respect for philosophy, saying that the
foolishness of God was greater than the wisdom of men. St
Thomas, at the end, may have come to the same conclusion.
At the age of forty-nine, while saying Mass, he fell into a
trance and thereafter stopped work on the *Summa*. When
asked why, he answered that in comparison to what God had
now revealed to him, all he had written seemed chaff. Less
than three months later he was dead.

6

Two Travellers:
St Paul and A.N. Wilson

A review of *Paul. The Mind of the Apostle*
by A.N. Wilson (Sinclair-Stevenson), first
published in the *Daily Mail*

IN THE WELL-TRODDEN ROUTE TO and fro from Christian faith, St Paul and A.N. Wilson are two travellers going in the opposite direction who nonetheless find a natural affinity during an overnight stay at an inn. Wilson, first an Anglican, then a Catholic, then an Anglican again, lost his faith some time ago in the divine claims made for the 'Galilean exorcist executed in *circa* the year 30, probably for sedition', the subject of his earlier work, *Jesus*.

Paul, by contrast, was an energetic persecutor of early Christians in Jerusalem until, on his way to Damascus to make further arrests, he was stopped by a blinding vision and the voice of Jesus. As a result, he became the most eloquent and energetic apologist for the risen Christ. Of particular significance was his insistence that Gentiles could follow Jesus without taking on the onerous observances that went with being a Jew. It was faith, not good works, that mattered – a teaching out of fashion in the age of Oxfam and Comic Relief.

We know a considerable amount about St Paul because two major sources have survived from the ancient world – St Luke's Acts of the Apostles, a history of the early Church with St Paul as its central character, and St Paul's own letters

to the different communities of believers in cities like
Corinth, Ephesus and Rome. It is from these sources that
Wilson delves into the mind of the Apostle, concluding that
he was 'one of the most important and influential figures
who ever lived' – not just 'a prophet of liberty whose vision-
ary sense of the importance of the inner life anticipates the
Romantic poets', but also the founder like Mahommet of a
world religion.

The genius of Paul, writes Wilson, 'was to mythologise
Jesus'. Following closely the thesis of Hyam Maccoby in *The
Mythmaker: Paul and the Invention of Christianity*, Wilson suggests that it was Paul who transformed the provincial healer
and preacher into the long-awaited Messiah, the Son of
God. Paul also 'invented' the Eucharist, 'the central mystery, the thread of continuity which stretches through all
lands and all times back to the origins of the Church itself'.
However, Paul did not intend to found a new religion and
things have certainly not turned out as he would have
wanted. 'Paul would have been amazed by the idea of the
Jesuits,' writes Wilson; and Anglicanism, 'had Paul lived to
see it, would have been for him the ultimate absurdity –
more ridiculous than any of the other forms of
"Christianity" which would have filled him with despair.'

To Wilson, however, it is not just the founding of a
Church that subsequently went off the rails that accounts
for Paul's true greatness. It is rather in his artistic achievements. He was 'one of the most stupendous religious poets
and visionaries whom the world has ever seen – on a par
with Blake, Dostoevsky and Simone Weil.' He quotes the
celebrated passage about love from Paul's first letter to
the Corinthians which is such a popular reading at church
weddings, but when he comes to Paul's masterpiece, the
letter to the Romans, he simply tells us to read it: 'Any
attempt to summarise it would distort it; any attempt to
draw it to its logical conclusions will get it wrong.'

It is not uncommon for those who lose their faith in God
to idolise Art. Wilson is quite right to recognise Paul's artistic genius, but his hypothesis that Paul invented Christianity
is unconvincing. It is patently clear from the Gospels that
Jesus was recognised in his lifetime as the Christ, the Son of

God. Wilson is unquestionably erudite: he has an encyclo-
paedic knowledge of the ancient world, and has made full
use of the kind of conjecture that passes for fact among
academics working in the flourishing industry of biblical
scholarship.

But he is opinionated and every now and then under-
mines his credibility with assertions that even a less knowledgeable reader will know are wrong. For example, to
support his claim that Paul invented the Eucharist rather
than Christ at the Last Supper, he states that it is 'unthink-
able' that 'a pious Jew such as Jesus would have spent his last
evening on earth asking his disciples to drink a cup of
blood.' Yet in Chapter Six of his Gospel, St John quotes
Jesus telling his disciples 'most solemnly' that unless they
eat his flesh and drink his blood they will not inherit eternal life: and, significantly, describes the consternation that
this saying provoked at the time.

It is the same with the question of Timothy's circumcision, described by Wilson with no real evidence as 'pure
fiction'. He too readily dismisses anything in the epistles
that contradict his hypothesis as 'later interpolations':
indeed, as the book proceeds Wilson seems increasingly desperate to establish that he is right and Paul was wrong about
Jesus. He is Paul before his conversion, using all his literary
talent and wide learning to hunt down believers. But there
is no escape from the faith at the heart of Paul's teaching,
and so Wilson fails in his attempt to move him to the
Pantheon of Romantic Poets from the Communion of
Christian Saints.

7

Screwtape Returns

First published in *The Catholic Herald,*
26 September 1997

IT IS NOW ALMOST TWENTY-FIVE years since I wrote *Alive,* the story of the young Uruguayans who survived an aircrash in the Andes by eating the bodies of those who had died.

Writing the book taught me many things about human courage and endurance; and also, incidentally, about how hard it is to know oneself. After reading the manuscript, a number of the survivors took me aside to complain about how they had been portrayed in my book. 'You have caught the others perfectly, Piers, but you have wholly failed to understand me.'

My own inability to see myself as others see me was brought home to me recently when I saw myself described in the brochure for October's Cheltenham Festival of Literature as 'a stern moralist'. This is not how I see myself, nor how I want to be seen. The moralist in our society is at best a busybody and at worst a threat. We dislike feeling guilty and so turn against those who trouble our conscience. Also, a stern moralist is expected to practise what he preaches, and I do not want my life put under scrutiny of any kind. Above all, it is bad for business. No one wants to read novels by stern moralists.

How did I gain this reputation? I have always been a Catholic but never a fanatic. My lifestyle is about as indulgent and hedonistic as the next man's. If my family sometimes regard me as a kill-joy, this is not because of my piety and asceticism but because I never seem to enjoy what other people regard as fun – football, sunbathing, restaurants, dancing. By and large, like Brendan Behan, I see myself as a 'bad Catholic'; or, to be less melodramatic, a mediocre Catholic. As a young man, I revered great saints like John Fisher and Thomas More; but my role models were the young heroes of French nineteenth-century novels like Maupassant's Bel Ami or Stendhal's Julien Sorel. One of the great advantages enjoyed by Catholics, it seemed to me in my twenties, was the sacrament of Confession. I pitied my poor Protestant friends who were so ill-equipped to sail close to the wind.

My novels, though they frequently had a moral denouement, were hardly works of Catholic propaganda. I have always felt that in fiction the Devil must be given his due. As a result many Catholic readers have been shocked by certain passages in some of my works: a priest once suggested that I should publicly repudiate an early novel because it contained scenes that might lead the reader into occasions of sin.

This makes me feel that my reputation as a stern moralist is wholly undeserved, and wonder what steps I should take to change it. First I consult my family, 'Learn to play tennis'. Then my friends, 'Learn to play bridge'. And finally a professional publicist from Screwtape and Co. His advice is more considered, more substantial.

1 Stop holding forth on moral issues in papers like the *Daily Mail.* What difference will it make to you if the government lowers the age of homosexual consent? Or if other people's marriages end in divorce? Their children may suffer, but then so do the parents. How does it help to make them feel guilty? Read the signs of the times. Wedding vows are part of our folklore. Life-long monogamous marriage is a thing of the past.

2 If you feel the compulsion to moralise in print, stick to issues that have little to do with our lives like land mines or third world debt. We are a nation of Mrs Jellybys: we like to feel indignant about injustice that takes place a long way from home and is beyond our control. Demonise historical figures like Hitler and Stalin, or politicians in faraway countries like

General Pinochet in Chile. Do not make virtue too difficult. It is easier to give a fiver to CAFOD or write to one's MP than to care for an incontinent parent with Alzheimer's. Or be chaste.

3 Stop going to Mass every Sunday. This gives the impression of rigidity if not fanaticism. Respect the Sabbath by reading the Sunday papers.

4 Express reservations about the Pope. His views on abortion and contraception are unacceptable to most in Britain, including a fair number of Catholics. And while it is part of his job to promote such unpopular teachings, it is hardly part of yours.

5 Speak out in favour of women priests, married priests and intercommunion. Encourage acceptance of Lesbians and Gays. Surely God has better things to do than fuss about who does what to whom in the privacy of their own homes?

6 Promote Catholic social teaching. It is almost impossible for the modern mind to conceive of good and evil, except as it affects the material interests of mankind. Paradise, promised by Christ to the good thief, is beyond their imagination. The Church makes more sense as an agency promoting better schools and shorter waiting lists in hospitals than something founded by Christ for the salvation of souls. A castaway on a desert island can be neither good nor evil. St Simon Stylites lived on top of a pillar because the Byzantine empire did not provide care in the community.

7 Avoid saying the rosary – at any rate in public. This is regarded as primitive and superstitious by non-Catholics and a fair number of Catholics too.

8 Stop reading the Bible. It only leads to trouble. Jesus and the Apostles lived before Vatican II and so some of their ideas are quite inappropriate for the modern world. St Paul's remarks about homosexuals in Romans 1 are a good example. But even Jesus sometimes comes across as a latter-day Savonarola. He seems to think that we are in real danger of damnation: Hell is mentioned over twenty times in St Matthew's Gospel alone. Anyone taking such a line today would be regarded not as a stern moralist but as a madman. Does anyone seriously believe that he might go to Hell?

9 The Old Testament is likely to lead you even further astray. The prophet Ezekiel says that if you fail to point out his wrongdoing to the sinner, you will be held responsible for that wrongdoing and be punished for his crime. This implies that you are somehow your brother's keeper. It trespasses on the sovereignty of his conscience which as we all know, thanks to Cardinal Newman, is inviolable and supreme.

10 Go easy on the veneration of the Saints. It is somewhat archaic to believe that they are sitting around in Heaven waiting for us to join them, ready to help you find your wallet or get rid of toothache. It is also unwise to look upon them as models for our behaviour. Most of them believed that outside the Church there was no salvation when now we know that there is very little difference between the world's great monotheistic religions. Today a St Dominic or a St Ignatius would come across as a fanatic. Even St Francis de Sales, considered easy-going in his time, disapproved of partying, flirting and sex before marriage. He would seem the sternest of stern moralists today.

11 Choose Christian injunctions that match the spirit of the day. 'Judge not that you be not judged'. 'Let he who is without sin cast the first stone'. In other words, mind your own business. Read the newspapers. Watch television. Play tennis. Learn to play bridge.

THE CHURCH

8

A Time of Trial

First published in *Come on In . . . It's Awful:
Collection of Essays Examining the Catholic Church,*
edited by Joanna Bogle (Gracewing, 1994)

THE SON OF AN ANGLICAN VICAR, well known as a humorist and man of letters, once described in an article how his inclination to become a Catholic ended abruptly when he went to Mass at the Carmelite church in Kensington and saw me join the file to receive Communion. I like to think that the inclination cannot have been a strong one, but it is a salutary reminder to Catholics that they themselves are often the chief obstacles to other people's conversion.

In the same way, there are Catholics baptised in infancy who stop going to Mass as adults because of the banality, even vulgarity, of the liturgy, or because the views preached by the priest in the pulpit are so far from their understanding of the Catholic faith. Tastes and opinions often go together: nostalgia for the Tridentine rite accompanies support for the teaching of *Humanae Vitae*, while zeal for Liberation Theology goes with folk masses and altars-in-the-round.

It is important, however, when airing one's grievances about the Catholic Church in England not to dwell too much on what is largely a matter of taste. The People of God are not all high-brows and grace does not make them immune from the vulgarity that pervades our culture. I regret the passing, in my lifetime, of many things – the mystery of the Tridentine rite, the beauty of certain prayers, the profundity of the Last Gospel which so impressed me as a child that I had learned it by heart by the age of ten. I miss the stirring hymns we used to sing, and dislike the monotonous ditties that have replaced them: but I have never wished to return to the use of Latin, and when I finally took the trouble to read them for myself, I was wholehearted in my assent to the teachings of Vatican II.

Truth comes before beauty, and I have always tried not to make too much of inessentials. English Catholics, after all, have always had to put up with ugly churches. As a child in North Yorkshire, I went to Mass either in a village hall or the back room of a pub. I was indifferent to the drab surroundings because of the momentousness of what I believed took place at the Mass, and I felt sorry for our Anglican neighbours whose fine churches were never visited by the living God. As Newman observed, 'after tasting of the awful delight of worshipping God in His Temple, how unspeakably cold is the idea of a Temple without that Divine Presence! One is tempted to say what is the meaning, what is the use of it.'

It is not, therefore, the ugliness as such that is awful in the contemporary Catholic Church, but rather the implications which lie behind some of the ugliness. Here one must beware of paranoia or conspiracy theories. As with a rash or a stomach ache, it is sometimes difficult to decide whether they are caused by something trivial or are the symptoms of a serious disease. A majority of church-going Catholics may prefer the facile ditties to the triumphant hymns; they may like their priest to face the congregation and project his own jovial personality like the host at a children's party, yet there have been times when I have suspected that 'Faith of our Fathers' was dropped from the repertoire not to suit the taste of the congregation, but because it was considered ecumenically incorrect, and that the priest was so effusive and friendly because he did indeed see the Mass as more like a children's party than the sacred re-enactment of Christ's sacrifice on the cross.

In time, these suspicions were confirmed. A parish priest told me that in his opinion there was no difference in either the Eucharist, or the validity of the orders, of Catholics and Anglicans, or, for that matter, Methodists either. Only the vested interests of powerful prelates in Rome prevented the reunion of the different Christian churches. A Jesuit friend said that he sat down at the same table each day with a Jesuit theologian whom he knew no longer believed in some of the articles of the Creed. In the past, those who lost their faith left the Church. Now they remain, either to keep a job or the better to take others with them.

This covert apostasy, often disguised as renewal, has been the true awfulness of the Catholic Church in England in my adult years. At its worst it has been a concerted attempt to persuade Catholics 'in the spirit of Vatican II' to abandon some of the central tenets of the Catholic faith. At best, it has been an exaggerated zeal for various worthy causes such as the unity of Christians or the welfare of the poor. In some ways, despite the references to new theologians, it merely followed on from the liberalism and modernism of the nineteenth century. Yet it has been more surreptitious – heretical, as one monsignor said of the Dominican Herbert McCabe's 'new catechism' – less in what it said, than in what it left unsaid.

Thus it came to be regarded as inimical to the cause of Christian unity to insist upon the Catholic teaching on the real presence of Christ in the consecrated wafer, 'the Great Presence,' to quote Newman again, 'which makes a Catholic Church different from every other place in the world'. It was the same with the Pope. Although many Englishmen had died to uphold his authority over the English Church, it became fashionable to suggest that it was an exaggeration of Vatican I which had been put right by 'collegial' teaching of Vatican II.

Beyond these attempts to accommodate Anglicans, there was a move to make Catholic teaching acceptable to those without Christian faith – to play down anything difficult or audacious or extraordinary in the teaching of Christ; to drop 'mediaeval' notions like Hell or the Devil, angels and even an afterlife; to replace the supernatural yearnings of the Christian life with clear natural objectives like overseas development and famine relief; to reduce the Cross to a

logo of one among other benevolent organisations like
Oxfam or Dr Barnado's.

At first sight, it seemed as if the source of this awfulness
was in the lay activists in the Church – some of them, as it
happened, former priests. It was clearly only a matter of
time before the bishops, who were charged by *Lumen
Gentium* 'to ward off whatever errors threaten their flock',
would confound them. This never happened: indeed, it has
seemed at times as if some of the English bishops not only
tolerated, but actually promoted this neo-Reformation, less
Christian by far than that of Cranmer and Bucer.

It is quite baffling, for example, that *Weaving the Web*,
described as a 'modular programme of Religious
Education', can have received a *Nihil Obstat* stating that it is
free from 'doctrinal or moral' error, for it presents the
Roman Catholic Church as just one among other Christian
churches, and Christianity as just one among other faiths.
There is no sense of a spiritual or supernatural dimension:
faith is presented on the one hand as a blend of custom and
folklore, and on the other as an efficacious ideology for the
emancipation of women, and the material development of
the Third World.

This phenomenon of a Catholic faith that is reformulated
in the name of renewal, is not confined to England and
Wales, but the Catholic Church in England has its own particular characteristics which to some extent explains why it
has been so easy for a few zealots to impose their perverse
concept of renewal on the Welsh and English People of
God.

First of all, where a group is divided, it is easier to rule.
Whilst we talk of 'the Catholic Community' as if all English
Catholics came from the same subculture, there are in fact
different and distinct Catholic communities that feel ill-at-
ease with one another, meeting only at Mass on a Sunday or,
by adopting particular parishes, not even then.

The groups with the greatest influence, and hence those
who contribute most to the climate of opinion among
Catholics, are those with both historic roots and an historic
role: firstly the Catholic aristocracy with its recusant creden-
tials; secondly the expatriate Irish, numerically the most

significant; and thirdly what one might call the Catholic intelligentsia, those who profess their faith with the pen.

Thanks largely to the dramatisation by Granada Television of Evelyn Waugh's *Brideshead Revisited*, the Catholic aristocracy, or upper class, is a popular topic for gossipy articles in newspapers and magazines. Almost anyone who went to one of the Catholic public schools like Ampleforth or Downside is supposed to belong to this elite circle, although a socio-economic analysis of the school lists would tell a very different story. However, the myth is sustained by the disproportionately large number of Catholics in the House of Lords.

It is generally assumed that all upper-class Catholics are recusant Catholics and that all recusant Catholics are upper class. This is not strictly true. There are some impressive instances of a family's loyalty to Rome going back to before the Reformation, but there are others like the Howards who chopped and changed. However, there are Catholics who are quite happy to be taken for recusants because it suggests a pedigree which some may not in fact possess. Indeed, there are some who flaunt their Papist connection even if the practice of their religion is limited to baptisms, weddings and funerals at the Brompton Oratory. They take pride in past persecution, and residual prejudice in the present day, but prefer to dwell upon Norman genealogies, rather than on the semitic origins of the Catholic religion. We were told as boys at Ampleforth that one of the trials we might have to face when serving in the army would be at church parade when the order was given: 'Fall out, Catholics and Jews'.

In this the upper-class Catholics are perhaps demonstrating their 'Englishness' to their wary Anglican compatriots, to whom all Papists are potentially spies for Spain. Another quality they are willing to flaunt is the philistinism that the English consider a mark of good breeding – above all an aversion to anything that might be thought pretentious or intellectual. They may have noticed that in churches other than the Brompton Oratory, the Mass was no longer in Latin and the priest faced the congregation, but they were

unwilling, even if able, to discern the orthodoxy or unortho-
doxy of religious ideas.

The role of these Old Believers, in the context of the
Catholic Church in England, is something like that of a
fishbone stuck in one's throat. It is not dangerous, but is
uncomfortable, and can best be dislodged by swallowing
unmasticated wholemeal bread. The consumer, in this
analogy, is the most numerous segment of the Catholic
community – *viz.* those who trace their origins not to
northern landowners in the sixteenth century, but rather
to Irish immigrants in the nineteenth, and who still have
both affinities and characteristics derived from their ethnic
origin.

Now, in theory there is no reason why the English and
Irish, as well as the more recent immigrants from Spain,
Italy, the Philippines and so on, should not make a holy
alloy of these different national metals in the melting pot of
the universal Church. However, history rudely intrudes to
the Devil's advantage. Unquestionably, over the centuries,
the English have not treated the Irish well, and as a result an
involuntary Anglophobia is now lodged in every Irishman's
DNA. At the same time, the English DNA is programmed
with that contempt which people always feel in order to
justify their bad treatment of their victims. Hence somewhere beneath the surface lurks the belief that the Irish
talk too much (the Blarney stone!), and that they are lazy,
sentimental, dishonest and always drunk.

One has only to read Dostoevsky to know that this mutual
aversion between nationalities is not confined to the Irish
and English: the Russians loathe the Poles, the Poles the
Russians, the Germans the Poles, and so on. To the dispassionate observer, the antipathy has no justification, but
there it is: *l'enfer, c'est les autres*. However, it is particularly
unfortunate when it comes to the Catholic Church in
England because, while as Christians we must all try to (and
if we fail, pretend to) love one another, we are constantly
waylaid by the tribal prejudices programmed into our DNA.
Those from Ireland, who, like the Poles, have historic reasons for regarding the Catholic Church as particularly their

own, cannot escape an involuntary feeling that the English in the congregation have come to the wrong place.

There is also a profound mistrust of those members of the laity with a higher education. Without a native aristocracy, the Irish had for centuries been led by their priests. Since it was not just their office, but also their education that lent authority to this ascendant class of clerics, it was understandable that they should be wary of those who might claim to know better. Thus, added to the widespread view that the English had no right to express views about the expatriate Irish community at prayer, was a profound and ingrained suspicion of intellectuals of any kind.

This brings me to the third component part of the Catholic community, the Catholic intellectual. What has he done to defend the Faith? Little or nothing. Rather like the English Church itself, his dim present contrasts sadly with his illustrious past. Cardinal Manning was an *eminence grise* at Vatican I; Cardinal Newman the posthumous patron of Vatican II; G.K. Chesterton an outstanding apologist; Evelyn Waugh and Graham Greene among the finest novelists of their day.

Of course, neither Chesterton nor Waugh were unblemished witnesses to their faith: the politics of the one and the social prejudices of the other are open to question. However, Waugh for all his snobbery was unquestionably 'a sign of contradiction'. It is significant that Noel Annan, in his book *Our Age* – a comprehensive apologia for the ethos that triumphed in the 1960s – should devote a whole chapter to Waugh's beliefs, seeing him almost as an Athanasius who kept the true faith alive, teaching 'the successors of Our Age how to rough us up'.

Greene is more problematic: his skill as a writer sometimes distracts us from the ambiguity, even perversity, of his theology. There is no question but that the repentant sinner has a place in the Church, not just at the back beating his breast like the Publican in the Gospel, but in a place of honour like the Prodigal Son. However, Greene at times appears to think less of heroic virtue and more of heroic vice, and there is some evidence that the faith that led to his conversion, and put the miraculous into a novel like *The*

End of the Affair, changed in kind in later life. It is no coincidence, I think, that his novel *A Burnt-Out Case* was written
around the time of Vatican II. There were no more miracles
in his subsequent novels. Instead, he espoused a kind of
Liberation Theology, saying shortly before the collapse of
Communism in Russia that the Pope would do well to take
some advice from the Kremlin.

Greene died a Catholic. Many of the Catholics who
became novelists in the next generation, while they could
not disguise the imprint of their Catholic formation, either
avoided questions of faith in the themes they chose, or
treated them to demonstrate their doubts. Bryan Moore's
The Black Robe and John Cornwell's *Strange Gods* both seek to
demonstrate the futility of Christian mission, and promote
a Rousseauesque notion of the noble savage. David Lodge,
in his early novels, ridicules the scruples of Catholics about
sex prior to Vatican II, and more recently depicts a former
priest finding salvation in erotic love.

There are a number of prominent journalists who are
practising Catholics, but few of their readers would know it.
Seeking to earn a living in a profession in which the
Catholic faith is widely regarded as an absurd superstition,
the Catholic journalist, by and large, disguises his religious
affiliation as a status-conscious shopper might remove the
label from a jersey bought at British Home Stores.

Some would say that this is not moral cowardice, or a sign
of lukewarm faith, but a cunning strategy to leaven the
world with a Christian ethos which would be impossible if
they were ever to mention Christ. In journalism as in broad-
casting, God belongs in the God-slot, and Catholic writers
who might jeopardise their standing as columnists and pun-
dits can always come out as Catholics in Catholic newspapers and magazines.

The Tablet is such a venue, in which there are often excellent articles by Catholic writers, journalists and academics.
But *The Tablet*, for all its journalistic excellence, does not
escape the charge of moral mediocrity. Indeed, in many
ways it exemplifies the intellectual malaise that has beset
English Catholicism in the past few decades. Its zealous
pursuit of certain objectives (ecumenicism, liberationism,

feminism, and moral relativism in sexual ethics) in what purports to be 'the spirit of Vatican II', has most assiduously combatted over several decades the true traditional teaching of the Catholic Church.

'Faith assures us', states the new *Catechism of the Catholic Church*, 'that God only allows evil if He can make good come out of it in ways which we will only fully understand in the world to come.' If God permits the Devil, as prince of this world, to tempt us with the glamour of evil, then, by the same token, he is permitted to tempt us by misrepresenting the good, in particular the good that is inherent in the Catholic Church.

There have been times when Catholics themselves have made his task easy: it is impossible to understand how Cathars, Lutherans, Jansenists or Communists flourished in their day without appreciating the scandalous spectacle of Christian theory and practice far apart. The wonder remains that, during the reign of a Pope like Alexander VI, so many remained loyal to the Church.

In my lifetime, the glamour of evil may be much as it always was – money, power and sex – but the scandal of corruption has been replaced by the apparent mediocrity of the Catholic idea. The enormous good done by the Church – by beleaguered priests in their parishes, by devoted nuns in hospitals and convents – has been hidden by the garish zeal of the iconoclastic reformers.

It has been a time of trial which thanks to God's grace may now be ending. The decision to ordain women exposed the over-optimism of the more fanatic ecumenists. The collapse of Communism in Eastern Europe, and the defeat of the Sandinistas in Nicaragua, has put the liberationists on the defensive. The publication of the *Catechism of the Catholic Church* will make it difficult in the future for catechists to pervert the teaching of the Catholic Church: and the Encyclical *Veritatis Splendor* will oblige bishops to stand up and be counted in defence of the Church's moral teaching.

There may even come a time when we will sing 'Faith of our Fathers' once again, if only to remind ourselves that despite the passing of centuries our beliefs remain the same. 'Robert Lawrence', wrote Henry VIII's Royal Commissioner of the Carthusian prior, 'says that there is one Catholic Church of which the Bishop of Rome is the head; therefore he cannot believe that the King is the supreme head of the Church'. With his fellow prior, Augustine Webster, he was sentenced to be hanged, drawn and quartered at Tyburn.

To the few Catholics who shared the Carthusians' convictions, the condition of the Church at that time must indeed have appeared awful. Among the Catholic bishops of England and Wales, only John Fisher was willing to stand up to the king. Some, like Cranmer, went over to the reformers. The new ideas of the radical theologians were in the ascendant. Yet when Thomas More saw the Carthusian priors pass under the window of his cell where he too was imprisoned, on their way to their execution, he turned to his daughter and said: 'Look, Meg, they go to their death as cheerfully as bridegrooms to their marriage.'

9

Modern Catholicism

A review of *Modern Catholicism: Vatican II and After*, edited by Adrian Hastings (SPCK), first published in *The Spectator*, 16 February 1991

It is now twenty-five years since the close of the Second Vatican Council, called by Pope John XXIII. In four sessions the 2,500 bishops passed sixteen decrees which radically affected the attitudes and practices of Catholics throughout the world.

The most immediate and visible changes were the abolition of Latin as the sole language for the liturgy, and the introduction of Communion in both kinds. The laity were no longer to be seen as an appendage to a priestly caste: the celebrant who had said Mass with his back to the congregation now faced 'the People of God'.

Equally significant were the changes in attitude enjoined by the Council fathers. Catholics were not to remain indifferent to the material condition of their fellow men, or to anathematise those who belonged to other religions. Above all they must strive to unite with other Christian denominations because Christ had prayed that 'all might be one'.

Although the Council led to both elation and anguish in the Catholic Church, one can only marvel today, in reading its decrees, at the manner in which it steered a difficult course between the Scylla of sclerosis and the Charybdis of modernism. Perhaps its decrees on the liturgy were imposed with an insensitive zeal – particularly in England where, for historical reasons, the Latin Mass was held in great affection; but the only flaws I can discern in the texts today are the use of the term 'world' in two contradictory senses; and in an over-optimistic reading of the 'signs of the times'.

The Church has misinterpreted them before, and one must remember that this was the epoch of 'flower-power' and Dr Spock. The war in Algeria was ending; that in Vietnam had not got underway. No wonder, then, that the Decree *Gaudium et Spes* felt able to talk of 'the birth of a new humanism, where man is defined before all else by his responsibility to his brothers and at the court of history'.

What remains difficult to understand – and will undoubtedly perplex future historians – is the way in which the Council was subsequently used to subvert the Catholic beliefs which it either explicitly or implicitly confirmed. As David Lodge has illustrated so well in his novels, Catholics suddenly behaved as if the Council had abolished Hell. In fact, it did nothing of the kind: indeed *Gaudium et Spes* implies that we might be damned for breaking the speed limit or tax evasion.

This collection of essays by forty leading Catholic scholars is a more learned expression of the same phenomenon. Presented as a 'comprehensive study' of modern Catholicism, its contributors come mostly from a particular group within the Church whose opinions, considered progressive in the era of bell-bottomed jeans, rarely match those of the Pope in Rome. *Caveat emptor.* When the editor, Adrian Hastings, once a priest and now Professor of Theology at Leeds, writes that the essays have 'avoided extremes', remember that Catholics can differ on what they mean by extreme.

The arrangement of the contributions is excellent: a brief history of the Catholic Church from Vatican I to the present; portraits of recent Popes by two former Jesuits, Michael Walsh and Peter Hebblethwaite; essays on the Conciliar documents, the institutions of renewal which followed the Council; aspects of Church life since the Council, and so on. Most entertaining are Hebblethwaite's essays: he has a touch of a Nigel Dempster when it comes to the Vatican's corridors of power. Remarkably restrained is his wife

Margaret's short essay on 'Devotion' ('sacred hearts and crowned virgins were on the decrease; golden sunsets, billowing waves, snow-clad mountain peaks and leafy glades took their place'). The Jesuit John McDade contributes a good essay on post-Conciliar theology, contrasting and comparing the writing of von Balthasar and Schillebeeckx. He comes down – inevitably but, one suspects, not entirely happily – in favour of Liberation Theology and Rahner's misty notion of a 'world Church'.

Most revealing is a section by F.J. Laishley, head of the department of Christian Doctrine at Heythrop College, on the Council's 'Unfinished Business'. With a barrage of intimidating jargon, he appears to advance the theory that the Council fathers did not know what they were *really* saying and therefore did not mean what they *actually* said, particularly about such things as celibacy, birth control, the Pope, or the status of the Roman Catholic Church.

This may be orthodox deconstructionism but it is not even heterodox Catholicism if the word is to have any meaning. To say that 'pluralism is a permanent feature of all theology' effectively denies not just the power of the Church to interpret Revelation but the authority of Revelation itself. It also leads to the absurd spectacle of Dr Laishley, supposedly acting in the spirit of the Council, discussing the exact position of the word 'quoque' in section 22 of *Gaudium et Spes* or the precise meaning of the word 'subsists'.

It is instructive to compare his piece with the cogent essay by Dr Edward Norman, the only Protestant contributor to the collection. He recognises that the Council's 'reformulations of faith were, in the event, surprisingly unitary and conservative'; and rather than abolish distinctions between the different Christian Churches, he admits that the Ecumenical dimension 'was not a priority . . . of the Council'; and that 'beneath the ecclesiastical courtesy . . . there was basically an unchanged landscape'.

If that is so clear to Dr Norman, how can the other contributors find a contrary 'spirit' in the Council? It is done either by ignoring whole chunks of the Council's teaching, or by distorting the meaning of certain paragraphs, or reading into them meaning which is not there. The best

expression of the absurdity to which this leads is the essay
on the Decree on Other Religions (*Nostra Aetate*) by Donald
Nichol, once the rector of the Ecumenical Institute at
Tantur. He concludes that 'the very inner logic of the
Council's various statements has gradually crystallized the
fundamental issue which now faces Catholic theologians
concerning what is called "the uniqueness of Christ".' If the
Church now accepts that there is truth in other religions,
'does it not follow that there is now no need for evangeliza-
tion?' Can it still insist upon 'the uniqueness of Christ'?

Since *Nostra Aetate* specifically states that 'the Catholic
Church . . . proclaims, and is in duty bound to proclaim
without fail, Christ who is the way, the truth and the life', it
is difficult to understand how someone who no longer
believes it can consider himself a Catholic or even a
Christian. The Council may have taught that everyone has a
right to his opinion, but there comes a point when dissent
destroys the coherence of any religion and reduces a
Church to a tower of Babel.

10

The Inquisition and Dr Küng

First published in *The Observer*,
8 November 1980

Hᴀɴs ᴋüɴɢ ɪs ᴛʜᴇ ᴇɴꜰᴀɴᴛ ᴛᴇʀʀɪʙʟᴇ of the Roman Catholic Church. By origin the son of a Swiss shopkeeper, by vocation a priest, by profession a teacher of theology at Tübingen University in West Germany, he gained fame through his many books and pamphlets which call for a radical change in Catholic beliefs and behaviour.

Those not trained in theology might find it hard to follow his long dispute with the German bishops and the Vatican on, for instance, whether 'Christ is one in substance with the Father': but it is not difficult to understand his rejection of papal infallibility, and his demands for the reversal of certain papal rulings on the celibacy of priests, the validity of Anglican orders and birth control.

The story of the struggle between Küng and the Church authorities is long and complicated, but it reached a climax at the end of last year when the Sacred Congregation for the Doctrine of the Faith withdrew Küng's *missio canonica* which is an essential qualification for his chair of Catholic theology at the university.

Now, nine months later, Küng remains at Tübingen – still a professor of theology but not within the Catholic faculty – a compromise arrived at by the university itself. He lives in a large house overlooking the town with a fine view of the hills on the far side of the river Neckar.

His study where he received me is not a monk's cell. It is large and low with elegant modern furniture, fitted carpets, and various *objets d'art* among the books which line the wall.

Nor does Küng himself look like a monk. Slim and sunburnt, dressed in beige slacks and a brown open-necked shirt, he appeared more like a successful tennis-player than a rebel priest. He has strong, curly hair swept back from a very Swiss face, but what struck me most about his appearance was the delightful, almost mischievous, smile which seemed to be its natural expression.

Before the Second Vatican Council Küng wrote a book called *The Council and Reunion* in which he had warned that 'the Council will either be the fulfilment of a great hope or a disappointment.' I asked him now, several years after the Council, whether he was in fact disappointed by what it had achieved.

No, not at all. This early book of his he now felt stands as a prophecy fulfilled. Most of what he had asked for had been done – the change in the liturgy, the use of the vernacular, the new role of the Bible, the status of the laity, and so on.

Then why, I asked, did he talk as if the Church was in such a bad way?

The Council, he said, had been the turning point he had asked for but the Church had not gone on from there. First Rome had put the brakes on over the issue of birth control. Most Catholics had expected what Küng called 'a positive answer' on this issue. The same had happened over clerical celibacy and divorce, so now the Church was in a state of crisis precisely because the curia in Rome was trying to impede the progressive movement started by the Council.

I expressed my doubts about this point of view and told Küng that in my opinion the Church had more integrity now than at any time in the past thousand years; and that many of those who were proud of the achievements of the Council were sceptical about the further agitation of enthusiasts. Did he think, I wondered, – given his call for greater democracy within the Church – that a majority among Catholics agreed with his progressive views?

Küng answered carefully. There was, he explained, a

small conservative wing to the right – men like Lefebvre – which he did not think was very strong; and then there was a more powerful wing – certainly intellectually more powerful – to the left, and in between the 'middle field' which was moving ('or would if they could') to the left on specific issues such as birth control, the admission of divorced people to the sacraments, clerical celibacy and the validity of Anglican orders.

If Anglican orders are valid, I asked Küng, is there any reason why an Englishman like me should remain a Roman rather than an Anglo-Catholic?

He shook his head. Although he considered that the different denominations were branches of a single Christian Church, he thought that changing denominations just caused ill-feeling. In his opinion we should all work for Christian unity from within the denomination in which we found ourselves.

'Some people,' I said, 'might say that you attach such importance to Christian unity that you dilute Catholic beliefs and blur the differences between the different churches.'

No, he said. Not blur the differences but transcend them. He gave as an example his attitude towards the papacy. You can affirm the importance of the see of Rome, even insist upon its pastoral primacy, but also want to limit it 'to the norm of the Gospel and not see it act in a worldly spirit'. One of the reasons, he thought, why he was so appreciated in England was that a great many Anglicans thought in the same way as he did. He was convinced, for example, that if the Pope during his visit to Ireland had talked to both Catholics and Protestants as a common pastor, and had not just whipped up the confessional enthusiasm of the Roman Catholics, he would have helped the two sides come together.

Turning to the question of clerical celibacy, I asked Küng whether the Pope had a point when he said that it was unfair to release priests from their vows if husbands and wives were held to theirs.

'No,' said Küng. 'I think that is not a valid point. I think that to be married is the natural way to be and it is not a special obligation.' It was, he thought, a human right, and it was referred to in ecclesiastical documents as such. The question was whether the Church had the right to make the special gift of celibacy – or 'charisma', as the theologians call it – a routine requirement for the priesthood. 'I have never denied that celibacy was a good thing,' he said with one of his charming smiles. 'If I had had a wife and family, I would certainly have written fewer books – which would probably have made them happy in Rome!'

'And you don't feel,' I asked, 'that perhaps priests are more demoralised when you write that we don't really need them, than by not being allowed to take wives?'

'I have never said that we do not need priests.'

I quoted from his book *The Church*: 'The believing and baptised Christian therefore needs in this ultimate sense no human mediator at all in order to find and maintain fellowship with God in Christ.' Had he not also said, I asked, that a Christian need not be a priest to celebrate the Eucharist?

Küng shook his head. Firstly, he said, it was a mistake to see the priest as mediator. Christ was the only mediator. What we needed were spiritual leaders in our parishes, and also bishops as spiritual leaders on the regional level.

Nor had he ever said that individual Christians could and should celebrate the Eucharist. The Eucharistic meal was and would always be something for the community. The only question was whether a community of Christians could celebrate the Eucharist if they had no priests, 'and that of course is a question which must be discussed and a lot of very knowledgeable people are thinking about it . . .'

'You concentrate your fire,' I said, 'on things like clerical celibacy and papal infallibility. We don't see much from you about issues which other Catholics regard as serious such as abortion or homosexuality.'

'Generally,' said Küng, 'I am . . . much more reluctant to take a stand on a lot of things than most people think. I think that the question of birth control is a relatively simple question and the Papal Commission in their greatest majority agreed that we have to change. The question of celibacy is also I think . . . a fairly simple question . . . but abortion is a relatively complicated question . . . I see that a lot of very good people are on both sides, so I haven't taken a stand on this. Also, I am not a specialist in this matter. I am not a moral theologian.' The same was true of homosexuality.

'You don't feel that either of these two things is evil?'

He shook his head. 'On the contrary, I protested recently against this general ban or condemnation of homosexuals or people who have abortions which the Pope made in the United States . . . I am sure Jesus would have protested too . . .'

'And does this polemical role you play,' I asked Küng, 'mean that you have become the leader of a movement within the Church?'

'No. I think this would be exaggerated.' A leader of a movement, he said, would mean organisation. He would have to become very political, and an organiser when he would rather remain simple and ordinary: and it was regrettable, he added, that newspapers like *The Observer* printed a photograph of him next to one of the Pope. 'And yet,' he said – looking at the photographs which were above the open letter he had written to the Pope – 'I cannot understand why the Pope is not ready to answer a letter like this, nor even to confirm that he has received it, and I cannot understand why he is still now not ready to talk to me . . .'

'He may feel,' I suggested, 'that you are slightly unfair to the Vatican in comparing yourself to Sakharov and by implication the Holy See to the Kremlin.'

Until now Küng had spoken with the calm deliberation of a tutor with his student – pausing only to consider his replies, and to drink the coffee and eat a mouthful of the Apfelstrudel which had been so generously provided for us both. Now his features tightened: he seemed to grow almost angry. He denied that he had compared himself to Sakharov, but only when asked had agreed that he saw certain parallels between Sakharov's experiences and his own.

'But you also talk about the Inquisition,' I said, 'which in England makes people think of burning heretics, when so far as I know you have not even been threatened with excommunication.'

'The Inquisition,' said Küng, 'is a precise term for a certain process which is used in Rome by the Holy Office, the
Holy Inquisition, for many centuries using methods quite
opposed to the legal formalities now established in all
civilised countries.'

'Yet all they wanted to know,' I said, 'was whether you
should go on teaching the Catholic faith, not whether you
should be excommunicated and burnt.'

'It is not thanks to them that they do not burn people any
more,' said Küng. 'They would if they could. And you can
burn people in different ways. You can burn them physically
and you can burn them spiritually.'

'But don't you concede,' I insisted, 'that the Church has
a right – even an obligation – to supervise the qualifications
of its teachers?'

'Who is the Church?'

'Well, the Vatican or the Sacred Congregation . . .'

'The Sacred Congregation is for me the Holy Inquisition,
and I am for the abolition of the Inquisition. There is no
institution in the Catholic world which has done so much
harm to orthodoxy as this terrible organisation which like
the secret police in Russia changes its name all the time,
and its methods slightly, but . . .' He did not finish his
sentence.

'And the Devil?' I asked. Did he believe in the Devil?

'I am against the personalisation which makes evil too
naive,' he said. 'We cannot go back to the imagination of
earlier periods. We have to take evil more seriously.'

'But didn't Christ talk about the Evil One?'

'Yes, but he spoke especially about demons, and demons
are different from the Devil. Satan, however, is another
thing. He was the great prince . . . but that's rather complicated and I have never been very interested in the Devil anyway. I am interested in God.'

The impression that Hans Küng left on me after the two
hours that we had spent together at his house was of sincerity rather than holiness; of knowledge rather than wisdom.
The breadth of his learning is demonstrated in the eight
hundred pages of his new book, *Does God Exist?*, but from

this vast canvas comes a picture of the Catholic Church and the Christian tradition quite different from my own.

He undoubtedly has great charm, and I could understand why he had such a following among Anglicans and 'progressive' Catholics, but it saddened me that he could equate with such facility the discipline of a Church to which he belongs by choice with the despotic methods of a totalitarian state; and that while he took on the whole bundle of causes of the Catholic Left such as the right of priests to marry or of women to become priests he had no particular view on other issues such as abortion which I would regard as more grave.

II

The Theology of
Benedict XVI

A review of *The Theology of Joseph Ratzinger.*
An Introductory Study by Aidan Nichols OP
(T. & T. Clark)

IN THEOLOGY AND AESTHETICS the means does not lead
to the end. Intellect and erudition cannot produce a work
of art, and one act of charity or simple prayer may bring a
soul closer to God than a doctorate in Thomist philosophy.
'Of what use is it to discourse learnedly on the Trinity,'
asked Thomas à Kempis, 'if you lack humility and therefore
displease the Trinity? Lofty words do not make a man just or
holy; but a good life makes him dear to God.'

These words are particularly apposite today when most
theology seems directed towards the debunking of traditional beliefs. Orthodox teachers labour in obscurity while
their unorthodox colleagues get their names in papers and
sell a large number of their books. In the Catholic Church,
in the years which followed the Second Vatican Council,
considerable mischief has been done by men like Küng,
Schillebeeckx, Boff, Segundo and even Rahner which has
led to some confusion as to what is and what is not the
Catholic faith.

Since the sixteenth century there has been a department
of the papal curia whose business it is to pronounce upon
the truth or falsity of theological pronouncements. Once
called the Inquisition, it is now known as the Congregation

for the Doctrine of the Faith and its Prefect is Joseph Cardinal Ratzinger who was, paradoxically, one of the radical young theologians who as assistant to Cardinal Frings of Cologne dusted out the Catholic Church during the Second Vatican Council. The son of a police officer in Lower Bavaria, he was ordained priest in 1951 and then taught theology in several German universities, including Tübingen, the home of Hans Küng, before being appointed Archbishop of Munich by Pope Paul VI.

Only four years later, in 1981, Pope John Paul II brought him from Munich to Rome. It is not difficult to see why, for in the years since the Vatican Council the poacher had turned game-keeper, breaking his ties with the review *Concilium* which was the standard bearer of liberal theology and speaking out in defence of traditional beliefs, notably, in 1985, in an interview with the Italian journalist Vittorio Messori which was subsequently published as *The Ratzinger Report*. This consoled the traditionalists but enraged the progressives who were preparing the ground for Vatican III. To them he embodied all that was worst in the pre-Conciliar curia: the police officer's son was now the heavy-handed police chief of the Catholic Church, dousing their enthusiasm for reunion with Protestant churches and silencing dissidents like Küng and Boff because they did not agree with his point of view.

Now the English reader can judge Ratzinger for himself for not only has a collection of his essays been published by St Paul Publications as *Church, Ecumenism and Politics* but the English Dominican Aidan Nichols has written a study of his theology. Nichols deliberately avoids becoming embroiled in the controversies surrounding decisions by the Congregation for the Doctrine of the Faith but concentrates rather on the evolution of Ratzinger's theological thought. He begins his book by saying that 'Joseph Ratzinger is very much a Bavarian theologian', and then gives a chapter on his Bavarian background. This is not of merely folkloric interest: there is an indisputable link between the national background and the theological views of both Pope and Prefect, and it is no coincidence that an easy-going attitude towards Christian belief springs more readily from pluralist

democracies like England or the United States than it does
from the naturally conservative and 'black' Catholic heart-
land of Central Europe. Undoubtedly John Paul II and
Cardinal Ratzinger see eye to eye on most of the issues fac-
ing the Church, and their 'reaction', if one can call it that,
marks a return of self-confidence to the Central European
Weltanschauung.

It would be a mistake, however, to think of Ratzinger as a
reactionary. Certainly the events of 1968 may have made
him more conservative just as those of 1848 tempered the
liberalism of Pius IX. What they seem to have reminded
Ratzinger of is the danger inherent in reason when it is cut
adrift from faith, and the danger inherent in faith when it
abandons the Magisterium of the Roman Catholic Church
and conscience 'becomes the principle of subjective obsti-
nacy established as an absolute . . .' At a time when it is
thought tactless to insist upon the claims to authority of any
one particular Church, let alone one particular bishop, he
is emphatic that the primacy of the See of St Peter is the prerequisite of Christian unity and forms an integral part of the
Church established by Christ.

In the English context such 'triumphalism', however cour-
teously expressed, seems an affront to the ecumenical spirit:
thus his essay entitled 'Anglican-Catholic dialogue: Its problems and hopes' is of particular interest. His fundamental
conviction is that neither Pope nor bishops have the right to
trim the doctrines of the Catholic Church to reach a compromise with other Christian denominations. 'The question
that is really at issue in the Church today has remained precisely the same as in the days of the Tractarians: the place of
authority and the value of dogma as opposed to private
judgement.'

Aidan Nichols's book limits itself to a respectful exposition of the different themes in Ratzinger's writings from his
early studies of St Augustine and St Bonaventure through
his role in the Council to his more recent preoccupations
with Liberation Theology. Inevitably, at times, this comes
across as a *resumé* and lacks the lucidity of the Cardinal's
own essays, so admirably translated by Robert Nowell. In
these he displays not just his philosophical and theological

skills, but also a considerable historical erudition. They are largely free from theological jargon and the style is that of a man who uses his incisive intellect with patience and humility.

What marks him out from other Church leaders is the clarity with which he perceives the inner logic of the Catholic religion, and the danger posed by well-meaning tampering with apparently negotiable articles of faith. This at times makes him seem even more audacious and 'triumphalist' than his adversaries would have us believe. If he refers back to an earlier era, it is not to the Church prior to the Second Vatican Council but to the Christendom of the Middle Ages when reason was exercised only in the context of faith and that faith itself was taught in its entirety. Most of the calamities of the modern era he ascribes to the Enlightenment when philosophers decided that man could work out his destiny without reference to God. What he hopes for in the future is a return of Christians' confidence in their transcendent vision of the human condition.

12

The Worlock Archive

A review of *The Worlock Archive* by Clifford
Longley (Geoffrey Chapman), first published
in *The Catholic Herald*, 17 December 1999

CLIFFORD LONGLEY IS WELL KNOWN AS A veteran correspondent on religious affairs, writing first for *The Times* and
now for *The Daily Telegraph*: his Friday columns manage to be
at the same time lucid, intelligent, stimulating and provoca-
tive. So too is this book. It is an investigation of the late
Archbishop of Liverpool, Derek Warlock, following permis-
sion by Warlock's literary executors, Canon Nicholas France
of the Portsmouth Diocese and Bishop Vincent Nichols of
Westminster, to peruse his files contained in cardboard
boxes stored in the former seminary at Upholland.

The book is not a biography. Almost half of it is made up
of the diary that Worlock kept during the Second Vatican
Council, first as secretary to the then Archbishop of
Westminster, Cardinal Godfrey ('Why is this man Godfrey',
the joke went, 'signing Monsignor Warlock's letters?'); then
as a *peritus* with a significant role in drafting some of the
Council's decrees. The diary, hard-going compared to
Longley's sparkling commentary, reveals that Worlock
began as a conservative who looked askance at the ecumenical initiatives of the then Archbishop of Liverpool,
John Heenan, and referred to the future Pope Paul VI, as a
member of 'the extreme leftist gentry'. His principal preoccupations in the early days of the Council were to secure
better treatment for the cardinals' secretaries – he was

actually struck by a Vatican official – and, rather than record Pope John XXIII's momentous speech at the opening ceremony, describes instead 'the behaviour of the ecumenical observers with their cameras'.

However, as the Council progressed Worlock changed sides; he became an enthusiast for reform and finally 'the very essence of Vatican II man' – to traditionalist Catholics the leader of the neo-modernist faction within the Catholic Church in England or, as one priest once put it to me, 'the spider in the centre of the web'.

Longley, a cafeteria Catholic *par excellence*, has no love for what he calls 'the self-righteous ultra-conservatives' within the Church who he says bombard the Vatican with 'a constant barrage of irritating, uncharitable, ill-informed and time-consuming complaints'; but his liberal sympathies stop short of writing a hagiography of the man who embodied the spirit of Vatican II. Worlock emerges as an opportunistic *apparatchik* – 'an administrative genius' who believed that 'if the party line changes, those faithful to it must change too'. He was 'self-righteous: sometimes he was a bully', and 'he could be unthinkingly cruel'. He 'was never a man to let modesty deny him his rightful place in history'; 'often assumed for himself the air of infallibility' and proceeded as if he alone truly understood the will of the Church following Vatican II, 'presenting himself as almost a Moses, bringing the tablets of stone down from Mount Sinai to the people'.

John Heenan, who succeeded Godfrey as Archbishop of Westminster, disliked Worlock and after reading this book it is easy to see why. The formerly conservative Worlock became an ultra-liberal and fostered the post-Conciliar movements that Heenan, once a liberal, feared would destroy the Church. Passed over for Westminster after the death of Heenan, Worlock found the appointment of George Basil Hume 'hard to bear'. He could be scathing about Hume 'and did not feel that the better man had won'.

To Longley, Worlock's intellectual arrogance had a dire effect on just the people who, in the spirit of Vatican II, he hoped to help – the Liverpudlian working class. Together with his Anglican opposite number, David Sheppard, he was

Old Labour, seeking to alleviate poverty and unemployment through high taxation and government spending. He failed to understand the dynamics of wealth-creation and, when sent Pope John Paul II's Encyclical *Laborem Exercens*, he responded by sending his own thoughts on the subject to the Vatican via the nuncio when, as Longley points out, a reading of the Encyclical might have produced a 'different, more profound and more constructive' analysis of the problems of Merseyside.

Longley absolves him of blame for the rapid decline of Catholic practice in the Archdiocese of Liverpool which is hardly surprising since Longley himself believes in many of the 'reforms' that so changed the Church in the space of a generation. He also fails to point out that the same culture of complaint permeated Catholic agencies such as CAFOD, set up by Worlock, or the Catholic Institute for International Relations.

Indeed, throughout this book one senses the tension between Longley the objective journalist and Longley the partisan of the alternative magisterium. He rebukes Worlock for failing to appreciate that the breakdown of marriage and family life was not simply a by-product of unemployment, but may be the result of 'feminism and elements of Marxism': and he appears to think that there might be more to be said in favour of *Humanae Vitae* than he once supposed; but nonetheless Pope Paul VI got it wrong. A celibate clergy cannot know 'the quasi-mysticism of sexual passion, ecstasy and union, the sense of being translated beyond time and space to another dimension where angels sing; the outer circle, surely, of the Beatific vision . . . A lover knows something of the Divine in the only way the Divine can be known.' This is surely dubious reasoning because sexual ecstasy is not experienced only by married couples. What about the transports of adulterous or fornicating lovers? Are they also blessed with a Beatific vision?

There are also flaws in Longley's analysis of history which not only takes up a significant part of his book but is also fundamental to his thesis that the Second Vatican Council in fact annulled much of the teaching of the Council of Trent. He states that the Council of Trent was 'a response' to the Protestant Reformation when modern historians such as Hsia and Mullet have shown that it was rather the culmination of a movement of Catholic renewal that pre-dated Luther. He considers the Decree on the Jews of the Fourth Lateran Council in 1215 which excluded them from public employment, confined them to ghettos and required them to wear yellow stars in public as the precursor of the Nazi anti-semitism. This fails to take into account the per-ceived threat posed to Christendom by Islam at the time: a better analogy would be with the internment of enemy aliens in Britain during the war. Even at its most intolerant, the Church never proposed *exterminating* the Jews; indeed when pogroms took place, they were often protected by the Church authorities. Nor was liberty of conscience wholly an invention of Vatican II: popes in the Middle Ages condemned the forced conversion of Jews.

Despite these shortcomings, however, *The Worlock Archive* is an invaluable contribution to our understanding of the Second Vatican Council and the inner workings of the Church in England in recent years. It is also highly relevant at a time when the archdioceses of Westminster and Birmingham are vacant.

13

Pilgrim Cormac

A review of *At the Heart of the World* by Cormac
Murphy-O'Connor (Darton, Longman and
Todd), first published in *The Catholic Herald*,
2 April 2004

CATHOLIC BISHOPS IN THE PAST HAVE COME in all
shapes and sizes. In France in the seventeenth century you
find the Archbishop of Bordeaux doubling as an admiral of
the fleet but also St Francis of Sales, a timeless model for a
good pastor. St Francis came to mind when I was reading
this book because, though Bishop of Geneva, he was obliged
by the Calvinists who ruled the city to live in Annecy over
the border in France. Was Arundel a kind of Annecy for
Cardinal Cormac Murphy-O'Connor when he was Bishop of
Arundel and Brighton – a charming town in beautiful coun-
tryside a safe distance from the horrors of the metropolis? It
was only in obedience to the request from Pope John Paul
II that he accepted the transfer to the Archdiocese of
Westminster.

Cormac Murphy-O'Connor is the son of an Irish doctor
who came to live in England with his wife and practised as a
GP in Reading. His mother who 'had a great influence on
me' 'was a very modern woman and much more adventur-
ous and open to developments than my father'. He had four
brothers and a younger sister. The family was devout and
their large house in Reading was a port of call for visiting
priests – even Monsignor Ronald Knox though the young
Cormac was not at home at the time. Cormac was sent to

boarding school at Prior Park College in Bath: 'they were tough years. Food was pretty rotten and I remember the bitterly cold winter of 1946-7.' As a boy he thought of being a doctor like his father or a concert pianist but when his father asked him what he wanted to be when he grew up, the young Cormac answered: 'I want to be a priest.'

Two of his brothers had been called before him and it required special pleading to persuade the Rector of the English College in Rome to accept a third Murphy-O'Connor. Cormac arrived in Rome in 1950 and remained there, with the exception of one visit home, until he was ordained in 1957. He was to spend fourteen years of his life in the Eternal City, first as a seminarian and later as the Rector of the English College.

The young priest's return to a working-class parish in Plymouth came as a shock but taught him many things such as the importance of the sacrament of marriage and family life. He also came to value 'small communities' within the parish which we see, many years later, in the groups formed in the current programme for spiritual renewal in the Archdiocese of Westminster, *At Your Word, Lord.*

It was also the time of Vatican II: 'a great deal was happening in the Church during the years after my ordination . . . they created enormous changes in the way in which we perceived ourselves and our Church.' 'As far as I was concerned, the years of the Second Vatican Council filled my heart with joy and hope.' Cardinal Murphy-O'Connor was and remains an enthusiastic proponent of the unity of the Christian churches and for sixteen years served as co-chairman of ARCIC (the Anglican–Roman Catholic International Commission). He has been, then, and remains a man of his time.

Le style est l'homme même. The Cardinal's book is modest, intelligent, wise and well written: great charm emanates from his prose. He deals with serious questions but leavens them with his good humour. He is judicious, quoting from Vatican II, Pope John Paul II, his predecessor Basil Hume and the Dominican mooted as a rival for the Archdiocese of Westminster, Timothy Radcliffe OP: but also some unexpected writers, that show wider reading, such as Timothy Garton Ash.

At times I sensed a certain caution as if he felt that Cardinal Ratzinger was peering over his shoulder. For example, he wonders, somewhat opaquely, about 'the extent to which the structures and procedures of the Roman Curia adequately respect the legitimate authority and responsibility at different levels of the Church': is this a call for Conciliar government or more Episcopal autonomy, or both? He also suggests that 'the Roman Catholic Church has a responsibility to put its own ecumenical house in order, at the same time as travelling down the road towards institutional unity with differing Churches.' One would like him to have spelt out quite what he meant by that.

The Cardinal touches on the horrors surrounding the scandal of paedophile priests – over which he personally suffered much vilification by the media; and he is so alarmed by the inexorable secularisation of our society that he feels we are 'on the edge of a cultural abyss'. Given this, the Cardinal's optimism may baffle some of his readers. Congregations dwindle, the Church's teaching on sexual morality is ignored, and one wonders how he can be so sure that 'there is very good reason to think that Christian unity will come about'. Surely as the co-Chairman of ARCIC for so many years he must have felt the unilateral decision of the Church of England to ordain women as a kick in the teeth?

'My faith is the greatest treasure that my parents bequeathed to me,' writes Cardinal Cormac Murphy-O'Connor, 'and the central aim of my life has always been to share this treasure.' No bishop can have a finer ambition than that. At the start of *At the Heart of the World*, he tells his readers how, on a visit to the Outer Hebrides, he came across a memorial to a missionary of the seventh or eighth centuries. 'Pilgrim Cormac,' read the inscription. 'He went beyond what was deemed possible.' We should all pray that our present-day Cormac will do the same.

LIBERATION
THEOLOGY

14

Rich and Poor

First published in the *Tablet* on 23 August 1986

THE CURRENT CRUSADE AGAINST POVERTY and famine seems a better object for Christian zeal than the armed crusades against the Saracens in the Middle Ages. Bob Geldof may lack the learning and eloquence of St Bernard of Clairvaux, and the emblems of CAFOD and Oxfam may be less colourful than the banners of Richard the Lionheart and St Louis, but by and large it seems probable that God prefers us to feed the infidel than slaughter him. The only anxiety I sense among Catholics is that the Church will be outdone by the secular agencies in this mass enthusiasm for large-scale corporal works of mercy.

However, just as the mediaeval crusades began with pious intentions but degenerated into brutal fiascos, so the campaign to feed the world, and to alleviate poverty in our own society, may by its obsession with the material condition of men obscure the essentially spiritual import of the gospel. The very prosperity which enables us to help others, and the importance attached to it in our developed economies, may either lead us to project our own esteem for comfort and convenience, and our terror of penury, onto others; or it may blind us to the spiritual value of poverty, or inhibit us, where we see it, from pointing out this value for fear of the charge of hypocrisy.

There is also a danger that the spiritual discomfort we feel at the discrepancy between our wealth and the poverty of others may lead us to distort economic truths to suit our moral convictions. No one doubts that a human being who is hungry or cold suffers, and that a fellow human being who ignores his suffering lacks compassion. No one can question, either, that Christ admonished the rich man who would be perfect to give all he had to the poor, and that the Church throughout the ages has encouraged and admired those who take a vow of poverty. What we must recognise, however, is that the two halves of this moral equation do not add up to an economic truth; and that when, for example, a man like Fr John Dalrymple writes in a pamphlet published by the Catholic Truth Society called *Following Jesus Christ* that 'it is difficult to become rich without making others poor', he betrays an elementary ignorance of economics which if it were to gain currency would not just impoverish us all but make Christians look fools.

To put the paradox at its simplest, if all those who are rich gave all they have to the poor there would be an immediate global recession leaving no one rich and everyone poor. The very surplus of wealth in the west which makes charity possible relies upon the thrift, perhaps even the cupidity, of western man; and the attempt to harness the generous impulses of well-meaning Christians to dramatic but simplistic political solutions to complex economic problems often compounds the problems themselves.

There is a second paradox, moreover, that in some instances denying oneself to give to others may do more spiritual good to the donor than material good to the one who receives. Charity breaks the elemental link between endeavour and reward. It may seem a scandal that there is a surplus of grain in Europe while Africans starve; but on reflection it is apparent that the peasant who has hitherto scratched a living from the Sahara will abandon his meagre husbandry if that European surplus is given to him *gratis* in a refugee camp or a shanty town. The best way to help the Third World, we now know, is not to dump our surplus food in its impoverished countries – except in the case of famine – but to stimulate their own agriculture through economic incentives, and develop their economies through trade. Ten pounds spent on coffee from Colombia, or on a transistor radio from the Philippines, may do more real good than ten pounds put in the Oxfam box.

Such economic truths are frustrating for the Christian because they destroy his assumption that by denying himself he is helping another. It is awkward to realise that whether on a global, national or local scale, it may be by encouraging consumption, and the labour and enterprise that are necessary to pay for it, that the prosperity is created which in time leads to a real and lasting rise in the standard of living among those who are currently poor.

Here we come upon a third paradox. In a society where the poor become richer, the rich tend to become richer still. This often seems to affront the Christian conscience more than absolute want because the inequality of material condition is deemed to be unjust. Certainly in Britain today, by global standards, there are no poor: and the Christian who equates justice with equality may find himself in the anomalous position of demanding or donating washing-machines and video-recorders in the name of Christ.

Even when it comes to the Third World there is a danger of confusing inequality with injustice. Take, for example, a priest from Skelmersdale in Lancashire who was posted to a remote parish in Peru and appeared on a television film on the Catholic Church (*Outside the Window*, BBC 2). After clips showing the *jeunesse dorée* of Lima lounging on speed boats, he described his attitude towards the inequalities of wealth.

> I don't for a minute believe that my role is to politically motivate the people in the area in which I live, but I believe that if I can contribute in any way to the growth and the consciousness raising of the people among whom I am living, a lot of whom don't even know that they live in Peru . . . a lot of them don't even know that they're poor . . . Now I think I have some responsibility to try and educate these people in the broadest sense, because the Church, it strikes me here, would seem to be the only agent for change down here, and the only hope and chance that our people have, because we're talking about a basically, radically unjust society, where

you can be in parts of Lima which are more sophisti-
cated than anything north of the Midlands in England.

This attitude seems to epitomise the kind of moral trap
into which many of those who thirst for justice seem to fall.
It assumes that the prosperity of some Peruvians is responsible for the poverty of the others, or that impoverishing the
few would enrich the many. It implicitly rejects the common
phenomenon that the poor become richer when the rich
become richer still.

Worst of all, however, it suggests that justice is not to be
found in Christ, and in the life hereafter, but in this world
through the expropriation of speed-boats in Lima. The
priest tells his parishioners that they are poor. He activates
their anger and stimulates their envy. His norm is
Skelmersdale, and the standard of living of his former
parishioners whose children send two-penny pieces to help
their fellow-Catholics in Peru. Anything more 'sophisti-
cated' outrages him. Yet the discrepancy in wealth between
the peasants in Peru and the worthy Lancastrians is just as
great as the discrepancy between the Lancastrians and the
Peruvian upper-classes. The Church is universal; charity
knows no boundaries; and it cannot be construed as more
unjust for a sophisticate of Lima to own a speed-boat, while
a peasant goes hungry, than for a citizen of Skelmersdale to
own a colour television or a Mini Metro.

Yet any global levelling of men's economic condition
would not only lead to the total and universal recession that
I have described, it could also only be brought about
through expropriation and coercion which can hardly be
deemed a suitable expression of Christian love. It is one
thing to urge men to the temporal works of mercy; it is quite
another to insist that divine justice demands a common
sharing of material goods. Quite to the contrary, the implication of Christ's teaching is that what we enjoy in this world
detracts from our reward in the next. The poor are blessed
not just if they choose to be poor but if they accept an involuntary poverty. The poverty of the monk, wrote St Francis of
Sales, 'has a very great excellency' but the poverty sent by
fate is more excellent still, first because 'she came to you not

by choice, but by the will of God, who has made you poor, without any concurrence of your own will', and second because it is true poverty. 'That poverty which is praised, caressed, esteemed, succoured, and assisted, is near akin to riches, at least, it is not altogether poverty; but that which is despised, rejected, reproached, and abandoned, is poverty indeed.'

It was not that St Francis hoped that all of us would be poor. 'To be rich in effect, and poor in affection, is the great happiness of a Christian; for by this means he has the conveniency of riches for this world, and the merit of poverty in the world to come.' But the man who finds himself poor in affect should not complain, for 'we never complain but of that which displeases us, and if poverty displease you, you are no longer poor in spirit, but rich in affection.'

To be poor in spirit is not easy, for all our worldly instincts are to comfort, prosperity and ease – but as Christians we should beware of the benevolence which suggests that these are our only needs – that not only can poverty be eradicated but also suffering and travail. The paradise we await is not a life on earth where robots do all the work while we devote ourselves to leisure – indeed it is possible, as Simone Weil suggested, that physical labour itself is a means of salvation. 'Through original sin,' she wrote in *The Need for Roots*,

> man placed himself outside the current of obedience. God chose as his punishment labour and death. Consequently labour and death, if man undertakes them in a spirit of willingness, constitutes a transference back into the current of supreme good, which is obedience to God . . .

'Physical labour is daily death . . .' she went on, yet 'Physical labour willingly consented to is, after death willingly consented to, the most perfect form of obedience.'

Our Pope too reminds us of the value of suffering in his Apostolic Letter *Salvifici Doloris.*

> It is suffering, more than anything else, which clears the way for the grace which transforms human souls. Suffering, more than anything else, makes present in

the history of humanity the powers of the Redemption. In that 'cosmic' struggle between the spiritual powers of good and evil, spoken of in the Letter to the Ephesians, human sufferings, united to the redemptive suffering of Christ, constitute a special support for the powers of good, and open the way to the victory of these salvific powers.

Certainly, Christ has taught man not just to do good by his suffering but also to do good to those who suffer; but in studying the faces of those who are poor in the Third World, and comparing them to those enjoying their material prosperity in the shopping centres or pleasure parks of the First, one is left in little doubt as to who are closer to God.

15

Catechists and Commissars

Published in truncated form as 'Taking Heaven
by Storm', in the *Independent Magazine* on
17 March 1990

LAST NOVEMBER IN EL SALVADOR, after twenty years of
civil war, the Farabundo Marti National Liberation Front
(FMLN) made an all-out attack on San Salvador, the capital
city. Fifteen hundred guerillas came down from the volcano
which overlooks some of the smartest suburbs. Others, in
the *barrios*, dug up weapons which had been hidden in
readiness for this offensive. Several areas of the city were
occupied, and mortars were fired at the President's home.
However, there was no general uprising against the government, and after ten days of fighting the guerillas withdrew.

Up to three thousand people were killed in the course of
this offensive, either in battle, or caught in the cross-fire, or
killed in cold blood. Most horrifying of all, to the outside
world, was the murder of six Jesuit priests, their housekeeper and the housekeeper's daughter. It happened on
the night of 16 November, on the campus of their University
of Central America. All the Jesuits were distinguished academics, five of them born and trained in Spain, but resident
in El Salvador for so many years that the Rector of the
University, Fr Ignacio Ellacuria, had become a national
figure. According to the provincial of the Society of Jesus, Fr
Tojeira, he was regarded by the President, Alfredo
Christiani, as 'the only critical and yet constructive political
opposition he had in the country'.

These Jesuits were neither the first nor the most notable Catholic priests to have been killed in El Salvador. Between 1977 and 1981, ten met violent ends, among them a Jesuit, Fr Rutilio Grande. Many catechists, church workers and members of the Christian base communities have been among the 70,000 slaughtered. In 1980 four American women missionaries were raped and then murdered by National Guardsmen. In March of the same year, the Archbishop of San Salvador, Oscar Arnulfo Romero, was shot dead with a single bullet as he was celebrating Mass.

To understand this apparent persecution of the Catholic Church in a Catholic country, one must go back to the deliberations of the Second Vatican Council, called by Pope John XXIII in 1963 in which there was a shift in emphasis from a purely spiritual and self-contained concept of Catholicism to one which was open to and appreciated what was good in the world at large.

In particular the material and the social aspirations of man were deemed good, and a commitment made to help the poor. 'The Church encompasses in her love all those who are afflicted by human misery, and she recognizes in those who are poor and who suffer, the image of her poor and suffering founder. She does all in her power to relieve their need, and in them she strives to serve Christ.'

Such solicitude for the unfortunate was not new. Numerous religious orders had been founded specifically to do charitable work. In the past, however, they had sought to alleviate the symptoms of suffering rather than do anything about the cause. Now, the Council suggested, 'the best way to fulfil one's obligation to justice and love is to contribute to the common good according to one's means and the needs of others, even to the point of fostering public and private organizations devoted to the bettering of conditions of life.' 'Thus,' said the fathers, with a certain optimism, 'there will arise a generation of new men, the moulders of a new humanity.'

None met this challenge with greater zeal than the members of the Society of Jesus. Founded in the sixteenth century by St Ignatius Loyala to combat the Protestant Reformation, the order had succeeded so well in the centuries which followed that Jesuits had become the power behind many a throne. In Europe they became the confessors of reigning monarchs and the tutors of future kings. Their missionaries went to India, China, Africa and the Americas, braving tempests and tortures to bring heathen souls to the one true faith. In Peking they became intimates of the Manchu emperors; in America it was a Jesuit who first discovered the Mississippi. In Paraguay they ruled colonies or 'reductions' of Christian Indians, described as 'the most remarkable example of a whole people transformed and exalted through Christianity that has been known since the Middle Ages'.

Their influence grew so strong that they became loathed and feared. 'Jesuitical' entered the language, meaning unscrupulous and crafty. Any means were justified by the end they pursued which was the greater glory of God. In the middle of the eighteenth century, they were expelled first from Spain and all Spanish possessions, and later from Portugal, France and Naples. In 1773 the Pope, Clement XIV, suppressed the order. In 1814 it was restored.

Most efficacious of all the Jesuits' methods was the education of the young. 'Give us a child until he is seven,' they would say, 'and he is ours for life.' In an age of *cuius regio, eius religio*, they concentrated their attention on the sons of future rulers. Theirs became the best schools and universities in the major cities of Catholic countries throughout the world. Their pupils were the future elite. In San Salvador, as in Paris, Prague, Warsaw, Washington or Madrid, the Jesuits catered for the children of the upper classes in their high school and University of Central America.

It was therefore the Jesuits who felt most chastened by the rebuke implicit in the decrees of the Council. Many of their pupils in San Salvador, when they graduated, became leading figures in the community – landowners, lawyers, doctors, businessmen and politicians. They always took their families to Mass on a Sunday and made sure that their daughters married lavishly in a church. But did they practise what they preached? Were they Christians in spirit as well as in form? 'Even though incorporated into the body of the Church,' the Council had warned, 'one who does not persevere in charity is not saved. He remains in the bosom of the Church, but in body, not in heart.'

Eager to mend their ways, and respond to the call of the Council, many Jesuits now espoused a new 'theology of Liberation' which not only justified but insisted upon a radical political expression of Christian faith. It had been born at a meeting of young theologians at Petropolis in Brazil in 1964, and claimed its most notable triumph four years later when the Catholic Bishops of South America, meeting at Medellin in Colombia, declared their 'preferential option for the poor'. Traditionalists claim that this merely reminded Catholics of an age-old commitment, but the members of what came to be called the 'progressive' or 'popular' Church saw it as episcopal approval of their collective, political and usually Marxist and revolutionary concept of salvation.

While the application of this theology was directed principally to the impoverished nations of the Third World, many of its leading theorists were in fact European, and many of their theories evolved in institutions like the Catholic University of Louvain in Belgium. A leading Liberation theologian among the Jesuits, Jon Sobrino, was a Basque who taught at the University of Central America (UCA) in San Salvador. All the students of the Society in Central America, in their training for the priesthood, learned their philosophy and theology at UCA, and many became zealous advocates of the theology of Liberation.

No country seemed more appropriate to put their theories into practice than El Salvador. A small, densely populated country, it was almost a caricature of a Central American banana republic. Of its five million inhabitants, most were *mestizos* (of mixed Spanish and Indian descent). The land could hardly sustain them, and what land there was, in the second half of the nineteenth century, had been enclosed to form plantations not of bananas but of coffee. Huge fortunes had been made by a few energetic and unscrupulous entrepreneurs. By the 1960s, more than half of the rural peasantry had no land. Sixty per cent of the land was owned by 2 per cent of the population. Nor was this disparity merely a matter of statistics. In the capital, San

Salvador, huge mansions surrounded by fortified walls stood side by side with makeshift shacks with no drains, no water, no light and often no food.

The country was ruled in the interests of the landowning oligarchy, the famous 'fourteen families', who, though they may have had the mentality of the Spanish *conquistadores*, were often more recent arrivals with names like Schwartz, Schmidt, Dalton and Hill. There was both an army and a national guard to protect the 'security' of the nation from external enemies as well as from 'enemies' within – in particular those who dared protest against political oppression or low rates of pay who were called Communists or subversives.

It was armed and financed by the United States in the interests of its own security. However, the officers were not drawn from the landowning families themselves, but from impecunious members of the middle and lower-middle class. These soon learned, like Mao-tse-Tung, that power comes out of a barrel of a gun. There began a succession of coups and counter-coups which, together with frequently fraudulent elections, provided El Salvador with its assembly and a head of state.

It was in this classic case of an unjust society that the progressive priests and their catechists went to work in the late 1960s, organising workers and peasants into unions, staging protests and inculcating in students their duty as Christians to work for a better world. In this they were opposed not just by the army and the police, but at times by their fellow clergy in what came to be known as the 'traditional Church'. These included not just prelates who preferred the company of landowners to that of the unwashed poor, but also conscientious pastors who felt that their flocks were being led astray. Many of the diocesan priests had had grave misgivings about Liberation Theology. They may not have had doctorates from European universities, nor have been able to argue with erudite Jesuits like Jon Sobrino or Ignacio Ellacuria, but they resisted the progressives all the same because of their temporal and material concept of salvation.

To circumvent this opposition from within the Church,

there arose the 'base communities', small groups of Christians who met together to study the Bible and decide for themselves, without the guidance of a priest, how to apply its teaching to their daily lives. The conclusions they reached invariably coincided with those reached by the Liberation theologians – to support, as the Council had commanded, organisations working for the common good – not bourgeois reformist parties like Duarte's Christian Democrats, but radical left-wing parties, and later the revolutionaries who had taken to the hills. For after the election of 1972, when power was denied to Duarte's Christian Democrats at the head of a united opposition, a guerilla group was formed, 'the Popular Liberation Force – Farabundo Marti', named after the Mexican revolutionary who had led a peasants' revolt in the 1930s. The FPL-FM, which was to evolve into the FMLN, had a specifically Marxist-Leninist ideology and set about assassinating politicians, landowners and army officers, and kidnapping or murdering the children of the landowning oligarchs.

The reaction of the army was a repression whose horrors continue to this day. The soldiers, often press-ganged from the peasantry, and originally trained by German advisers in the Prussian tradition, dispatched suspected guerillas, sometimes with no interrogation and invariably without due process of law.

To the Jesuits committed to the progressive Church, it was a case of the imperialist leopard showing its true spots. The greater the repression, the more zealous became their commitment to the people's cause. However, they still faced the opposition of the bishops, among them the then Archbishop of San Salvador, Luis Chavez y Gonzalez.

The priest who at the time was secretary to the Bishops' Conference of El Salvador, Mgr Freddy Delgado, describes the crisis which arose when the Archbishop dismissed a French priest, Father Bernardo Boulang, for engaging in political, not pastoral work. The progressive priests rallied to his defence. The Jesuit Father Ellacuria said that to expel Father Boulang was to stop the kind of authentic pastoral work that the church should have been doing in the past. A group of twenty-seven progressive priests protested to the

Archbishop but Monsignor Chavez y Gonzalez stood firm and Father Boulang was expelled.

There was a further fracas when the bishops of El Salvador, at the end of 1972, decided to wrest control from the Jesuits of the diocesan seminary in San Salvador of San Jose de la Montana. It had become so politicised that some of its students had been recruited into a Marxist-Leninist cell by the director of the National University, Dr Fabio Castillo. (Two of these, Octavio Ortiz and Ernesto Barrera, were among the priests later killed by the armed forces.) Protests were organised but to no avail. The Jesuits left the seminary of San Jose de la Montana and went to live either in private houses, base communities, or at UCA. There the most progressive Jesuits shared one house, the less progressive another, while the old traditionalists were banished to El Carmen in Santa Tecla.

What this taught the progressive Jesuits, according to Mgr Delgado, was the importance of having a bishop, or better still, an archbishop sympathetic to their point of view. Their opportunity came with the appointment of Mgr Oscar Arnulfo Romero to the see of San Salvador. He had hitherto been considered a conservative pastor but there were traits to his character which gave the progressives reason to believe that they might convert him to their cause. According to the Bishop of Santa Ana, Mgr Marco Rene Revello, on the very day his appointment was announced, a meeting was called of forty progressive priests, led by Ignacio Ellacuria and Jon Sobrino (and including the diocesan priests Fabian Amaya and Ricardo Urioste), to 'analyse' the appointment of Mgr Romero. A list was drawn up on a blackboard of his strengths and weaknesses. In his favour it was agreed that he was an honest man, a man of the Church, a man of prayer and a charitable man. Against him, they wrote that he was ambitious for power (he was said to have admired both Mussolini and Pius XII while studying in Rome); that he was an insecure man who was afraid to stand alone; and that he was an inflexible man who, once he had made up his mind, would not change it.

They decided that their first step should be to stimulate his ambition by showing how, if he joined with them, he could become a great figure in the Church. Secondly, because he was so insecure, they would surround him and keep others away. Thirdly, if they could get a fixed idea into his head, then they would have him in their power.

They selected a committee of five diocesan priests to ask for 'a dialogue' with the newly appointed archbishop. They met with him the day after his appointment, and insisted that the officials of his episcopal curia should be sent away. Two nuns stood at the door to make sure they were not interrupted. Mgr Revello, the Bishop of Santa Ana, who had got wind of what was happening, came to warn Mgr Romero, but was not admitted. In his view, Romero decided that his diocese would be ungovernable if he did not throw in his lot with the progressives.

Thereafter, every Monday, the Jesuits Ignacio Ellacuria and Jon Sobrino, would meet with the diocesan priests Jesus Delgado, Fabian Amaya and Ricardo Urioste to decide which of them would contribute what to the Archbishop's sermon on the following Sunday. On the Thursday they would meet again to put the different sections together, and on the Friday the homily would be given to Mgr Romero. This was not only preached from the pulpit, but broadcast throughout the country on the Catholic radio. On 24 March Romero pronounced that 'no soldier is obliged to obey an order to kill if it runs contrary to his conscience'. The next day he was killed.

Today, ten years later, the division between the progressive and the traditional Church remains as pronounced as ever. To the progressives Mgr Romero is the archetypal martyr of the modern age, 'the greatest figure in the Latin American Church', a Jesuit told me, 'for half a century'. The Bishop of Santa Ana, however, sees Romero not as a Christian martyr but 'as a hero who died for a cause'. To the current Archbishop of San Salvador, Mgr Arturo Rivera Damas, and his coadjutor Bishop, Mgr Rosa Chavez, Romero was certainly a martyr and they continue to speak out against the abuse of human rights. Mgr Rosa Chavez warned me, however, that I should distinguish between the homilies of a pastor and the opinions of a theologian. Ellacuria had been killed for his opinions, Romero for performing his duties as a priest.

The same distinction was made by Fr Jesus Delgado, now parish priest of the church next to the seminary of St Jose de la Montana. A priest in the exercise of his pastoral duties must sometimes conceal his opinions. Though himself enraged at the disparity between rich and poor in his own parish, where hovels with no plumbing stand in the shadows of the satellite dishes on the rooves of the fortified villas of the rich, he expresses his opinions through example by encouraging the poor to dig their own drains, and the rich to pay for the free breakfasts which he gives to the hungry children of his parish every Sunday after the 7 a.m. Mass. One of the ladies who helped him said to me approvingly: 'We have a very fine priest. He helps the poor but keeps out of politics.'

Such discretion in El Salvador, I soon learned, showed not just modesty but common sense. Traditionalists as well as progressives were afraid to express their opinions. I was told that Francisco Peccorini, a professor of philosophy and former Jesuit, who had been the only man with the intelligence to counter the arguments of Ignacio Ellacuria on the televised debates about the state of the nation, had been assassinated by the FMLN. According to Mgr Barreiro, the current Secretary to the Bishops' Conference, all the apologists for the Right had either been killed or had fled abroad. Mgr Freddy Delgado, the brother of Father Jesus and a member of the Government's Human Rights Commission, lived in fear of his life. After writing a pamphlet exposing Communist manipulation of the Popular Church, fellow priests in the FMLN had sent a unit to assassinate him. It is not difficult, in El Salvador, to know where the sympathies of a priest lie. A portrait of the Pope betrays a traditionalist; a portrait of Romero a progressive. In the office of Father Rogelio Pedraz, the Jesuit in charge of the publishing press at UCA, there did not even seem to be a crucifix, only a portrait of Romero. He described very vividly his conversion to the cause of the Popular Church through his experience of oppression in Latin America. He defends the violence of the guerillas on the grounds that 'in this country, no one will give anything unless it is taken from them'. And if the Church is being used by the Left, 'Well, it was used by the Right in the past, so let the Left have a turn.'

If other priests resist the cult of Romero, it is not because they doubt that he was a good man. They feel it is being exploited to lead gullible people away from God. 'The progressive groups,' said Mgr Tovar, the Bishop of Zacatecoluca and now President of the Bishops' Conference, 'have reached a point where to enable a man to escape poverty they demean the idea of salvation. They value only the temporal, but man has a soul as well as a body.'

This was confirmed by a young man from a base community, whom I met in a *barrio* to the north of the city. He found it hard to believe that there was life after death. Aged in his early thirties, he had been given leave by the FMLN to come to San Salvador to visit his wife and baby. He came from a family of *campesinos*, and as a student had joined the Revolutionary Student Movement. For two years he had worked in a factory, and for five more had studied for the priesthood in the seminary of San Jose de la Montana. He had decided not to be a priest partly because he had to earn money for his family, partly because he had doubts about some of the teachings of the Church.

In 1980 he had joined a Christian base community which, after a process of 'consciencization', decided to support the FMLN. In 1985 he was captured by the armed forces, tortured and then released. He was almost captured again a month before the November offensive when the police raided his house and seized his car and television. His wife was betrayed during the offensive, arrested, but later released. He now lived in a guerilla camp in a war zone, but found it easy enough to go to and fro from San Salvador.

He described his base community as a small group of people who met to study the Bible, and learn from it how God works through history to liberate the poor. They were taught to appreciate their responsibilities toward the church and the world, answering such fundamental questions as 'What am I?', 'What does it mean to be baptised?' or 'What can I do to change society?' Invariably the conclusion reached 'by the most mature' was to support the FMLN.

The specifically religious aspects of the life of a base community differed so radically from those of the traditional Church that he did not believe that there could ever be a compromise between the two. First of all, the base communities believed in a collegiate, not a hierarchical church. A priest could take part in their discussions, but he spoke with no more authority than anyone else. He had no special privilege either, and must take his turn to do the cooking. Certainly, he would be the one to consecrate the host, but, if there was no priest they would distribute already consecrated hosts, and if there were no consecrated hosts, they would bless *tortillas* and distribute them instead.

Their principal task was to evangelise – to spread the Good News. What was the Good News? That they were working for a better future where there would not be a few who had much, but all would have something – food, shelter and jobs. Each would till his own land and enjoy the fruits of his labour. There would be peace not just as an absence of war, but as a condition where the causes of war did not exist.

Was this what he meant by the Kingdom of Heaven? It was halfway there. Did he know if such a society already existed? They were being built. Where? He had read that in Russia and in Cuba they were building such a society. Had he also read about the changes that were taking place in Russia and Eastern Europe? Yes, but he understood that these were merely reforms of the Marxist system.

There were two girls with him, both members of the base community movement. One was a full-time proselytiser, working in the provinces of Usulatan and San Miguel in the central region of the country. She was a Catholic but worked with Lutheran groups as well, and did not think that there were any significant differences between the two religions. She evangelised at Masses and meetings, or simply by going door to door. The most important mission of the Church, she thought, was to make individuals aware of social and political changes, and bring them to see the importance of unity in relation to justice, equality and peace.

Could peace be brought about by violence? She thought

deeply before answering. Not violence as such, she said. But one tends to evaluate deeds on their merits, and in that context being critical did not mean to condemn.

I asked if all base communities sympathised with the FMLN. She wriggled in her seat. One had to make a distinction, she said, between levels of maturity in the different base communities. Some were very new. Politically, they had not come of age. And when they do? They support the FMLN.

Now the Spanish priest who had introduced us, joined our discussion. Like the Jesuit, Fr Rogelio Pedraz, he was small and slight, with a severe look on his face. He told me, somewhat derisively, that while people in Europe talked about Liberation Theology, here they lived it. The poverty one can see and share, changes one's thinking. By analysing social reality – the plight of the poor – one sees that there is nothing for which any one person is to blame. It is the *structures* of a society that are sinful, and it is by collaborating with these structures that we sin. The evils of the structures of Salvadorian society brought poverty, exploitation and death.

'And the FMLN?' I asked. 'Isn't that also a structure which brings death?'

The priest looked down at his papers.

'Lives are lost every day,' said the girl.

'I saw planes bomb villages,' said the priest. 'Furthermore, the FMLN is not a structure . . . '

'And its violence is incidental,' said the girl. 'The evil caused by capitalism is historically different.'

I told them that I had recently visited Lithuania, a very Catholic country, where people took a contrary view.

'There are different kinds of poverty,' said the priest. 'What is clear is that capitalism produces poverty . . .'

'But in Western Europe,' I suggested, 'even the poor have been made richer by the success of the capitalist economies.'

'That is sin! The consumer society is sinful. The Pope has condemned it. The values of the First World are dead. People think only of earning more to spend more. There is injustice – people without houses, people without jobs, people up to their necks in debt. Things should not be so. People should feel like the children of God. They should make their own history, and live like brothers, caring for the weak, the old and the poor.'

'As in Cuba?'

'No. There is no such society here on earth. But we must fight for it.'

'With violence?'

'Yes! Because Jesus said, "the kingdom of heaven has been subjected to violence, and the violent are taking it by storm."'

The impression I formed from this encounter, that the Christian base communities doubled as cells providing recruitment, propaganda and support for the FMLN, was confirmed by a wry old Maryknoll father from New York State who had been working in Central America for twenty-five years. He took me to Zacamil, the scene of heavy fighting during the offensive, where government forces had looted and desecrated a chapel used by the local base community. 'I did notice,' he said, 'that on the day of the offensive many of the young people went off to fight for the FMLN. They were romantic kids who thought the fighting would last for a couple of days. Now some have gone to train in Chalatenango, but most couldn't face it and have gone abroad.'

At St Antony Abad, an impoverished suburb to the north of San Salvador, there was a notable absence of young men at a Mass held by the base community. When I asked the English nun, a Poor Clare, who had taken me there, where they were, she laughed nervously and did not reply. The sermon, given by an Irish Jesuit, who, she said, had 'come for an experience', was not a homily from the pulpit but a discussion with the whole congregation. All agreed that they should evangelise, but, a girl complained, many were now afraid to join the base communities because of the political commitment it involved. They were turning, instead, to the Pentecostalist sects because they knew that at their services they would be safe from harrassment by the armed forces.

There was a meeting, that Sunday, in a stadium in San

Salvador of the born-again Christians of the Elim Church. It was founded with two families in San Salvador thirteen years ago by the pastor Sergio Solorzano. Now it had 30,000 members and there were 30,000 more in the stadium. They were all neatly dressed, the women in pretty dresses and with *mantillas* over their heads, the men wearing jackets and ties. There were 3,000 stewards, all in uniform, and many with walkie-talkies. The service was like a pop concert, with catchy, melodic hymns, ending with a virtuoso tirade by Sergio Solorzano, calling upon everyone to turn to Jesus. Above an army helicopter circled the stadium taking aerial photographs. Below the audience wept, and cried 'Glory, Allelujia', among them the Minister of Agriculture.

The organisers welcomed me with open arms. 'Thank God you have come,' a lady said to me. 'We want you to tell the world that there is no persecution of Christians in El Salvador.' 'Do you know,' she went on, 'why San Salvador did not fall to the Communists during the November offensive? Because all these people here were praying, praying each day that they would fail.'

'Not by the sword,' thundered the pastor, Solorzano, 'but by the word of God shall you be saved . . .'

The most common charge levelled at the progressive Church, by traditional Catholics and the sects alike, was that it preached hatred of their enemies when Christ had said that evil should be overcome by love. 'If you attack someone, you cannot convert him', I was told by a pious lady who lived in the elegant suburb of Escalon where the guerillas had dug in during the offensive. 'If the bishop Rosa Chavez wants the rich to help the poor, castigating them is not the way to go about it. God told us to love, and to forgive, our enemies. One must hate sin, but love the sinner. He who has not sinned, let him throw the first stone . . . We have only to change people's hearts, and the injustice of society will disappear.'

She was particularly bitter about foreign journalists who came to El Salvador with their minds made up in favour of the FMLN. It was the foreign priests, too, who incited the gullible *campesinos* to rebellion. No wonder so many

Catholics were joining the Pentecostalist sects. They left Mass agitated and angry: the sermons of the sects brought peace to their hearts.

Equally critical of the progressive Church was an Italian Salesian who had been working in El Salvador for twenty-seven years. It was the custom of his order, founded by St John Bosco in the nineteenth century, never to offend and to forgive all; but it was galling, all the same, to hear it said by the progressives that it was only at Medellin in 1968 that the Catholic Church had discovered its option for the poor. The Salesians had been working in Central America for almost 100 years, educating the sons of the poor. They had schools throughout the country, and technical institutes which gave vocational training. In a country of high unemployment, all their pupils were offered jobs a year before they graduated – not just for the skills they had learned, but because of their sound Christian formation.

This, he thought, was by far the best way for priests to exercise their option for the poor. While the Salesians planned a new institute in Soyapango which would eventually turn out 40,000 qualified students every year, the Jesuits, the base communities, those who belonged to what he called 'Romero's Church', encouraged the young to join the FMLN and destroy the infrastructure of the country, burning plantations, blowing up buses, bridges, pylons and power stations. As a result the gross national product had fallen to the level of 1965. Coffee production had halved and cotton production was down by 90 per cent. To pay for this destruction, prices were raised. The standard of living had fallen for everyone, including the poor.

The Franciscans too, he said, had been quietly working for the poor long before the invention of Liberation Theology. They ran orphanages and homes for handicapped children, but, like the Salesians, were subject to enormous 'psychological pressure' from their coreligionists in the progressive Church. They disapproved of their co-operation with 'sinful structures' by raising money from private enterprise and USAID, and wished to intimidate those whose lives refuted their theological line. A Franciscan, Father Spezzotto, wrote a letter predicting that he would be

killed for preaching against a violent solution to social problems. Sure enough, he was assassinated. The Salesians
believe it was by the FMLN. For this reason the Salesian I
spoke to did not want me to mention his name. 'It isn't easy
to speak out,' he said. 'When I tell my bishop in Italy what
is happening, he doesn't believe me. The great untold story
is of the persecution of the traditional Church.'

There are bishops in El Salvador who share this point of
view, but it is difficult for them to denounce the political
involvement of the progressive Catholics without appearing
to side with the death squads of the right. So polarised is
opinion in El Salvador that there is little weight or space in
the centre. Paradoxically, the President, Alfredo Christiani,
is widely considered to be a moderate and conscientious
man. 'Even Fr Ellacuria,' said the Bishop of Zacatecoluca,
Mgr Tovar, 'was coming closer to the position of the current
government.' He had come to see 'that Marxism had not
improved the life of the country. On the contrary, how many
mutilated babies, how many deaths, had it produced?' It was
one thing, however, for an intellectual to modify his
opinions; quite another for him to modify the hatred of the
bourgeois capitalists inculcated by progressive priests over
the past twenty years.

Carlos Baron, a pious Catholic, removed his son from the
Jesuit school because he was marked down in his essays if he
strayed from a Marxist line. Later the headmaster left to
become a spokesman for the FMLN. 'Some of the priests
have lost their faith,' said Baron, 'and no longer believe in
the afterlife, but they continue to work in a social context.'

Another pious businessman, who has used some of the
profits from his chain of department stores to set up charitable foundations, helping not just the families of his 1500
employees but also funding clinics and orphanages as well,
admits that in the past the Church was too insensitive to the
plight of the poor. The rapaciousness of the *conquistadores*
was deeply embedded in the national psyche. Politics was
thought to be merely another, slightly seedy, branch of business. *Manga la guava* was the generally accepted ethic: if you
have a fruit in your hand, eat it.

Most disillusioning for him, as a Christian moderate, was the Presidency of the Christian Democrat, Duarte. Although tortured at one time by the military, and permitted to lead the opposition to victory in the elections of 1984 only as a result of intense pressure from the United States, Duarte then failed on every count. He appointed his cronies as ministers who turned out to be not only corrupt but also inept. He failed both to control the army and to end the war with the guerillas. And the land reforms which he enacted were a fiasco – the co-operatives turning out to be both corrupt and inefficient.

It was because of this that half a million Salvadorians – 53 per cent of those who voted, chose ARENA in the 1988 elections – the party founded by the man accused of ordering the murder of Romero, the notorious Major 'Bob' d'Aubuisson. However, d'Aubuisson was not the leader. It was Christiani. And Christiani's inaugural address was described by Fr Ellacuria as 'surprising for the moderation of its overall tone, and for its moderation in most of the specific issues addressed'. Ironically, too, some of the ministers he appointed were able professionals, educated by the Jesuits before the era of Liberation Theology. Negotiations were started with the guerillas to end the war, but ended with the November offensive and the murder of Ellacuria and the other five Jesuits at UCA.

This atrocity was such a disaster for Christiani and the ARENA government that it was assumed by Mgr Tovar to be the work of the FMLN. He added, at the time: 'I don't dismiss the idea that there may be certain individuals who use violent methods in certain restricted circles of the extreme right'; and now, after the arrest of Colonel Benavides, he concedes that his hypothesis fails, although he still believes that the murder was not planned by the army 'as an institution'.

Major Chavez, a spokesman for the Armed Forces, agrees. He referred to the killing of the Jesuits as a 'repugnant deed' and would be sorry if it turned out that it was Colonel Benavides who was responsible. However, by putting himself into the shoes of Colonel Benavides, he could understand how it might have happened. On the second day of the offensive, his son had suffered a breakdown which had reduced him to a vegetable. For years, now, he had seen and heard the progressive Jesuits on television – particularly, Fr Ellacuria – appear to justify the violence of the Communist terrorists who at that very moment, using innocent civilians as a shield, were attempting to seize power by force.

For years the Jesuits had been preaching hatred of the rich, inciting young people to take to the hills; and now, just across the road from the military compound where many of the officers lived, they sat in their ivory tower at UCA, publishing books sympathetic to the guerilla cause such as *I Was Never Alone* by 'Commandante' Nichia Diaz, and waiting, no doubt, for the moment when, like the three Catholic priests in Nicaragua, some of them would become Ministers in a government of the FMLN.

The Armed Forces, Major Chavez insisted, were on excellent terms with the traditional Church. Mass was compulsory on a Sunday in all the garrisons in the country. There were also compulsory classes in human rights. It was nevertheless frustrating to know that gullible *campesinos* who had always looked up to their priests, were being directed through 'consciencization' to fight for the Communist cause. It was well known that the base communities supported the FMLN. It was known, too, that foreign church workers – priests and lay catechists – came to the country to assist the guerillas.

Others, outside the Armed Forces, shared this point of view. 'The long Salvadorian conflict,' wrote La Prensa,

> has been a stage for the direct interference of foreigners who, in the most diverse guises, from simple adventurers to religious missionaries, have come to our small and convulsed country to 'experience' the drama of the Third World . . . Many of these noxious characters are dressed themselves in the garb of humanitarian piety, supposedly 'accompanying' the most humble in their pain, but in reality giving personal and material help to subversion.

Most frustrating, for the Salvadorian government, is the vast network abroad of organisations which support the political activists in the different churches, and cry 'persecution' whenever they are attacked. In Britain there is the CIIR which propagates their point of view. In the United States there are journals like the *Central America Report*, a bi-monthly journal 'of the Religious Task Force in Central America', with three Jesuits on its steering committee, which seeks to persuade public opinion that harassment of church workers amounts to a persecution of the Church.

A notable case was that of Jennifer Casolo. During the November offensive, according to Major Chavez, a captured guerilla named six houses in San Salvador where arms had been hidden by sympathizers. One of these caches was in the garden of a 28-year-old American, Jennifer Jean Casolo, who had worked in El Salvador for five years, organising tours for visiting Christians. Found buried in her garden, in the presence of an official from the US Consul, were grenades, explosives, detonators and 20,000 rounds of ammunition for AK 47 and M-16 rifles.

Jennifer Casolo was arrested, as were the others in whose homes such dumps had been found. The case was prepared against her. Then, suddenly, it was announced that there was 'insufficient evidence to convict her'. She was released from custody and flown back to the United States.

The Salvadorians, of course, remained in custody, and this reveals another paradox – that the Europeans and North Americans, who purport to be working for the brotherhood of man, in fact apply a double standard which values one of their lives more highly than that of a Salvadorian. During the offensive, the deaths which made the headlines were those of David Blundy, a British journalist, and the six Jesuits, five of whom were European. The five journalists who worked for the *Centro de Informacion Nacional,* and were captured and then executed by the FMLN, were not considered newsworthy in the northern hemisphere. They were, after all, *mestizos,* and were killed by the wrong side.

It is difficult, when visiting El Salvador, not to be drawn into the conflict and take sides. My brief, in any case, was not to analyse the political situation but to investigate the apparent persecution of the Church. The answer to that, as I discovered, depended upon what was meant by the

Church. Undoubtedly, many convinced Christians – including many Jesuits, and most of those in the base communities – feel that to live according to the gospel they must throw in their lot with the FMLN. The Archbishop of San Salvador, and his coadjutor, Mgr Rosa Chavez, with the mantle of Romero on their shoulders, feel that they must speak out for the right of these Christians to bear witness to their beliefs in this way.

Others, like the President of the Bishops' Conference, Mgr Tovar, fear that the Catholic Church is being used as a cover for political activists who want to impose by force a 'dictatorship of the proletariat', and in doing so have brought unparalleled misery to the Salvadorian people.

My own instinct, in the end, was to agree with this latter point of view. It was not just the cogency of Mgr Tovar which convinced me but the views of the other traditionalists like the Salesian who had been working for the poor a century before the invention of Liberation Theology or the decrees of Vatican II.

I was also subject to an experience of the kind which inevitably affects one's point of view. Many journalists who have visited El Salvador since the death of Mgr Romero have seen the bodies of those tortured and killed by the death squads of the right. This has led them, understandably, to sympathise with the FMLN. One of the American journalists whom I met in El Salvador told me with great enthusiasm what the guerillas had achieved in the November offensive. They had shown that they were a force to be reckoned with; and by occupying choice suburbs of San Salvador like Escalon, they had shown the middle classes that the army could not protect them. As a result, there was now an exodus of skilled professionals. The country's capital had already gone. The economy was in a downward spiral. And all this had been achieved with only slight losses to the hardened cadres: most of those killed had been recent recruits.

Who were those recent recruits? As the FMLN retreated after the offensive, thirty-two guerillas, cut off from the main force, had claimed sanctuary in the church of El Calvario in downtown San Salvador. Two months later they were still there. When I visited the church, a group sat disconsolately behind iron railings on the steps of the church beneath a huge red banner demanding free passage to a safe haven. On the walls there were smaller posters showing a guerilla holding a child with the slogan: 'For the sake of your children, all against ARENA'.

The officer in command of the unit surrounding the church allowed me to talk to these guerillas through the railings. Among them there was a group of three boys. One was aged twelve. He served as a runner. The other two were sixteen. One had had his leg amputated at the knee after stepping on a land mine. He wore a white trainer on his single foot from which he had peeled off the emblem – 'Nike' or 'Cobra' – and had drawn instead, with a ball-point pen, the initials FMLN.

I asked him for how long he had been fighting with the guerillas. He said for two years. I asked if his parents knew. He said that they did, and that they approved, but that they did not know where he was.

'Are there many boys of your age?'

'Yes. Most of us.'

'And why do you do it?'

'We like the life with the guerillas. We like the fighting.'

As I left the church, I wondered why it should be that a People's Army should depend upon teen-age boys to do the fighting and take the losses. If the progressive Church was really fighting to establish the Kingdom of Heaven on earth, why must it be a children's crusade?

As I flew back to London, I read in *La Prensa Grafica* that the thirty-two guerillas from the church of El Calvario, among them twelve minors, were to be flown out to Cuba, the demi-paradise they had been promised, and for which so many had died.

HISTORY

16

Truth and Fiction in The Da Vinci Code

A review of *Truth and Fiction in the Da Vinci Code*
by Bart D. Ehrman (Oxford University Press),
first published in *The Spectator,* 18 December
2004

SHORTLY BEFORE THE PUBLICATION OF Dan Brown's *The Da Vinci Code* in Britain, the publishers, Transworld, kindly sent me an advance copy of the hardback edition. I glanced through it, recognised the recycled nonsense of the 1980s' best-seller, *The Holy Blood and the Holy Grail,* and sent it off unread to the Oxfam Shop. It seemed to me unlikely that the public could fall for the same trick twice. How wrong I was: the novel was rapturously received in the United States, has sold more than 18 million copies in forty-two languages and has spawned a dozen commentaries – among them Bart D. Ehrman's *Truth and Fiction in the Da Vinci Code.*

Bart Ehrman is a serious scholar: he chairs the Department of Religious Studies at the University of North Carolina at Chapel Hill but is at pains to point out that, while this is 'the buckle of the bible belt', he is not a blinkered, born-again Christian. He rigorously confines himself to his area of expertise – early Church history – and eschews comment on tangential aspects of *The Da Vinci Code* such as the role of Opus Dei or the Templar Knights.

The 'facts' behind Dan Brown's novel are that Jesus of Nazareth had a child by his wife Mary Magdalene whose descendants became the Merovingian kings of France. This truth was ruthlessly suppressed by Christ's male apostles and the early fathers of the Church. Apocryphal gospels which give Mary Magdalene her due were excluded from the New Testament by order of the Roman Emperor Constantine: instead, Mary Magdalene – the 'divine feminine' – was demonised as a whore.

However, the truth was preserved by a secret 'Priory of Sion' and the crusading Knights of the Temple found documents that proved it under the Temple Mount in Jerusalem. These documents, together with the remains of Mary Magdalene, are the Holy Grail. Coded allusions to it are found in the songs of the troubadours and Leonardo da Vinci's famous painting of the Last Supper. The fictional plot turns on a race in the present day to find the Grail and reveal it to the world – unless, of course, the crazed assassin of Opus Dei gets there first.

So far, so good: all is fair in love, war and fiction. But one of the reasons for the novel's appeal is Dan Brown's contention that his characters' theories are based on fact. It is to counter those claims that Ehrman was persuaded by his editor at the Oxford University Press to put him right, and he does so patiently, comprehensively and in the kind of simple, step-by-step style that he no doubt adopts for his students in North Carolina. Jesus' life was *not* recorded by 'thousands of followers'. It is *not* true that eighty gospels were considered for the New Testament, or that Jesus was not considered divine until the Council of Nicea, or that the Emperor Constantine commissioned 'a new Bible'. The equation of Mary Magdalene with the woman of ill-repute in the Gospels was only made by Pope Gregory the Great in the sixth century. Jewish decorum did not disapprove of celibacy: the Essenes were celibate. The Dead Sea Scrolls make no reference to Jesus, nor do the Nag Hammadi documents tell the story of the Grail or emphasise Jesus' human traits: 'quite the contrary'.

To add to Ehrman's catalogue of Brown's disinformation from my area of expertise (sales of my book *The Templars* have risen dramatically thanks to *The Da Vinci Code*) I might add that the Templar church in London, like all Templar churches, was not 'perfectly circular in honor of the sun' as Sir Leigh Teabing claims in Brown's novel, but in imitation of the church of the Holy Sepulchre in Jerusalem. Nor did Pope Clement V kill 'hundreds of Knights Templar' on 13 October 1307, burn their bodies at the stake and throw their bodies 'unceremoniously into the Tiber River'; they were arrested in Paris and other French cities by King Philip IV of France in defiance of the Pope who vehemently protested. Nor could the Pope have thrown the bodies into the Tiber: he was residing at the time in the Angevin city of Poitiers.

If so many historical claims made by the characters in *The Da Vinci Code* are untrue one is left wondering about its author, Dan Brown. Is he ignorant, cynical or lazy, or perhaps a bit of all three? No doubt he saw promising material for a thriller in *The Holy Blood and the Holy Grail:* and no doubt the story taps into today's anti-Catholic prejudice and feminist paranoia. But by counting on the ignorance and gullibility in his readers he implicitly insults them. With, say, 2.5 readers for every copy of the book (I read my son's paperback) that makes almost 50 million dupes. Quite an achievement.

Bart Ehrman does not seem to mind. He is at pains to point out that off campus he is a regular guy who likes the movies *The Last Temptation of Christ* and *The Life of Brian* 'almost without reserve'. He finds *The Da Vinci Code* as a work of fiction 'intricate, compelling, spellbinding' and, perhaps because he lives in that buckle of the Bible Belt, is not bothered by Brown's slanders against Opus Dei and the Catholic Church. He also fails to pick up on a crucial contradiction: how can a Church criticised for Mariolatry be said to have suppressed the 'divine feminine' in Christian teaching? However, Ehrman is right that the novel's success may stimulate a wider interest in the history of the early Church and even for those who have not read *The Da Vinci Code* I would recommend this book.

17

Christians and Jews

A review of *A History of Christianity* (Weidenfeld
and Nicolson, 1976) and *A History of the Jews*
(Weidenfeld and Nicolson, 1987)
by Paul Johnson

PAUL JOHNSON IS AMONG THE MOST talented and
trenchant journalists in Britain today. He has a natural feeling for words and uses them with the urgency of a prophet.
He was once a socialist – he edited the *New Statesman* – but
then, like St Paul, he had a vision which changed his life. He
saw Britain as a New Jerusalem freed of state constraints and
now, in his columns, he is one of the foremost apologists for
Mrs Thatcher's Conservative Britain.

Johnson was raised a Catholic – he was educated by the
Jesuits at Stonyhurst – and he has retained from his past an
interest not just in religion but in the way in which millenial
ideas have influenced human behaviour – usually for the
worse. Twelve years ago he moved on from his political preoccupations which had led to a study of Queen Elizabeth I
and a polemic against the Common Market called *The
Offshore Islanders* to write *A History of Christianity* which dwelt
largely upon the cruelties and follies of the Western
Church. 'A Christian with faith,' he wrote, 'has nothing to
fear from the facts' but whether he was such a Christian was
left unclear. Now, after some potboilers and a polemical
History of the Modern World, he has produced *A History of the
Jews*, written in the same style as his history of Christianity
but treating his subject with much greater respect. Indeed,

reading the two histories together, one gets the impression that he would rather have been born a Jew than a Christian because the Jews were the first 'to rationalize the unknown' and are the 'pilot project for the entire human race'.

One cannot discount a twinge of bad conscience behind pro-semitism. Johnson, like any contemporary historian, writes in the shadow of Holocaust yet must remember praying condescendingly as a child for the *perfidis Judaeis*. 'Almighty, eternal God, who doest not withhold thy mercy even from Jewish unbelief . . .' His *History of the Jews* is thus a symptom of the change in Catholic attitudes towards heretics and infidels which came about at the Second Vatican Council – itself partly the result of Catholic remorse at what happened during the Second World War.

Thus he exemplifies the tolerance which is now the predominant dogma of all religions – at least in the western world – and both his histories are partly to be understood as an attempt to redress the wrongs done by Catholic anti-semites in the past. Like Pope John Paul II, who now refers to the Jews as 'our older brothers in the faith', Johnson, while working on his *History of Christianity*, became aware for the first time in his life of the magnitude of the debt Christianity owes to Judaism. 'It was not, as I had been taught to suppose, that the New Testament replaced the Old; rather, that Christianity gave a fresh interpretation to an ancient form of monotheism, gradually evolving into a different religion but carrying with it much of the moral and dogmatic theology, the liturgy, the institutions and the fundamental concepts of its forebear'.

It is fascinating, in reading Johnson's *History of the Jews*, to realise just how early in history – or prehistory – the mould was set for the shape we are today. 'Thou shalt not commit adultery', for example, is a tall order, even for civilised man, let alone for the semi-barbarians of the second millennia BC. Yet the Israelite conviction that there was an all-knowing and all-seeing God who punished the transgressions of man against man was a necessary foundation for the evolution of concepts such as the liberty of the individual or the rights of man. 'Indeed the Mosaic code,' writes Johnson, 'is a code not only of obligation and prohibition but also, in an embryonic form, of rights.' Thus those who scoff, from a comfortable distance in history, at the way in which the Jews slaughtered Jews, or the Christians Christians, or the Christians Jews; or who suggest, like Robin Lane-Fox in *Pagans and Christians*, that we were better off as pagans, should bear in mind that without faith in a living God the taking of innocent human life might have no greater moral significance than killing an innocent chicken.

As Johnson points out, however, the Jewish equation of social and theological morality did not make for an easy life. 'In Mosaic legal theory, all breaches of the law offended God. All crimes are sins, just as all sins are crimes. Offences are absolute wrongs, beyond the power of man unaided to pardon or expunge.' It was this concept which led to the crucifixion of Christ ('We have our own law,' said the Jews to Pilate, 'and by our law he ought to die, for pretending to be the Son of God') and later to the Christian persecution of the Jews.

The dogged fidelity of the Jews to their sense of election was in one sense their undoing and in another their salva-tion. It is an extraordinary and unparalleled phenomenon that a tribe from prehistory should remain an identifiable people in the twentieth century – distinctive not just as Israelis in Palestine but as Jews throughout the world. Their exclusivity, however, meant that they could not expand at a time when, says Johnson, 'Ethical monotheism was an idea whose time had come. It was a Jewish idea. But the Christians took it with them to the wider world, and so robbed the Jews of their birthright.'

So too did Islam, and both Christianity and Islam took from Judaism not only a belief in the one true God, but the conviction that this God intervened in human affairs to their advantage. Just as he helped the Israelites escape from Israel by opening up the Red Sea, so he helped the spread of Christianity by having the Romans remove the kingdom of Israel from the map of the ancient world. To Eusebius, writing in the third century, it was patently clear that Jerusalem was razed by the Romans to punish the Jews for killing Christ, and the defeat of the Crusaders on the horns of Hittim was equally clear proof to Saladin that Allah was on his side.

Johnson, of course, is too English and objective to come down on either the Jewish or Christian side and state whether or why God changed his mind about which religion he was backing. But it is hard, reading his history of the Jews, to disguise the abrupt change from majesty to pathos as we move into what the Israelis call the 'modern era'. The reign of Herod, as Johnson says, 'is an episode in Jewish history with which Jewish historians, no less than Christian ones, have found it difficult to come to terms'; but one has only to see Masada, or what remains of Herod's Temple in Jerusalem, to know that the man who massacred the innocents represented something spectacular; and that even though the diaspora communities continued to flourish after 70 AD, the Jewish people were set on a course of wretched decline which reached its nadir in Central Europe during the Second World War.

There were brilliant moments in this lamentable exile – in Spain in the Middle Ages, for example – but in general the Jews were doomed because of the triumph of that Jewish heresy, the Christian religion. The two could not co-exist happily together because the claims of the one were by definition anathema to the other. Both believed in a Messiah and either he was Jesus or he was not. The Christians, so long the top dogs, are now seen as the oppressors but from the perspective of the early Church it was the Jews who started the persecution – not just by crucifying Jesus but by stoning St Stephen, executing St James and doing what they could to get rid of St Paul. 'You stubborn people,' says Stephen in the Acts of the Apostles. 'You are always resisting the Holy Spirit, just as your ancestors used to do. Can you name a single prophet your ancestors never persecuted? . . . You who had the Law brought to you by angels are the very ones who have not kept it.'

That the Christians should get their own back when the boot was on the other foot was perhaps only human but it is all the more reprehensible because Jesus had enjoined them to rise above 'an eye for an eye and a tooth for a tooth', forgive their enemies and turn the other cheek.

What is so notable, in reading both of these histories, is just how un-Christian the Christians were in their hey-day – particularly towards the Jews – from St John Chrysostom in the fifth century through to St Vincent Ferrer in the fourteenth. Power undoubtedly corrupts. 'It was Jeremiah,' writes Johnson, 'who was the first to perceive that powerlessness and goodness were somehow linked', and came close to the notion that 'the state itself was intrinsically evil'.

It was St Augustine, however, who towards the end of the third century thought to replace the disintegrating Roman Empire with the City of God – a Christian society here on earth. From this came the concept of a Holy Roman Empire which was established by the triumph of Charlemagne. It persisted throughout the Middle Ages and 'never before or since,' writes Johnson, 'has any human society come closer to operating as a unity, wholly committed to a perfectionist programme of conduct. Never again was Christianity to attempt so comprehensively to realise itself as a human institution as well as a divine one.'

The attempt failed. Although popes like Gregory VII tried to establish a spiritual ascendancy over the temporal powers, a theocracy never existed. 'It was the kings, not the bishops,' Johnson tells us in his *History of Christianity*, 'who governed Spain and with it the Spanish Church. The position did not change in any essential throughout the Middle Ages.' Even the Spanish Inquisition 'was essentially an organ of royal power, one of whose functions was to "protect" the Spanish Church from the influence of outside agencies' including the papacy which protested against it.

The victims, of course, of this attempt to create a political Christendom were those like the Jews who were not Christians in the first place and courageously refused to be converted. What is hard to understand, however, is why prejudice and discrimination against them survived so long after Christians had abandoned their attempts to build the City of God. Johnson puts this change of heart in the mid-seventeenth century.

> The two decades of the 1640s and 1650s form one of the great watersheds in the history of Christianity. Up

to this point, the idea of the total Christian society, embracing every aspect of man's existence, still seemed attainable; and masses of men were prepared to wage war, to massacre, hang and burn to realise it . . . With the 1650s we get a change: war and suffering are replaced by exhaustion and doubt, and the European mind seems to sicken of the unattainable objective, and focus on more mundane ends.

The Jews should have been the beneficiaries of this change but they had to wait for legal emancipation – in France until the revolution of 1789 and in Germany until well into the nineteenth century. In the United States there was never any institutional discrimination but in England Jews were not allowed into Parliament until 1858 so Disraeli could not have been prime minister if his father had not had him baptised. On the Continent many of the newly emancipated Jews tried to shed their Jewishness and mingle with the crowd. Some, like Marx and Heine, 'turned on their Judaism with contempt and anger'. Heine put Jewishness along with pain and poverty as one of the three great evils of life.

Unfortunately, just as the gates of the ghetto were opened and assimilation seemed to make sense, the new pagan religion of nationalism excluded Jews once again, not for their religion but for their race. Under the Spanish Inquisition a Jew could at least convert to the Christian religion: a rabbi in Valladolid, converted by St Vincent Ferrer, went on to become Bishop of Burgos. But no baptism could make a Jew into an Aryan, and the racist ideologies which became fashionable in the late nineteenth century, and fitted so well the nationalistic spirit of the era, excluded Jews more rigorously than Christianity had done.

This is why the Jews who abandoned their religion were so often drawn towards the internationalist ideologies of Socialism and Communism. 'Jews,' writes Johnson, 'were prominent in every revolutionary party, in virtually every european country, just before, during and immediately after the First World War.' As we know from his *History of the Modern World* these 'missing rabbis' who became millenary ideologues are Johnson's *bêtes noirs*. But to him they are the 'non-Jewish Jews' and so cannot be blamed on their people. Marx, Trotsky, Zinovief, Eisler, Luxembourg, Landauer, Toller and Bela Kuhn were all the Esaus among the Israelites who sold their birthright for a mess of revolutionary pottage; while men like Herzl, Ben Gurion, Stern and Begin are the Jewish Jews who led their people back to the Promised Land.

When he comes to the state of Israel, Johnson takes no sides but describes it as such a close run thing that it is hard not to see the hand of Providence in its creation. He considers the year 1881, when pogroms in Russia drove tens of thousands of Jews to emigrate to the United States 'as the most important year in Jewish history since 1648, indeed since the expulsion of the Jews from Spain in 1492 . . . It was as though history was slowly solving a great jigsaw puzzle, slipping the pieces into their place one after another. The large-scale emigration of Jews to the United States was one piece. The next piece was the Zionist idea.'

Johnson claims credit for the British too. 'Between 1827 and 1839, largely through British efforts, the population of Jerusalem rose from 550 to 5,500 and in all Palestine it topped 10,000 – the real beginning of the Jewish return to the Promised Land.' Yet clearly, like Jeremiah and the other prophets of ancient Israel, he has misgivings about the corrupting effect of power. 'Samuel . . . saw clearly that the monarch, or as we would say the state, was in irreconcilable conflict with the rule by the Law.'

It is also in irreconcilable conflict with Christian historicism but then Johnson, in his earlier *History of Christianity*, never tries to justify his own religion. He never excuses the excesses of the Christian fanatics: there are no non-Christian Christians. The best that can be said for Luther or Torquemada is that they were as beastly to one another as they were to the Jews. Men slaughtered one another in the name of Christ until that watershed in the mid-seventeenth century when they started to slaughter each other for other reasons. Even then the different Christian denominations remained fiercely antagonistic until the Second Vatican Council when the Catholic Church acknowledged that there was good to be found in other religions and even in no religion at all.

What Johnson does not say is that in doing this the Catholic Church was freeing itself for the first time from a vital part of its Jewish inheritance. '*Odium Theologicum*', as he admits, 'was not a Christian innovation. It was part of the Judaic heritage, along with the concept of heresy and the anathema.' The model for the Crusader or the Teutonic Knight can hardly have been Jesus who blessed the meek and the peace-maker, but rather Samuel, Saul or David and the other triumphant warriors from the Old Testament who did the work of Yahveh with the sword.

Instead, in describing Vatican II, Johnson alights upon the controversies which made the headlines at the time – the intrigues of the curia or the controversy over contraception. This is symptomatic of a flaw in both his histories: they are written in a breathless, helter-skelter style of a journalist with a deadline. He gives us a mass of facts but takes short cuts which leave out significant nuances. He writes, for example, that the wealthy Jewish community was 'massacred at York in 1189' when in fact it committed mass-suicide in 1190 when besieged in the royal castle – a tragic echo of the mass-suicide of the Essenes at Masada.

A more serious flaw is the absence of any attempt to get under the skin and empathise with the religious figures of the past. He sneers at their excesses as if confident that the educated Englishman of the late twentieth century inevitably knows best. He accepts without question all the fashionable speculations of the contemporary biblical exegesis. 'We probably know more about the History of Jesus than [St Paul] did', he writes, 'despite the interval of nearly two thousand years.' Thus St James was 'the younger brother of Jesus' and so Mary, by implication, not the ever-virgin of Catholic belief.

If Johnson still considers himself a Catholic, he does not say so. Nor has he much good to say for the religion in which he was raised. 'Christianity has not made man secure or happy or even dignified.' The best that can be said for it is that 'it is a civilizing agent. It helps cage the beast.' He never appears to consider that its claims might be true but stresses, on his own admission, 'its failures and short-comings, and its institutional distortions.'

Thus he presents his readers with audacious over-simplifications such as: 'the essence of the Counter-Reformation . . . was Spanish power. It was not a religious movement'; and he swallows whole a number of historical clichés. For example he scoffs at Pius XII for seeing Bolshevism as a greater threat to the Church than Fascism in the late 1930s which certainly, with hindsight, seems absurd: but fails to mention that in Spain in 1936 eleven bishops and seven thousand priests were massacred by Communists at the outbreak of the Spanish Civil War. He also condemns the same Pope for not specifically denouncing the deportation and extermination of the Jews but fails to say that when this was done in Holland by the Archbishop of Utrecht it only led to the deportation of baptised Jews who until then had been exempt.

The tone of both histories is to be wise, and to sneer, after the event, but despite these failings they have one outstanding virtue: they infect the reader with Johnson's fascination with transcendental ideas. 'Give us a child until he is seven,' the Jesuits used to say, 'and he is ours for life.' A non-Christian Christian, like a non-Jewish Jew, is marked for ever by his religion.

18

Misunderstanding Islam

First published in *The Spectator* on
8 January 2000

A PARADOX MARKS THE OPENING OF THE new millennium for members of the Christian religion. On the one
hand, the fact that the anniversary of the birth of Christ was
celebrated throughout the world shows the universal historical ascendancy of the Christian religion; on the other,
Christ's message of peace to all men remains widely ignored.
Indeed, many of the endemic conflicts arise from religious
differences, particularly between Christianity and Islam. In
Nigeria, Egypt, Sudan, Indonesia, Bosnia, Kosovo, Cyprus,
Chechnya, Lebanon and the Philippines blood is being
shed by the warring partisans of Muhammad and Christ.

In response to this paradox the leaders of the Christian
churches have adopted a penitential stance. The
Archbishop of Canterbury, flanked by members of other
Christian denominations, publicly apologised for the sins
committed in the name of Christ following the example set
by Pope John Paul II last September when, at a general audience in Rome, he said that the communal implications of
sin impel the Church to ask pardon for the 'historic sins of
her children'.

What are these historic sins? Last week's act of contrition
by the British church leaders was somewhat vague: it mentioned Christians' past indifference to the institution of
slavery; to Christian racism, specifically Christian anti-
semitism. While in Rome the Pope has set up investigations

into the role played by the Catholic Church in the Inquisition, the Reformation and the Crusades; according to reports last week, Pope John Paul II is planning to mark the beginning of Lent by issuing a solemn apology for the past sins of the Catholic Church.

To many outside the Church, such an apology is long overdue. For example, in Britain, Dr Zaki Badawi, chairman of the Council of Imams and Mosques, has demanded that the Catholic Church should apologise for the Crusades. 'Hopefully an apology would also mean repentance,' he said. 'We hope that the word "crusade" will disappear from our language because it is something that rankles enormously with Muslims.' This view of the Crusades is not confined to Muslims: the celebrated Crusade historian, Sir Steven Runciman, judged that the Crusades 'were a tragic and destructive episode . . . a long act of intolerance in the name of God, which is the sin against the Holy Ghost.' An Anglican expert on Islam, the Revd Colin Chapman, agreed with Dr Badawi: 'The Crusades,' he said, 'are such a major stumbling block in the minds of many Muslims . . . the Christian community [should] recognise the enormity of what was done in the name of Christ.'

As a result a committee was formed by the main Christian denominations to draw up an apology to mark the 900th anniversary of the First Crusade in 1998. A draft was presented to the committee but the members could not agree. No statement was issued. No apology was made. What blocks a consensus? One of the difficulties is that a younger, post-Runciman generation of historians such as Jonathan Riley-Smith now dismiss the hitherto accepted view that the Crusaders had been greedy younger sons intent on pillage. 'Few historians,' wrote Riley-Smith, 'appear to believe in them any longer.' Instead the First Crusade should be understood more as a pilgrimage under arms involving considerable material sacrifices with little expectation of anything other than spiritual gain.

Indeed, a look at a broader sweep of history reveals that, while the growth of Christianity in the first three centuries after Christ had been wholly pacific, Islam from its inception had been a religion that spread the Word by force. The

Prophet Muhammad himself had led raids on rival tribes in Arabia and after his death his father-in-law, Umar, had led the armies of Islam in a lightning campaign of conquest against the Christian Byzantine Empire. Islamic armies conquered the Christian territories of Palestine, Syria, the whole of North Africa, and most of the Iberian peninsula, Sicily, Sardinia and southern Italy. A Muslim base was established on the coast of France in the modern La Garde-Freinet, and in 846 a Muslim expeditionary force made a move on Rome itself, sacking St Peter's basilica, then outside the city walls.

Islamic expansion into Christian Europe was only stopped in the West when a Muslim army was defeated by Charles Martel at Poitiers in 732; and in the East with the raising of the Turkish siege of Vienna in 1683. Far from being instances of aggression, the Crusades were seen by Christians at the time as wars both in defence of Christendom and for the liberation of fellow Christians under Muslim rule.

It was almost certainly the political and mercantile imperialism of the West European powers in the *nineteenth* century that accounts for the mistaken impression in the minds of many Muslims today that it is Christianity that is the predatory religion. And such are the sensitivities of Muslims that it becomes difficult and even dangerous to dispute the point of view. The French historian, Paul Fregosi, who described the Prophet Muhammad as a political and violent man in his book *Jihad in the West*, and suggested that this explained the violence at the root of many Islamic societies today, had his contract cancelled by the publishers Little, Brown. He accused Little, Brown of backing off for fear of a *fatwa*; Little, Brown replied that they had merely decided not to publish 'a bad book'.

Within the Catholic Church itself, the penitential stance taken by Pope John Paul II is questioned. Can there be a contradiction between the desire to make amends and a respect for truth? Does it perhaps feed the historical paranoia of some Muslims and justify a double standard on human rights? Critics point to the persecution of Christians in Muslim countries such as Algeria and Sudan; to the

denial of religious freedom in Saudi Arabia where the saying of Mass is a criminal offence. At last month's synod of
European bishops in Rome, Giuseppe Bernadini, the
Catholic archbishop of Izmir in Turkey, warned of Islam's
growing challenge to Christianity. 'The dominion,' he said,
'has already started with petro-dollars, used not to create
jobs in poor countries in North Africa and the Middle East
but to build mosques and cultural centres in Christian
countries . . . including Rome, centre of Christianity.' 'Who
cannot see in this,' he added, 'a clear programme of
expansion and reconquest?'

There can be no doubt that, as the Archbishop of
Canterbury put it last week, Christians 'have often fallen far
short of the example given us by the Prince of Peace in our
treatment of others'. Nonetheless, Christians today, like
their coreligionists in the Middle Ages, must recognise that
in those parts of the world where Islam has become domi-
nant, Christian communities have dwindled and died. In
the Holy Land itself, there is an exodus of indigenous
Christians who feel that they have no future in the country
that saw the birth of their religion. Early in this new millennium, if present trends continue, the only significant body
of Christians to be found worshipping in the Church of the
Holy Sepulchre in Jerusalem will be the pilgrims flown in on
jumbo jets.

19

A New Look at the Crusades

THE PREVAILING VIEW OF THE Crusades has, until now, been damning. The philosophers of the eighteenth-century Enlightenment, who dismissed Christian belief as superstition, ridiculed these wars fought in the name of Christ. The Scottish sceptic David Hume thought them 'the most signal and most durable monument to human folly that has yet appeared in any age or nation'. Denis Diderot's *Encyclopédie*, published in 1772, said they were inspired by greed, imbecility and 'false zeal'. The same strain of contempt continues through Edward Gibbon's *Decline and Fall of the Roman Empire* to our near contemporary, Sir Steven Runciman, who concluded his monumental *History of the Crusades* with the judgement that they were 'nothing more than a long act of intolerance in the name of God, which is the sin against the Holy Ghost.'

Are these judgements fair? And, more pertinently, can they be sustained by the evidence available to dispassionate historians? Following the events of September 11, it has been the clear objective of Osama Bin Laden – an objective aided by the careless use of the word 'crusade' by President Bush – to present the Allied Armed Forces as Christian crusaders intent on destroying a rival religion, Islam. His call resonates in the Muslim mind, because the brutality of the Latin warriors in the Holy Land is well established in the collective memory of the Arab peoples (they think of Richard Coeur de Lion as a West European might think of Genghis Khan or Attila the Hun); and because this collective memory is fused with a resentment against the 'imperialistic' incursions into the Middle East of western nations that followed the collapse of the Turkish Empire in 1918.

This pincer movement of sneering historians on the one hand and resentful Arab Muslims on the other has led to an apologetic attitude towards the Crusades by modern Christians – exemplified at the turn of the millennium by an 'apology' by Pope John Paul II. It is worth noting, however, that the Vatican's own panel of historians refused to endorse this apology, saying that it was the product of what they called 'anachronism': viz. judging the past by the standards of the present and therefore failing, as the conscientious historian should, to empathise and understand.

The first point to be made in defence of the Crusades is that they were initially a response to Islamic aggression. Islam from its inception had espoused the use of force. Where Jesus had died for his beliefs, the Prophet Muhammad had wielded a sword. Though Christianity was later to be exploited for political ends, the Christian religion as such had, in the first three centuries of its existence, spread peacefully – thriving, in fact, on the blood of its martyrs. I say this not to score a point in favour of Christianity but to emphasise an historical truth: the spread of Islam from the Arabian peninsula to south-western France in the eighth century, and to the gates of Vienna in the seventeenth, came as a result of conquest by Islamic armies.

The First Crusade was a response to one phase in this Islamic expansion. Christendom was then divided into the western 'Holy Roman Empire' – for various reasons largely led by the popes in Rome; and the eastern Byzantine Roman Empire with its capital in Constantinople. Towards the end of the tenth century, the Seljuk Turks, fighting in the name of Islam, invaded the Byzantine Empire and threatened Constantinople. The Byzantine Emperor called for help from the west, sending his ambassadors to a Church Council in Piacenza. The Pope, Urban II, responded with a call to arms at Clermont in France the following year.

What modern historians such as Professor Jonathan Riley Smith of Cambridge University have now established is that the motive of the knights who responded to this call was not greed for material benefits but a craving for spiritual ones. They believed – as do Catholics today – that the Pope had inherited the powers given by Christ to St Peter to 'bind and loose' – in this case to compensate them for their services as warriors by letting them off the punishment due for their sins in the world to come.

The prospect of booty, and even of establishing principalities which they could then rule, was an added incentive, but at the time was hardly controversial: it was universally accepted that to the victor should go the spoils. However, the expense of mounting such a complex expedition, and the extremely poor odds in favour of survival, made material profit implausible as a motive for going to war.

Of course, nothing is black and white. It is possible that Pope Urban not only wanted to help the Byzantine Emperor but also liked the idea of getting the quarrelsome Frankish knights to stop fighting one another and fight the Muslims instead. He was also skilled at 'spin': to motivate the crusaders, he made their objective the liberation of the holy city of Jerusalem, already at that time a place of pilgrimage for European Christians.

The First Crusade was also marred by many atrocities such as the massacre of the Jews in the Rhineland and after the taking of Jerusalem: these were recognised as such and condemned by Christian churchmen at the time. The sack of Constantinople by the Fourth Crusade was also a scandal though the judgement of Sir Steven Runciman, writing post-Auschwitz, that 'there was never a greater crime against humanity', exposes the irrational animus against the Christian religion of this influential Crusade historian.

It also prompts us to question whether the post-Enlightenment era of human history has been quite as enlightened as we like to think. Were the Middle Ages really so bad? We may look back with horror to the Inquisition, the Wars of Religion and the Crusades; but do they compare so unfavourably in the scales of human suffering with the trenches, the gulags and the concentration camps, products of the supposedly enlightened twentieth century?

Today, as throughout human history, ideological zeal is often used to justify the amoral pursuit of selfish interests.

We in the west may feel confident that on balance our values of liberty and democracy are superior to those of fundamentalist Muslims such as Osama Bin Laden: but can we be wholly confident that our rulers are clear in their own minds where the demands of justice and national self-interest coincide – and where they diverge?

Islam, by contrast, from its inception, had espoused the use of force. Where Jesus had died for his beliefs, the Prophet Muhammad had wielded a sword.

SEX AND MARRIAGE

20

Wine and Kisses

First published in *Crisis Magazine*,
11 January 1995

THE RECENT CONTROVERSY IN England and Wales over sex education in Catholic schools has exposed the considerable difference among Catholics on the approach that should be taken to what John Paul II has called the 'aphrodisiac culture' of the west. One party seems to believe that the traditional teaching of the Church on sexual morality is no longer credible. The other believes this teaching is an important 'sign of contradiction' that should be unfurled like a banner in the Church's confrontation with the modern world.

Nor is the difference limited to the question of sex education alone. There is a suspicion among what one might loosely call 'traditionalist' Catholics that the Bishops of England and Wales (Scotland has its own Bishops' Conference) lean towards the unorthodox in areas like ecumenism and catechetics, and are less than whole-hearted in their support for the stand taken against dissident theologians by Cardinal Ratzinger and Pope John Paul II in Rome.

Why should such suspicions exist of a body of apparently holy, sincere and conscientious men? The first reason is a lack of concrete information as to what the bishops actually believe. The idea of 'communion' has made it obligatory that they should speak with one voice, and they do this through agreed statements issued by the Bishops' Conference. It causes consternation on the rare occasions when a bishop (usually Maurice Couve Murville, the Archbishop of Birmingham) steps out of line.

The other way in which they disseminate their teaching is through their agencies like the Catholic Institute for International Relations, the Department of Christian Doctrine and Formation, or the Catholic Education Service. When objections are made to the apparently unorthodox teaching of a particular document, such as the bibliography accompanying the pamphlet *Education in Sexuality* published by the Catholic Education Service, the critics are told that the bishop nominally responsible had not actually read the offending books that were recommended in his name.

There are further straws in the wind that cause dismay to those in Britain who believe in the Church's established teaching. At a recent national Catholic 'event' at the Barbican conference centre in London, a panel chosen by the Bishops' Conference to discuss the state of the Church included Dr Jack Dominian, who has called over the years for a change to the Church's teaching on sexual morality. 'It is my personal view,' he wrote in his *Proposals for a New Sexual Ethic,* 'that the Church is not right in its attitude to masturbation . . .' and there is 'a profound reason for reassessing the moral categories of fornication and its meaning'. It is said that no one on the panel was prepared to defend the teaching of *Humanae Vitae.*

Then there is the case of Clifford Longley, a Catholic columnist on *The Daily Telegraph* who last year was invited to prepare a paper to assist the Bishops of England and Wales on retreat in Cumberland. Without doubt, Longley is an able journalist and a mellifluous writer; it is said that he is admired by Cardinal Hume; but it is the same Longley who wrote in an anthology to which I also contributed, *Why I am Still a Catholic*: 'I share none of the Roman Catholic Church's attitude on contraception, divorce, abortion and religious education of my children.' This was some years ago; but there is evidence that even today Longley's position has not much changed; and so the confidence placed in him by the bishops is hardly likely to reassure suspicious traditionalists that their pastors can tell the difference between a sheepdog and a wolf.

The question of sexual morality is perhaps the most acute because the Church's teaching on this question is indisputably rejected in good conscience by large numbers of otherwise loyal Catholics. Most commonly, married couples ignore the teaching of *Humanae Vitae* on contraception while their children ignore the Church's strictures against premarital sexual relations. Moreover, a climate of opinion exists in Britain, as in the United States, that considers it bigoted to condemn homosexual relations, and psychologically damaging to the young to label masturbation a sin. Equally, it is deemed offensive to the increasing numbers of children living in one-parent families to suggest that the two-parent family is a God-given norm. It is this climate of opinion that is reflected in the books recommended for further teaching in 'Education in Sexuality'.

This list was subsequently rescinded, but one excuse made for its initial inclusion was that the books in question were for the guidance of Catholic teachers, not the children themselves: but as a former Professor of Moral Theology at the Beda College in Rome wrote in *The Catholic Times*, 'many Catholic teachers of deep faith and great integrity . . . are, nonetheless, surprisingly ignorant of even fairly basic moral doctrine and its justification. They are entitled to help and detailed guidance.'

It is the lack of such guidance in the pamphlet itself that has led to the suspicion that Bishop Konstant, the Chairman of the Catholic Education Service, was using proxies to express his own unorthodox opinions. This has been emphatically denied. It is pointed out that Bishop Konstant was one of the episcopal authors of the *Catechism of the Catholic Church* in which the Church's traditional teaching is clearly restated. Nor do any of the other Bishops of England and Wales openly question the Church's teaching as has been known in the United States. Indeed, when necessary they will restate it: for example, when a bill was placed before Parliament to lower the age of homosexual consent, Cardinal Hume was unambiguous on the Church's teaching on the immorality of homosexual acts as opposed to the homosexual condition.

However, it is also possible that the Cardinal's tolerant

temperament, and his particular kind of spirituality, has led to a *strategy* that, being only half-understood, gives rise to some of the present confusion. In a revealing sermon he preached in Westminster Cathedral last September, he called for a fourfold witness – through holiness, through faith, through love and through the liturgy. 'See how those Christians love one another' should be the cry of the secular world. This seems to suggest that evangelisation is to be effected through a form of osmosis: there was no place, he said, for *stridency* in the Church.

Considering the riots provoked by St Paul in Ephesus, one is entitled to wonder whether such a strategy would have been effective in the early Church; and whether the switch to Roman Catholicism of one royal duchess and a number of Anglicans disenchanted over the ordination of women can be seen as a mark of signal success midway through the decade of evangelisation. But this option for a non-polemical witness, like the cautious tone of the Cardinal's statement on homosexuality, may also suggest how defensive many bishops feel about some aspects of the Church's teaching, particularly the question of sexual sin.

Certainly, the unambiguous statements made by the Pope on these questions rarely find an echo in the Catholic cathedrals of England and Wales. Almost never is reference made to Pius XI's Encyclical on marriage and sexual ethics, *Casti Connubii*, published in 1930, the year in which the Lambeth Conference of the Church of England decided that artificial contraception was no sin.

Rereading *Casti Connubii*, one is struck by how pertinent the Encyclical still is to the situation we face today. It demonstrates that our present predicament is not the consequence as some suggest of the sexual revolution of the 1960s, but was already present in the decades following World War I. If one makes allowances for the odd archaism, and for the unfashionably confident, polemical, even strident tone taken by the Pontiff, one can recognise that what is now *more so* was, even then, *the same*.

It is worth quoting at some length.

It is not now only in secret, or in the darkness, but openly and without any sense of shame, that the sanctity of marriage is treated with derision and contempt. The spoken and the written word, theatrical performances of every kind, novels, love-stories, humorous talks, cinematograph films, broadcast talks – all the latest inventions of modern science are used to this end. On the other hand, divorce, adultery, and the most shameful vices are glorified or, at any rate, depicted in such colours as to make them appear free from all blame or infamy. Books are published, impudently advertised as scientific works, but often in reality having nothing more than a veneer of science to recommend them more easily to the notice of the public. The doctrines they contain are proffered as the marvellous products of the modern spirit, a spirit described as single-minded in its search for the truth and emancipated from the prejudices of former times. And among these old-fashioned prejudices they count the doctrine which we have expounded on Christian marriage.

The advocates of the new doctrines . . . claim that the laws, institutions and customs by which marriage is regulated, having been established only by the will of men, are subject to that will alone, and therefore can be made, changed and abrogated at man's desire . . . The power of generation, they maintain . . . can be used outside the limits of wedlock as well as within them, and without any regards to the end of matrimony. It follows that the licentiousness of an unchaste woman would enjoy practically the same rights as would the chaste motherhood of a lawfully wedded wife.

Following the lead of these principles, some have gone to the length of inventing new types of union which they suggest as being more suited to the conditions of the modern man and the present age. In these they see so many new kinds of marriage: the temporary marriage, the experimental marriage . . . eliminating the indissoluble bond . . . and excluding offspring, unless the parties choose later to transform their cohabitation and intimacy into a fully legalised marriage.

There are some even who demand legal recognition of these monstrosities, or at least want them to be tolerated by public usage and institution. It does not seem to occur to their minds that in such things there is nothing of that modern 'culture' which they vaunt so highly; that they are, in fact, abominable corruptions which would result even in civilised nations adopting the barbarous customs of certain savage tribes.

From the perspective of the mid-1990s, Pius XI seems somewhat like King Canute, railing against the incoming tide. Unquestionably, 'the temporary marriage, the experimental marriage, the companionate marriage, excluding offspring, unless the parties choose later to transform their cohabitation and intimacy into a fully legalised marriage' describes precisely the kind of liaisons entered into in blithe good conscience by innumerable young Catholics today.

Again, it was not just to Popes like Pius XI that such a development was foreseen. In 1920, in his novel *Death of a Hero*, the English writer Richard Aldington dismisses marriage as 'a primitive institution, bound to succumb to the joint attack of contraceptives and the economic independence of women'. Philosophers like Bertrand Russell advocated 'trial marriages' for students who had already turned away from the moral precepts of the world's monotheistic religions to embrace those of modern prophets like Karl Marx, Bernard Shaw and, in particular, Sigmund Freud. 'Most modern people,' wrote C.E.M. Joad, the Professor of Philosophy at London University in the 1930s, in his *Guide to Modern Thought*,

> have a nodding acquaintance with the theories of Freud. They suffer from 'inferiority complexes', 'sublimate' their desires and are victims of 'neuroses', while young men, anxious to evoke suitable responses from the young women they desire, exhort them to get rid of their 'repressions'. This popular employment of the terminology of psychoanalysis corresponds to and reflects the wide area of its influence.

He went on:

> Religion has lost its old dogmatic assurance, or, in so
> far as it retains it, palpably loses hold of the modern
> mind . . . while in the sphere of morals the contempo-
> rary generation increasingly refuses to subscribe to the
> sexual restraints and taboos of the last . . . It is notori-
> ous today, that heavenly rewards no longer attract and
> infernal punishments no longer deter with their pris-
> tine force; many people are frankly derisive of both,
> and, seeing no prospect of divine compensation in the
> next world for the wine and kisses that morality bids
> them eschew in this one, take more or less unanimously
> to the wine and kisses.

But psychoanalysis, as Joad recognised, has affected man's
attitude to the actual moment of passing experience more
directly than through the scepticism which it has engen-
dered in regard to the traditional, inhibitory morality. To
distrust of the old doctrines of prudence and prohibition it
adds a positive doctrine of the *obligation* to experiment, with
the result that many young people regard self-expression as
a primary duty, and count repression, at least in theory, as
the only sin.

In Britain, where there is a greater scepticism about
psychoanalysis than there is in the United States, those un-
familiar with the work of Freud have frequently assimilated
his ideas through the work of D.H. Lawrence. Lawrence was
deeply influenced by Freud, and reverence for Lawrence,
first promoted by the Cambridge academic F.R. Leavis,
dominated the English Literature faculties in the universities and polytechnics in Britain in the 1960s and 1970s,
forming the minds of a whole generation of students who in
turn went out as lecturers and schoolteachers to form the
minds of the generations that followed. In this way it came
to be accepted without question that sexual restraint was
both psychologically injurious and morally wrong.

How, given this climate of opinion, should the Church
defend, or even promote, chastity when even among
Catholics the word itself frequently provokes derision, if not

outright disgust? Paul VI tried in *Humanae Vitae* to ask people to ponder the intrinsic significance of the sexual act – its potential to engender another human being with an immortal soul – but has been undermined by the 'rehabilitation' of sexual love as an end in itself by psychologists like Dr Dominian.

It is not that Dominian denigrates marriage; quite the contrary; but he represents a tendency found among Catholic specialists on sex education to present the Church's teaching as a 'vision' or an 'ideal', not a norm. Yet if one looks closely at what is revealed in Scripture about sexual relations between men and women, it is clear that while celibacy may be regarded as a particular vocation, chastity is integral to human nature as such. Christ commends those who become eunuchs for the sake of the kingdom: in considering divorce, however, he does not just forbid it or condemn it but points out that it is impossible. 'From the beginning of creation God made them male and female . . . the two become one body.'

This suggests that somehow marrying is intrinsic to the sexual act itself. In reading the account of the first, aboriginal marriage between Adam and Eve in the book of Genesis, one is struck by the erotic nature of Adam's cry: 'This, at last, is bone from my bones and flesh from my flesh!' St Paul, too, like Christ, refers back to Genesis when warning the Corinthians against consorting with prostitutes. 'As you know,' he wrote, 'a man who goes with a prostitute is one body with her, since *the two*, as it is said, *become one flesh.*'

John Paul II points out in *Mulieris Dignitatem* that the book of Genesis 'constitutes the immutable basis of all Christian anthropology', but there is an aspect of its account of the marriage of Adam and Eve which he does not discuss in that Apostolic Letter; yet it is one, it seems to me, that is central to our understanding of chastity.

Eve, the woman, is given by God to man as his 'helpmate': as St Paul puts it in 1 Corinthians, woman was made 'for the sake of man'. The gift is not woman in the abstract, or women in the plural, but *one* woman, Eve: and it is this one woman that is flesh of his flesh. Thus the sin in the transitory encounter – the love affair that either precedes or follows another love affair, that may or may not turn into a long-lasting relationship, or even a marriage, is (1) that it is taking God's gift on trial like a piece of merchandise from a shop; and (2) that it is an act of infidelity to the one woman given, or to be given, by God; or, in the case of a woman, to the one man to whom a woman is or will be given by God; and so is in essence the same as adultery.

This extrapolation by means of biblical exegesis is confirmed by the way in which men and women who break up after a 'relationship', or husbands and wives who divorce, so often find themselves unable to make the clean break in their own minds that they expect to follow the legal rupture and the actual separation. A form of commitment or engagement remains, either in the form of an abiding hatred or a lingering love. As old Prince Bolkonsky says to his son Andrei in *War and Peace*, one cannot unmarry.

But is the fractured heart the worst that is to be feared from the 'serial monogamy' that has become the norm today? What of St Paul's teaching that 'the wages of sin are death'? As Professor Joad recognised in the 1930s, 'infernal punishments' weigh little in the balance against the wine and kisses. If few people believed in damnation in the 1930s, fewer still do so today. As a result, if adultery, for example, is still regarded as a sin, it is not because it is a breach of one of the Ten Commandments but because it is perceived as a cause of unhappiness to the deceived spouse, or it endangers the stability of family life and so the welfare of the children.

But does Scripture warrant this sociological calibration of sin? If a man so much as *looks* at a woman lustfully, Jesus warned his disciples, 'he has already committed adultery with her in his heart', adding soon after that 'if your right eye should cause you to sin, tear it out and throw it away, for it will do you less harm to lose one part of you than to have your whole body thrown into hell.' If one works on the assumption that Christ meant what he said; and if, as I have suggested, all forms of unchastity are really one, fornication and adultery two sides of the same coin, then 'the temporary marriage, the experimental marriage', like the adulterous liaison, must surely incur the risk of damnation.

21

Reconciliation

First published in *The Guardian* on
12 September 1995

ONCE, WHILE VISITING DUBAI, I met an attractive woman from Lahore who, after going to university in England, married a man chosen by her parents. Now a fat and balding businessman, he was sitting on the other side of the room as she told me she had only met him on the day they were engaged and had not been alone with him until after they were married.

I asked her if she regretted not marrying for love. She laughed. 'Once, I used to wonder what it might have been like, but now, when I look at my friends who *did* marry for love, I feel relieved that I did not.'

I was then conducting some haphazard research for a book on marriage, which was commissioned, written, but never published: it turned out to be wholly unsatisfactory. The failure was frustrating. It seemed clear to me then, as it does now, that a happy marriage is the key to a happy life – not just for the husband and wife, but also for their parents, their children and, in the imprint it leaves on the children, their descendants for many generations to come.

Less clear is what makes a marriage happy, or how a marriage can recover from the misery and acrimony caused by infidelity. Despite the permissive ethos of our society, and the *prima facie* implausibility of an exclusive, life-long sexual union, the adulterous act remains an enormity for the one betrayed – as devastating in its psychological effect as the birth of a sibling or the death of a parent. Whether or not we are disappointed, irritated or bored by our husbands and wives, they are nevertheless figures upon whose total loyalty and commitment we have come to depend.

Clearly, different people react to the discovery of betrayal in different ways. When Elisabeth Pepys found her husband with his hand under the skirt of her maid, Deborah Willet, she sulked and raged – but, recorded Pepys, made love with him 'with more pleasure to her than I think in all the time of our marriage before'. The advice of Pepys's contemporary, Sir George Savile, First Marquis of Halifax, to his married daughter Elisabeth was to pretend not to notice her husband's affairs. 'Do not seem to look or hear that way; if he is a man of sense he will reclaim himself; the folly of it is of itself sufficient to cure him.'

I came across a number of marriages in the present that had survived adultery by either the husband or wife by following this advice: rivals have been seen off simply by being ignored. However, few are now capable of exercising such self-control. The more common reaction is to rage, sulk, reach for the bread-knife, or storm out of the house. The stiff upper lip gives way to inspired invective. Both parties become obsessed with their suffering, demonising the other in interminable conversations with their friends. Rarely will they listen to reason. Even the most liberal-minded are unable to extend the tolerance they feel in theory to the actual behaviour of their husband and wife.

The explanations put forward by counsellors and therapists for what has gone wrong may be accepted in theory, but have no impact in practice. A husband convinced that he has been punishing his wife because he was neglected as a child is still beastly to his wife and nice to his mother.

At times, the insights of the psychotherapists, however valid, can actually impede reconciliation by removing the concept of right and wrong. The old Judeo-Christian ideas of marriage and morals were both simple and clear. The husband and wife, swearing lifelong fidelity before God, became 'one flesh', but were nevertheless susceptible to temptation and the false promises of Satan. Infidelity was a sin, but upon repentance sins could and should be forgiven.

The Bible is filled with images of the cuckolded Yahweh forgiving 'adulterous' Israel.

Today, the aggrieved spouse is told that infidelity is not a sin, but the symptom of a psychic malfunction in the subconscious for which no one can be held to blame. The cuckolded husband learns that his wife is an ersatz mother chosen to enable him to resolve conflicts remaining from his childhood; the deceived wife that her husband is an ersatz father whom she has overburdened with her demands that he do better than the real one. To C.G. Jung, a young man was likely to fall for a woman who best corresponded to his own unconscious femininity, and so marry 'his own worst weakness'.

Such diagnoses inevitably undermine our confidence that we know what we are doing when we get married, but they are now generally accepted by therapists, counsellors and even priests. The Diocesan Tribunals of the Roman Catholic Church will now annul marriages on the grounds that the immaturity of petitioners made them incapable of giving informed consent. I know of one mother of six children who claimed that her marriage was invalid because she was so madly in love with her husband on the day of her wedding. Thus, Ambrose Bierce's definition of love in his *Devil's Dictionary* as 'a temporary insanity cured by marriage' is complemented with a new theological definition of marriage as 'a sacrament invalidated by passion'.

Playing down the significance of the adulterous act itself will also make a true reconciliation more difficult. Many may say that they would rather their husband or wife had a drunken one-night stand at the office party than that he or she fell chastely in love with another person. But, in reality, we feel a visceral revulsion at the idea of our husband or wife naked and ecstatic in the arms of another person. Marriage brings into play our lowest impulses, as well as our highest aspirations. We ignore our base instincts at our peril. Brute jealousy should always be given its due.

Moreover, making light of infidelity is not always what it seems. Many a complacent husband who has interpreted his wife's indulgent attitude towards his affair as a tribute to his prowess later discovers that she has welcomed it as an excuse for behaviour of a similar kind. I also noted that husbands who too readily forgive their wives earn only their contempt. In the 1970s, there was a publisher, frequently unfaithful to his wife, who, when he discovered that his wife was sleeping with a young journalist, flew into a terrible rage, threatening to ruin the journalist and divorce his wife. Impressed by this evidence of the strength of her husband's feelings, the wife promised to give up her lover if her husband would forgive her, but felt that to bring about a true reconciliation she must tell all. She confessed that the journalist was not the first; she had also slept on several occasions with her husband's most eminent author, Q. 'Q? You really had an affair with Q? Did he write you letters? Have you kept them? Don't leave them in their envelopes. Lay them flat in a folder, otherwise they will split along the folds.' So impressed was he by the first lover that he forgave her for the second. Six months later, the wife took up with a third, and a year after that they were divorced.

To bring about a lasting reconciliation, a married couple might consider the lady from Lahore whom I met in Dubai, looking upon their marriage less as a relationship between two people and more as a good in itself – a good in which fidelity is of the essence, a good that depends upon fidelity to survive.

The most obvious benefit from such detachment would be the stability and quality of their family life. Remaining together 'for the sake of the children' is usually portrayed as a bleak compromise, and so it may be if it means no more than a kind of internal divorce – living under the same roof but not sharing the same bed. 'Sex is not everything,' wrote Robin K. Skynner in *One Flesh: Separate Persons*, 'but is a catalyst for many other things, and, since so many other things must be right for it to function well, also a touchstone for the quality of the total relationship. . . . The emotional atmosphere one senses in a house where it is right is one of calm and peace, yet also of lightness, fun and humour, and everything moves easily. Above all, the children sense it and are happy for it, though they do not necessarily know what they sense, any more than they know, or care, about the cost of the good food that nourishes them.'

There is, therefore, much to be said for a reconciliation that returns so far as possible to the *status quo ante*. It will not necessarily follow some kind of dramatic scene we see on television: beware the candlelit dinners or weekends in Paris. It is as likely to take place over time, often in a particularly English fashion, without anything specific being said.

Imperceptibly, both men and women move on from that immature condition in which they see their husband or wife only through the prism of their own psyche and use them principally to satisfy their own psychic needs. They cease to blame them for life's shortcomings and, like the Marquis of Halifax in the seventeenth century, come to accept that recognising 'our common weaknesses and defects contributes more towards the reconciling of one to another than all the precepts of philosophers and divines'.

22

Sex, Predestination and the Working Wife

'THERE IS A MORAL AND RELIGIOUS, as well as a material environment,' wrote the historian R.H. Tawney, 'which sets its stamp on the individual, even when he is least conscious of it' so that even in an agnostic age our attitudes can be influenced by some forgotten precept of religion which has 'survived as a sentiment long after it was repudiated as a command.'

Take, for example, the doctrine of justification by faith, or predestination, which was one of the main doctrinal differences between Luther and Calvin on the one hand, and the Catholic Church on the other. Luther's revolt against the Pope began with his repugnance at the sale of indulgences to finance the building of St Peter's basilica. This led him on to question the right of the Church to forgive sins through the sacrament of Reconciliation. He became convinced that the soul did not reach Paradise by doing good deeds or by having the bad ones forgiven in the confessional. It was faith in Christ and faith alone which led to salvation.

For scriptural authority Luther referred to St Paul, the Apostle of the Gentiles. In the early years of the Christian Church he had opposed those Jewish Christians – among them some of Christ's original disciples – who taught that a Christian must first be a Jew – that he must be circumcised and keep the Law of Moses. To St Paul it was absurd that after Christ's sacrifice on the cross a man's supernatural destiny should be affected by whether he ate shellfish or had a foreskin. What mattered was the inner disposition of a man. 'The real Jew,' he wrote, 'is one who is inwardly a Jew, and the real circumcision is in the heart – something not of the letter but of the spirit' (Romans 2:29). It was not by obedience to the law that men were to be saved; rather it was 'by faith we are judged righteous and at peace with God, since it is by faith and through Jesus that we have entered this state of grace' (Romans 5:1–2).

This rejection of the old law was misinterpreted even in St Paul's day, perhaps because he overstated his case. 'For me there are no forbidden things' – intended to mean no doubt that he could travel on the Sabbath or eat pork if he chose – was taken in Corinth to allow trips to the brothel – an interpretation St Paul took pains to counter (1 Corinthians 6:12). There were sects in the sixteenth century, like the Anabaptists of Munster, who took the same view as the errant Corinthians in the first, deciding that since they were saved through faith they could indulge with impunity in orgies of sex and slaughter.

The more sober denominations which emerged from the Reformation were generally noted for their decorous behaviour; for though good deeds themselves did not earn salvation, faith was inevitably expressed in virtue and virtue was living in obedience to God's commands. There remained, however, an underlying conviction that since faith was a gratuitous gift of God which *predestined* those to whom it was given to Heaven, the behaviour of those who had it – the Elect – must be compatible with salvation.

Calvin in particular – the most legalistic of the great reformers – taught that from the beginning God had allotted some men and women a place in Heaven and others a place in Hell. All men deserved to be damned, since the whole nature of man since the Fall was 'utterly devoid of goodness . . . a seed-bed of sin' which could not but be odious and abominable to God. Thus those who went to Hell only got what they deserved. Those predestined to Heaven were not being rewarded for the good they would do, but were the involuntary beneficiaries of the gratuitous and irresistible gift of God's grace.

This may seem abstruse theology to the modern mind, but to the Puritans of the seventeenth century – those, for example, who fought in Cromwell's armies or sailed on the *Mayflower* – it was the principal difference between them and the wretched Papists who first wallowed in sin and then sought to buy their way back into God's favour with indulgences, pilgrimages, mortification and confession. The Puritans, justified by their faith, had no need to confess because they did not sin. Their virtue was the outward sign of their election: sin gave away one who was damned.

As a result, those who were convinced that they had been chosen lived lives of consistent and often heroic rectitude; but those with little faith, who merely found themselves born into a Puritan society, were bound to conceal their human frailty or else betray themselves as one of the damned. Appearances became all-important in Puritan communities. While those living in a Catholic tradition – in Italy, for example, or Spain – could live out a cycle of sin and repentance, rising and falling with the regularity of a pump almost according to the season, those living in a Puritan tradition – in Scotland, say, or in New England – were obliged to show a uniform virtue, or justify whatever shortcomings became common to the community as compatible with predestined salvation. Sexual transgressions, when exposed, led to social ostracism. Those who succumbed to the weakness of their flesh had to keep their sin hidden from public view for the woman taken in adultery was not simply told to 'go and sin no more' but was marked with the Scarlet Letter.

In Catholic countries, by contrast, sins of the flesh were not seen as evidence of a fatal disease, like pustules of the bubonic plague, but rather like the sign of some minor infection like influenza or the common cold. It was easily cured by a visit to the confessional and a dose of penance. The difference is well illustrated by the life and work of two writers, both obsessed with women – the French novelist Stendhal and the Scotsman James Boswell. Though neither were pious practitioners of any religion, the attitude of both men to sexual love was indelibly coloured by the religious traditions of the societies from which they came – Stendhal by the casuistic Catholicism of Continental Europe, Boswell by the Puritanical Calvinism of the Scottish lowlands.

Boswell was obsessed with sex, and expressed his obsession, largely through furtive encounters with prostitutes.

His diaries, like those of Samuel Pepys, refer almost exclusively to the mechanics of copulation. 'Girolama. Quite agitated. Put on condom: entered. Heart beat: fell. Quite sorry but said "A true sign of passion".'

The 'Girolama' he referred to here was Girolama Piccolomini, the wife of the mayor of Siena where, to Boswell's astonishment, adultery was accepted as a fact of life. It was the same easy-going attitude to adultery that captivated Stendhal when he arrived in Italy with Napoleon's armies. Stendhal was not a Catholic – indeed he was implacably opposed to the teachings of the Catholic Church: 'The prolific source of vice and misery which follows marriage nowadays is Popery . . .' Yet it was the Catholic concept of sin and repentance that made possible the easy-going *moeurs* of Northern Italy where 'The man who dances attendance on a woman is always a good friend of the husband'.

If we move now to the present day we find the same contrast in attitudes towards sexual sin – the easy-going hypocrisy in the Catholic cultures of France, Italy and Spain; together with the tormented vacillation between repression and justification in the Protestant cultures of Northern Europe and North America – particularly in the United States, where the Puritanism of the founding fathers seems to have entered the national consciousness as a defining feature of what it was to be an American. Even the Catholic Poles, Irish and Italians who flooded into America in the nineteenth century became affected by it. No one believes in the abstruse doctrine of justification by faith any more – few even know what it means – but the idea of predestination is so thoroughly integrated into the concept of what it was to be an American that the very term 'American' became one of moral approbation: men and women would argue, for example, over whether abortion was American or UnAmerican. To be American was to be one of the Elect and – since democracy was also an American value – what was done by the majority of Americans must be compatible with salvation.

This, I believe, explains the greater tendency among

Americans to sanctify their adultery through divorce and remarriage rather than acknowledge the sin – however leniently – by an open, adulterous liaison. It also explains why the sexual revolution in America became something of a crusade, making yesterday's sinner into today's saint: for given the Puritan mould, it was inevitable that once it was established by Kinsey that most Americans ignored the Christian precepts on sexual morality, it became equally clear that sexual morality could not be a prerequisite of salvation. No one, it seemed, had practised what they preached – yet no fire and brimstone had rained down from Heaven. Quite the contrary, the United States was at the acme of its power and influence, so the Kinsey report seemed to give *carte blanche* to Americans to go on as before without any need to dissimulate.

The prosperity of the United States brings up another aspect of Puritan belief which came from the alliance of the reformed religions with the rising class of merchants and businessmen. The decline of Spain and the poverty of a Catholic country like Ireland, as well as the decline of the Catholic nobility as a class, convinced the Puritan merchants of England, Scotland, the Netherlands and the United States that 'the Lord prospered their doings'. Tawney describes their image of themselves, in *Religion and the Rise of Capitalism*, as of 'an earnest, zealous, godly generation, scorning delights, punctual in labour, constant in prayer, thrifty and thriving, filled with a decent pride in themselves and their calling, assured that strenuous toil is acceptable to Heaven, a people like those Dutch Calvinists whose economic triumphs were as famous as their iron Protestantism'.

To them prosperity was a sign of predestined salvation: poverty a mark of the damned. In effect this meant a return from the morality of Christ, who had blessed the poor, to the morality of Moses. 'Keep and observe what will make you prosper' was as pertinent an adage to the God-fearing merchants of the seventeenth century as it had been to the nomadic tribes of Israel.

This link between Puritanism and capitalism has been

described by several historians – notably R.H. Tawney and Max Weber. What I wish to suggest here is that the same heresy – surviving as a sentiment long after it is forgotten as a command – drives the contemporary feminist to leave the home and pursue a career.

It was the American sociologist Thorstein Veblen who exposed the complex measures that 'men and women will employ to establish their worth and status'. As the members of the society made in the Puritan mould lost faith in the precepts of their religion, they retained nonetheless its values in a degenerate form. Thus the Puritan's admiration for the thrift and labour which made a man prosperous is replaced by the prestige of prosperity itself. Indeed, as Veblen wrote, 'labour comes to be associated in men's habit of thought with weakness and subjection to a master'. The Elect must therefore demonstrate that they need not work and they do this in the most arbitrary manner. In rural communities where most men and women work in the fields, a sunburnt complexion denotes low status: young ladies therefore shield themselves from the sun with parasols. Fifty years later, however, when fashion is set by the urban communites where women work in factories and have grey faces, it becomes a mark of social prestige to have a brown skin. It demonstrates the hours of idleness a woman has at her command.

Among the very rich, men themselves would lead lives of conspicuous uselessness – hunting, yachting, skiing, playing tennis. 'But as we descend the social scale,' wrote Veblen,

> the point is presently reached where the duties of vicarious leisure and consumption devolve upon the wife alone . . . It is by no means an uncommon spectacle to find a man applying himself to work with the utmost assiduity, in order that his wife may in some form render for him that degree of vicarious leisure which the common sense of the time demands.
>
> The leisure rendered by the wife in such cases is, of course, not a simple manifestation of idleness or indolence. It almost invariably occurs disguised under some form of work or household duties or social amenities,

which prove on analysis to serve little or no ulterior end beyond showing that she does not have to occupy herself with anything that is gainful or that is of substantial use . . . the greater part of the customary round of domestic cares to which the middle-class housewife gives her time and effort is of this character.

The principal complaint of the early feminists like Mary Wollstonecraft was not so much that women were exploited, as that women were idle – and because they were idle, bored and frustrated. In the twentieth century this idleness spread from a small section of polite society from which Mary Wollstonecraft came, to the population at large because men – largely to please women – invented machines to lighten their labour in the home. More money and ingenuity was devoted to the development of domestic aids than to anything else except perhaps the machinery of war; so that now there is barely a gesture made in the kitchen which is not done with the help of some machine.

These developments, however, only added to the time which lay heavy on women's hands. As Ivan Ilych put it in *Gender*, 'Tap water put an end to her carrying the jugs to and fro, but also to her meeting friends at the well.' Her husband was absent at his office from dawn to dusk: so too were his friends. No wonder that Betty Friedan's suburban housewife suffered from acute boredom.

Betty Friedan's feminist, however, who decides that she 'can find identity only in work that is of real value to society – work for which, usually, our society pays' does not escape from the charge that her career is still, in Veblen's terms, 'vicarious leisure', first because no work can be of greater value to society than the raising of a family; and second because the mother who works must employ someone else to perform her household duties. 'Who will do the cooking for the child who still comes for lunch?' asked Fidel Castro. 'Who will nurse the babies or take care of the pre-school child? Who will cook for a man when he comes home from work? Who will wash and clean and take care of things?' The answer, in feminist theory, is that men and women will share these tasks, but in practice women in the west, like women in Eastern Europe, are not only averse to the motherly man, but are loath to abandon the standard of living which comes from their husband's full-time job. The children are therefore taken on by a mercenary who because of her lesser intelligence or education, or because of some other disability such as the absence of a work-permit, will labour for a wage that the working mother can pay out of her own salary.

Thus in Veblen's terms the working mother's job is a mark of prestige, for it implies sufficient intelligence, education and application to earn enough money to employ others to do the 'menial' tasks of the home. As a result other mothers who do not work feel implicitly demeaned. They no longer meet their friends at the day nurseries or in the park, but exchange pleasantries in halting English with Austrian au pairs or Haitian housekeepers. They plummet in their own estimation; and though instinctively averse to the idea, feel that they can only keep their end up if they too take a job.

In this way the harvest sown by a Puritan dogma in the sixteenth century is reaped four hundred years later by those who are quite unaware of the source of their sentiments. To the Catholic mind, however, this by-product of heresy must seem as pernicious as the heresy itself; so to Pope Pius XI, the

> social emancipation [which] would free the wife from the domestic cares of the children and family, enabling her, to the neglect of these, to follow her own bent and engage in business and even in public affairs . . . is a degradation of the spirit of woman and the dignity of a mother; it is a total perversion of family life, depriving the husband of his wife, the children of their mother, and the home and the family of their ever-watchful guardian.

23

Men

A review of *Men. A Documentary* by Anna Ford
(Weidenfeld and Nicolson) and *Men: the male
myth exposed* by Mary Ingham (Century),
first published in *The Times Literary Supplement*,
29 March 1985

DESPITE THE ELOQUENCE OF Simone de Beauvoir and
the wit of Germaine Greer, it never occurred to me until
now that feminism was taken seriously. To suggest that
women are oppressed or exploited by men seemed as
absurd as to say that lionesses are oppressed and exploited
by lions. We are all subject to the exigences of our species.
Men are men. Women are women, and books by feminists
only illustrate the point made by Schopenhauer that they
'never get beyond the subjective point of view'.

Now men and women alike are punished for their patron-
ising neglect of feminist apologetics, for here are two books
by two women who feel no need to argue the feminist case
because they write on the assumption that it is won. Both are
graduates from northern universities: Mary Ingham has a
degree in social science from Liverpool, Anna Ford a degree
in social anthropology from Manchester. Both see society as
a sum of its 'sub-cultures' and use words like 'chauvinism',
'traditional' and 'stereotype' with particular and pejorative
meanings. Anna Ford's book is described as a documentary
– a term taken from the world of television where she
worked for some years – notably as a reader of the News at
Ten. At first sight this seems an honest-enough description

since it reads like the transcript of a series of programmes on BBC 2 or Channel 4. The disadvantage of such a form is that the printed word demands more concentration than the word spoken over an image on the screen. It is not the same to be introduced on the page to 'Giles, an insurance broker', or 'Piers, a dentist', as it is to see the expression on a filmed face – particularly if one has been told in advance that 'In order to allow these men to speak frankly without fear of identification, all names and locations and, in most cases, the surrounding circumstances have been changed.'

Many of the transcribed interviews are also onerous to read because most people express themselves badly and have banal perceptions about their own lives. *Men* never achieves the cumulative impact of a book like Studs Terkel's *Working*. It is most effective as an eye peeping through keyholes at those aspects of our lives we usually keep to ourselves – something which Anna Ford seems to appreciate since the chapter on 'Sex' is the longest in her book and gives value for money to the reader-as-voyeur.

Almost from the start we see the subtitle, 'a documentary', as a ruse to give the book an air of objectivity and disguise the fact that it is not an investigation but a tract. The author assures us at the outset that she 'approached the subject with an open mind' and only wrote the book because she was 'as intrigued as ever about what made people, but in particular men, tick'. But no sooner has she said this than she gives away her feminist preconceptions with phrases like 'Despite being a woman in a patriarchal society' or 'The Mother, often a prisoner of child-bearing' or 'perhaps they had not discussed a fairer division of time off from household chores.'

This presents her with a dilemma, because few of the men she interviews seem to conform to 'chauvinist' type. Her ideology may demand that she criticise men; her research leads her to pity them. 'My overall impression,' she writes,

> is that the world men inhabit, and from which we women are often excluded, is rather bleak. It is a world full of doubt and confusion, where vulnerability must be hidden, not shared; where competition, not co-operation, is

the order of the day; where men sacrifice the possibility of knowing their own children and sharing in their upbringing, for the sake of a job they may have chosen by chance, which may not suit them, and which in many cases dominates their lives to the exclusion of much else.

Or, as a fashion designer, 'Cyril', puts it: 'I don't think women always realise what a grind a man's life can be.'

Nor, it seems to me, do women always realise the extent to which they elicit in men the very behaviour Anna Ford finds objectionable. It is easy enough to say that a husband should sacrifice his ambition at work for domestic bliss, but often it is the wife's material expectations, and the link between her esteem and his achievements, that lead him to work late at the office. It is the man who is unsure of his own masculinity who objects to changing the nappies – chiefly because so many women think it an 'unmanly' thing to do. Women may be sexually harassed by men. Men are often emotionally harassed by women; and even if, as Anna Ford suggests, they 'ceaselessly spar with each other in public . . . like stags battling for supremacy before the herd', they nonetheless 'like joining clubs and spending time together', wish that they could be 'left alone' by their wives and children, and often escape at weekends to relax among other men at the football stadium or the pub.

Because of her celebrity as what the French call a *speakerine*, Anna Ford's *Men* has had more attention than Mary Ingham's *Men*, and her dust-jacket is decorated with a full-plate photograph of the author by David Bailey whereas Mary Ingham, quite properly more modest about her appearance, has only a passport-size photograph inside on the flap of the dust jacket. Nature, alas, as our feminist authors should realise, is not always fair; for Anna Ford is also a better writer than Mary Ingham. The sincerity of her endeavour and the honesty of her judgements come through in her decent, functional prose. All it lacks is any wit or humour which I would have thought a prerequisite for any study of the sexes.

No doubt men, to Anna Ford, are no laughing matter: or

perhaps a sense of humour cannot survive a course in social science at a north-country university, for Mary Ingham lacks it too and where Anna Ford only occasionally lapses into sociological jargon, Mary Ingham writes largely in this style. 'But what about men who aren't in a couple role relationship?' She uses fewer transcripts than Anna Ford, and principally illustrates her argument with references to other people's books. Her conclusions, however, are much the same as Anna Ford's or, to be fair, since her book was published last summer, Anna Ford's are the same as hers. 'Men have got to start questioning themselves, admitting their lack of skill in making relationships, their fear of closeness to women, to other men and in a very basic sense to themselves.'

Like Anna Ford she seems to assume that the complementary qualities in men and women, which bring and keep them together, should be replaced by an ambisexual interdependence. If only they did more kissing and hugging and chatting about their feelings, all men's 'chauvinism' would disappear. This seems to me unlikely: it is precisely the macho Mediterranean who cuddles his children yet treats his wife as a chattel and practises the infamous 'dual morality'.

It is also undesirable since the more the sexes grow like each other, the less they will need one another to the detriment of family life. The counterpart to the house-keeping husband is the working wife who delights the Gradgrinds and Don Juans because she is so easily led into low-cost labour and the adulterous bed. As Ivan Illich points out in his excellent book *Gender*, 'Up to now, wherever equal rights were legally enacted and enforced, wherever partnership between the sexes became stylish, these innovations gave a sense of accomplishment to the elites who proposed and obtained them, but left the majority of women untouched, if not worse off than before.'

On a familial level, too, the replacement of the complementary qualities of the two sexes with like ones only leads to the disintegration of marriage. As the marriage therapist H.V. Dicks put it in *Marital Tensions*,

For success in marriage there must be present in each partner a clear and definite sense of *sexual identification* . . . The male parent is typically equipped to fight, hunt, build, manipulate, roaming outside the home *for* the home. The female parent gives expression more typically than her man, to tender and protective emotions, and responds to those of her offspring, staying close to them . . .

'All my own clinical experience,' wrote the marriage therapist A.C. Robin Skynner, 'extending now over more than twenty years, has certainly convinced me that, other things being equal, the optimal pattern for family functioning is one in which the *father* in general accepts the ultimate responsibility and the authority which goes with this.' The threat we face is therefore less from chauvinist husbands who bully their wives into ironing their shirts and cooking their suppers, than from harridan wives who drive their husbands into passivity, indifference and escape from the hell-hole of the home. If any policy was to be pursued for the public good, it would be one to protect rather than diminish the authority of the husband and father.

WRITERS

24

The Catholic Novelist in a Secular Society

Talk delivered at the Jagielleon University,
Cracow; excerpt published as 'The Decline
and Fall of the Catholic Novel', *The Times*,
29 March 1997

I WANT TO CONSIDER THE DILEMMA of the Catholic
novelist in a secular society of the kind that exists, I would
suggest, in Britain today. I approach this theme less as a
critic than as a working novelist who, like the authors I shall
discuss, has been given the label 'Catholic' both because of
the content of my novels and because of my publicly stated
beliefs.

Let me begin in 1850, the year in which a hierarchy of
Catholic archbishops and bishops was re-established in
England and Wales. There were, at this time, a number of
notable conversions from the Church of England to the
Church of Rome; and it was from this moment that there
also arose a remarkable partnership between the Roman
Catholic Church and the art of fiction. The first Archbishop
of Westminster, Cardinal Wiseman, wrote a popular historical novel called *Fabiola*, a story of early Christian martyrs;
and perhaps the most distinguished convert from the
Church of England, Cardinal Newman, one of the greatest
stylists of the English language, wrote two novels – one, *Loss
and Gain*, an account of a conversion not unlike his own; the
other, *Callista*, like Wiseman's *Fabiola*, a story of conversion
and martyrdom in the ancient world.

A number of able and distinguished Catholic writers

followed the example of these churchmen, using novels as a means to convey the insights of their faith. Some were unashamedly apologetic, such as R.F. Benson's *Come Rack, Come Rope*; others had a less obvious but nevertheless distinctive Catholic colouring – novels by authors such as Frederick Rolfe, Ford Maddox Ford, Hilaire Belloc and G.K. Chesterton. But it was with the advent in the 1930s of two convert novelists, Evelyn Waugh and Graham Greene, that the Catholic Novel became a recognisable entity with the informed public in Britain.

What is notable about Waugh and Greene is that the specifically Catholic content of some of their novels did nothing to impede their popularity or the critical acclaim. Greene's *The Power and the Glory, The Heart of the Matter* and *The End of the Affair*, all deal with Catholics and depict God as an invisible but active character in the narrative.

Certainly, Greene developed a particular perspective on questions of sin and grace which might have alarmed Cardinal Wiseman if not Cardinal Newman; but nevertheless in a novel written in a wholly realistic idiom such as *The End of the Affair* there is described the miraculous saving of a man's life as a result of a woman's prayer. The price she must pay for this divine intervention, as those familiar with the novel will know, is the renunciation of her lover. The heroine is married; adultery is mortal sin.

Such renunciation is paralleled in Waugh's ornate novel, *Brideshead Revisited*. Again, it is written in a realistic idiom and contains the miraculous repentance of old Lord Marchmain on his deathbed – described as God's twitch on the line – which in turn leads to the realisation by the two lovers, the hero, Charles Ryder, and Julia, Lord Marchmain's daughter, that they cannot marry: both have been married before.

Brideshead Revisited, published in 1945, was an enormous popular success. Some critics found it too Catholic; others objected to its setting among the English aristocracy; but by and large the public accepted the estimate of Waugh's friend, Nancy Mitford, that it was 'an English Classic'. The same was true of Graham Greene's *The Heart of the Matter*, published in 1948, and *The End of the Affair*, published in

1950. Both were highly charged, uncompromisingly Catholic novels with the sin of adultery centre stage. Both were immediate best-sellers in Britain and the United States, and entered into the mainstream of contemporary English literature.

Could the same happen today? I think not. Although anything is possible within the whimsical idiom of *magic* realism, it would be considered quite ridiculous to portray a miracle within the idiom of realism as such. Nor would contemporary readers, or contemporary critics, show much patience with a hero and heroine who renounce one another simply to comply with the teaching of the Catholic Church. Today, such self-denial could only be portrayed as a form of eccentricity or neurosis.

This is not, I think, because the general attitude among *bien pensant* intellectuals towards the kind of Catholicism that found expression in these novels by Waugh and Greene has radically altered. Atheist critics at the time disliked the overtly Catholic aspects of the novels, and much of the controversy that followed the publication of *The Heart of the Matter* was in fact among Catholics: Waugh described the idea that Scobie might kill himself for the love of God as 'either a very loose poetical expression or a mad blasphemy'.

Nevertheless, the audience for these novels would broadly speaking have been Christian in outlook, willing to accept the possibility of God's miraculous intervention in everyday life as in *Brideshead Revisited*, and to believe that Scobie in *The Heart of the Matter* might be damned to Hell for all eternity. Britain was a Christian nation in which the majority, although not Catholic, accepted the basic tenets of Christian teaching and, for all the concessions that were already made to human weakness when it came to questions like divorce, remained in favour on moral and social questions of the Christian norm.

Today, no such consensus exists in Britain because, in the course of the 1960s and 1970s, the British, like many other peoples in the western world, abandoned these Christian standards of social behaviour. This is seen particularly in the changes made to legislation on social questions which had hitherto been based loosely on Christian teaching. Now the only principle behind legislation became tolerance – the unfettered right of the individual to do as he or she pleases in so far as it did not infringe upon the rights of another individual: as a result, homosexual acts were decriminalised, and divorce and abortion became available virtually on demand.

There were a number of reasons for this change in our moral attitudes. Time does not permit me to give them in full or in detail. There was, for example, a delayed reaction to the atrocities committed by the Nazis during World War II. In Britain, where the Jews were seen as the principal, and even the sole victims of Nazi genocide, the Catholic Church, and particularly Pope Pius XII, have been portrayed as passive and even indifferent witnesses to this spectacular evil.

Another reason for the abandonment of Christian values was the adoption during this period by many members of the British intelligentsia of Marxist-Leninist ideas, and the dissemination of these ideas down from the universities into our teacher-training colleges and schools. As an example, let me cite Terry Eagleton, now professor of English at Oxford University. He was born and was raised a Catholic but, as he confessed to the Irish writer Colm Toibin, moved from Catholicism to Trotskyism during this period 'with ease'.[1]

A third reason for the loss of a Christian consensus in British life – and this is of particular relevance to the Catholic novel in England – is what has been called 'the sexual revolution'. This cannot be analysed in a few words, but without a doubt a combination of a number of social, economic and technological developments such as the ability of women to earn their own living or to receive support from the state, the widespread availability of contraception, and the decriminalisation of abortion are among the causes. Clearly, once the pragmatic disincentives to sex outside marriage were removed, the traditional Christian teaching could no longer count on society's support. Free love became the norm and there came into being what Pope John Paul II has called 'the aphrodisiac civilisation of the west'.

To English Catholics during this period, it was one thing to endure the ridicule of rationalists for their superstitious beliefs, but quite another to miss out on the fun simply to avoid a notional torment in a world to come. As the narrator notes in a novel by David Lodge, the most successful Catholic novelist in the generation that followed Waugh and Greene, 'the liberal hedonistic spirit has achieved irresistible momentum as much within the Church as without, and young Catholics now reaching adulthood have much the same views about the importance of sexual fulfilment and the control of fertility as their non-Catholic peers'.[2] Clearly, not just British society but British Catholics had changed, and David Lodge himself was to become both the foremost chronicler and apologist for this reversal in attitude among Catholics towards sexual morality. Born in 1935, he was raised in a conventional Catholic school, was a student at the time of Vatican II, became involved in the movement for reform and renewal, and subsequently described them with comic genius in novels such as *The British Museum is Falling Down*, published in 1965, and *How Far Can You Go?* published in 1980.

To Lodge, the birth-control controversy was a crucial focus for the Catholic dilemma about attitudes to sexuality. His heroes and heroines suffer inordinately from the strains imposed by continence; he even suggests, in *The British Museum is Falling Down*, that the use of the rhythm method caused the conception of a handicapped child. He leaves his readers in no doubt but that he regards the Church's traditional teaching on sexual morality to be wrong.

Clearly, such a message was music to the ears not just of non-Catholic readers, but also of Catholics who wished to join in the sexual revolution. But what becomes clear from this and some of Lodge's subsequent novels is that even before a crisis arose within the Catholic community over the question of contraception, there had been no proper understanding, let alone acceptance, of chastity as a norm of Catholic behaviour, or even as an ideal. After all, the only issue treated by the Encyclical *Humanae Vitae* was whether *married couples* should be permitted to use artificial methods of contraception; yet the overwhelming rejection of the papal teaching among Catholics was quickly extended from the issue of birth control to the Church's teaching on sexual morality as such.

To Lodge's characters, the Church's prescriptions are seen simply as somewhat arbitrary rules that should be circumvented as far as possible without falling into mortal sin: hence the question in the title of his novel, *How Far Can You Go?*

In other words, if one takes Lodge's heroes and heroines as exemplars of English Catholics of their time, it is pertinent to ask whether they were not so much seduced by the lax values of a secular society as liberated from the constraints of traditional Catholic teaching by a new understanding of the Catholic faith?

Here I should like to pause to consider the significance of the Second Vatican Council and its effects upon Catholic writers in England.

It is common today to describe the debates in the Council as a struggle between liberals and conservatives from which the liberals emerged triumphant. However, if one takes the trouble to actually read the Council's decrees, it is hard to find evidence to justify such a claim. In reality the differences were between the conservatives and *arch*-conservatives. As a result, there is nothing to be found in the decrees themselves to explain, let alone to justify, the turbulence that followed the Council – these changes made 'in the spirit of Vatican II' – unsettling, for better or worse, so many Catholics. More than fifty thousand priests left the priesthood – among them, the university chaplain in one of David Lodge's novels.

But rather than continue with Lodge, our chronicler of those troubled times, I should like to return to consider the effect of the Council on the two Catholic novelists with whom I started, Evelyn Waugh and Graham Greene.

Waugh saw it as a total disaster. He was wholly out of sympathy, particularly with the liturgical changes. He loved the Latin Mass in the Tridentine rite and was alarmed by the theological changes implicit in many of the supposed reforms.

On Easter Sunday, 1965, he took stock in his diary of what had been accomplished thus far:

> A year in which the process of transforming the liturgy has followed a planned course. Protests avail nothing. A minority of cranks, for and against the innovations, mind enormously. I don't think the main congregation cares a hoot. More than the aesthetic changes which rob the Church of poetry, mystery and dignity, there are suggested changes in Faith and morals which alarm me. A kind of anti-clericalism is abroad which seeks to reduce the priests' unique sacramental position. The Mass is written off as 'a social meal' in which the 'people of God' perform the consecration. Pray God I will never apostatize but I can only now go to church as an act of duty and obedience . . . I shall not live to see things right.[3]

His premonition proved right. This was the last significant entry in his diary. He died exactly a year later, on Easter Sunday, after attending Mass with his family.

Graham Greene, by contrast, appears to have embraced 'the spirit of Vatican II'. Like Waugh, he regretted some of the liturgical changes but he disagreed with the teaching on birth control of *Humanae Vitae*; backed the revolutionary movements in Central America inspired by Liberation Theology; and admired the writings of theologians like Hans Küng, Edward Schillebeeckx and Karl Rahner.

As Thomas Woodman of Reading University has noted in his work *The Catholic Novel in British Literature*, Greene's novel *A Burnt-Out Case* specifically 'addresses itself to Karl Rahner's influential notion of "anonymous Christianity".' Querry, the hero, is a famous architect who has lost his Catholic faith and comes to work in a leper colony in Africa. There he attends a sermon with the atheist doctor who runs the colony in which the priest preaches that everyone in the world is a Christian to the extent that he is loving and merciful. 'That would make us both Christians,' Querry says to the doctor. 'Come away before you are converted.'

The same kind of thinking is evident in Father Rivas, the priest in Greene's novel *The Honorary Consul*, who denies that he has left the Church by taking up arms with the socialist guerillas: 'How can I leave the Church? The Church is the world. The Church is this barrio, this room. There is only one way any of us can leave the Church, and that is to die.' If we remember that George Orwell criticised Greene's earlier novel, *The Heart of the Matter*, for 'the fairly sinister suggestion that ordinary human decency is of no value', and the value drawn from the same novel by the critic John Carey was that 'it is better to be an erring Catholic than a virtuous pagan', then it will be seen that Greene's views had radically changed. Certainly Greene, in the last decades of a long and productive life, spoke out in public more for the social mission of the Church – and in the context of Central America a specifically political and even violent mission – than he did for the old mystical and sacramental Church. He even suggested when in Moscow shortly before the collapse of the Soviet Union that the Vatican could learn much from the Kremlin.

He did not deny what one might call the metaphysical aspects of his involvement with Catholicism but made much more of his doubt than his faith, refining it with statements that some found profound and others merely paradoxical, even perverse, such as the remark he made to his friend, the Spanish priest, Fr Leopoldo Durán: 'The trouble is I don't believe in my unbelief.'

Whatever the travails of his soul – and this is an area where it would be improper for a critic to enquire – he did not lead the life of a conventionally observant Catholic, and did not want to be described as 'a Catholic novelist'. Yet the fact remained that because of his celebrity as a novelist, and because of the Catholic themes of those earlier novels, he was perhaps the most prominent Catholic layman in the English-speaking world; and his well-known disregard, both in theory and practice, for the Church's traditional teaching on sexual morality was unquestionably appealing to those Catholics who were caught up in the sexual revolution in the way I have described. David Lodge, as a writer of a younger generation, is a case in point – someone who not only admired Greene as a writer, but someone who was undoubtedly encouraged to find that the master shared his own views about what was meant by the spirit of Vatican II. Some now describe this as a form of Pelagianism; certainly, it has been generally accepted by a generation of Catholics in Britain that their own conscience should be not just the *final* but *only* arbiter of right and wrong; and that a subjective sense of love overrides any constraints imposed by Church Law.

Let me take an example of what I mean from Lodge's most recent novel. Here the middle-aged hero in the course of a kind of psycho-spiritual therapy (*Therapy* is the title of the novel) catches up with his first girlfriend, now a middle-aged woman making a pilgrimage to Santiago de Compostela. She is a Catholic. She is married, but as a result of cancer has had a breast removed. The two make love once they reach Santiago. To Lodge the compassion expressed in this act transcends any sin that might once have been considered implicit in its adulterous nature. We have come a long way from both *Brideshead Revisited* and *The End of the Affair.*

Of course, both the subjective judgements apparent in this and other novels by David Lodge, like the moral conundrums that are expressed in the later novels by Graham Greene, appeal to a society where moral relativism is the norm. And by and large most other novelists coming from the Catholic community have since the 1970s presented their readers with novels about *losing* their faith rather than gaining it. Often the message is in the title as in John Cornwell's *The Spoiled Priest* or Jill Paton Walsh's *Lapsing.*

Less appealing – indeed wholly obnoxious in many quarters – is the work of the Catholic writer who still holds the Church's traditional beliefs. If he becomes known not just as a Catholic novelist, but as an *orthodox* Catholic novelist, then he not only limits his appeal among readers: he is even seen as an enemy of enlightenment and progress. As Bryan Appleyard wrote in *The Independent* last September, Catholicism confronts the liberal consensus that prevails in Britain today. 'The truth is that Catholicism is not a problem for the contemporary liberal, it is *the* problem . . . To the modern imagination, Catholicism is the biggest enemy of all. As a result, "I hate Catholics" is quite commonly heard in otherwise civilised circles . . .'[4]

A good example of the kind of pressure that can be brought to bear on writers who offend against this liberal consensus was given last week in an article in the *Evening Standard* by Howard Jacobson who described how the managers of Waterstone's had banned a biography of the northern comedian, Bernard Manning, because his humour was deemed 'racist'.

However, Jacobson did not consider that 'racism' was the only offence which led the young Commissars of Political Correctness to ban books from their shelves. His own books, he wrote,

> have been thought policed out of West London in their time . . . I don't think racism was the offence exactly. Comparing notes with other writers who were conspicuously missing, and looking hard at writers who were conspicuously *there*, we took sex to be the matter. We weren't gay enough. There was a whiff of Insufficient Gay Reverence Syndrome about us.[5]

My own experience of Waterstone's would seem to support Jacobson's contention. My novel *A Patriot in Berlin* was on the in-house best-seller list at Hatchard's book store in Piccadilly but was difficult to find in the branches of Waterstone's in London's West End. My suspicions that this was the result of public pronouncements in favour of papal teaching on contraception and women priests or, more pertinently perhaps, against the lowering of the age of homosexual consent, had been dismissed by my publishers as paranoia: Jacobson's findings would suggest that they are not.

However, the problem goes beyond the prejudices of a homosexual mafia in the book trade. The Catholic writer has to acknowledge that today's non-Catholic reader may be put off his fiction by his Catholicism. In an exhibition on Modern British Fiction mounted last year by the British Council, and sent around the world, I was placed in a subsection called 'The Moral Maze' with Graham Greene and P.D. James. 'Religious crisis in Graham Greene and incipient Tory Anglicanism in P.D. James,' said the commentary written by Alastair Niven of the British Arts Council, 'pale beside the strong Roman Catholic conviction of Piers Paul Read. Perhaps this moral certainty, even in novels where problems of conscience are genuinely invoked, accounts for Read having failed to gain the popular following of the other two.'[6]

Some years ago, an American critic Philip Flyn made the same point. 'The Catholicism that provides Read's fiction with its moral center could prove to be the artist's liability, narrowing the subjects or circle of readers he can touch.'

Of course such an orthodox Catholic author may have his loyal following among his own Catholic community. Should he be content with them? The disadvantage here is two-fold. He is preaching to the converted. He is hiding his light under a bushel. The specific insights afforded by his faith will not reach those who do not share it: his art will be lost to the wider world.

Second, his work might not be appreciated even by the kind of Catholics who share his belief. In Britain and America there is seldom a correlation between piety and literary sophistication. Many Catholics were shocked by the novels of both Waugh and Greene. Greene was severely criticised by the then Archbishop of Westminster for *The End of the Affair* and his novel *The Power and the Glory* was placed on the Index in Rome. Waugh, who generously donated his foreign royalties to the local churches, on occasions had them returned by bishops shocked by the sexual candour of his novels.

An alternative strategy is for the Catholic novelist to follow a *via media* with an oblique approach to Catholic themes. Thomas Woodman of Reading University, whom I quoted earlier, writes that 'the better British Catholic novelists often follow the French in making crafty use of the device of the sceptical third-person narrator . . . and seem even more careful to preserve the saving ambiguity of the possibility of alternative explanations.' I myself have done this on a number of occasions and in the case of an early novel, *Monk Dawson*, had the dubious satisfaction of being congratulated by a Russian critic during the Soviet era for demonstrating so clearly that Christian belief was a form of insanity.

The difficulty here is that, while such ambiguity may be artistically fruitful, it demands a certain restraint and control which, in some writers, may impede the flow of inspiration. Particularly as the social norms in western society increasingly diverge from Christian principles, the Catholic conscience will be more seriously affronted by what it witnesses in everyday life. One sees in *The Thanatos Syndrome*, the last novel by that fine Catholic novelist from the United States, Walker Percy, a shrill, one might even say hysterical, denunciation of the evils of his age.

It also poses a problem for the Catholic writer when the Church's teaching comes under attack. I have described ours as a pluralistic society, and moral relativism as the norm; but moral relativism does not mean moral indifference. Quite to the contrary. There is any amount of ethical debate. We have seen how Marxism still flourishes among our intelligentsia, particularly in the universities. There is also humanism, feminism and environmentalism which fight it out with Christianity in the columns of newspapers and on television. In certain subcultures such as education or the media we frequently find a new orthodoxy of supposedly progressive attitudes often described as 'political correctness'.

In this continuing national debate, the Catholic writer has a choice of two courses of action. He can remain silent like those early disciples of Our Lord, described by St John in his Gospel, 'who did believe in him . . . but they did not admit it, through fear of the Pharisees and fear of being expelled from the synagogue: they put honour from men before the honour that comes from God';[7] or he can speak out in favour of specifically Catholic perspectives on questions such as the family, the free market, sex education, euthanasia, pornography, the role of women, the morality of homosexual relations, and particularly abortion, and in the process risk alienating not just non-Catholic critics but potential readers too.

The third possibility for the Catholic novelist in a secular society is to dissociate his faith from his art, deciding that, in the words of Hilaire Belloc, he will be 'God's spy in the world'. He peacefully pursues his career; his convictions remain a private matter; he does not broadcast them either in his life or his work.

That, I suspect, will be the course chosen by most Catholic writers in the future, and it will almost certainly mean the end of the Catholic novel that flourished in Britain from Cardinal Newman to Graham Greene. This will not be the result simply of the prudence of Catholic writers, but also of the less distinctive nature of post-Conciliar Catholicism as such. As Thomas Woodman says at the end of his perceptive study of Catholic fiction:

> The old ideology had absolutized the Church and over-simplified its relationship with the world. It had nevertheless provided the vantage point for a distinctive vision and critique. There is some question whether the new versions will be able to do the same, and doubts have been expressed not only about the future of Catholic fiction but even about whether a distinctive Catholic contribution of any kind will continue.[8]

For society, however, perhaps more serious than this loss of a literary genre is the end of any witness to the very idea of objective truth. To quote Bryan Appleyard once again:

> 'We agree to differ' [becomes] the standard form towards which all conflicts in a liberal society tend. And, finally, because of the aridity of such a conclusion, even the energy to differ expires. Unable to create a solidity for himself, liberal man lapses into a form of spiritual fatigue, a state of apathy in which he decides such wider, grander questions are hardly worth addressing. The symptoms of this lethargy are all about us. The pessimism, anguish, scepticism and despair of so much twentieth-century art and literature are expressions of the fact that there is nothing 'big' worth talking about any more, there is no meaning to be elucidated.[9]

'The tolerant society,' Appleyard warns,

> can easily decline into a society that cares nothing for its own sustenance and continuity. The fact that the

democracies constantly seem to have a crisis in their schools is important – it is a symptom of a crucial uncertainty about what there is to teach, about whether there is anything to teach.

A society in which there is no agreement on moral principles, or on objective truth in the moral sphere, is a society heading for trouble. 'In communism,' wrote the French philosopher Alain Besançon,

> the contrary of the truth was the lie, and the lie was the very nature of communism. In democracy, the contrary of the truth is the meaningless, and the meaningless is a menace to democratic life. The relativity of truth, its reduction to opinion, the progressive weakening of opinion, create a metaphysical void in which modern man suffers . . .[10]

The question for the future is therefore this. Will the Catholic novelist in the next millennium increasingly dissociate his faith from his work? Or will he, as Besançon demands, combine his faith with his talent to 'help democracy heal itself from the deficit of truth'?

NOTES

1. *The Signs of the Cross. Travels in Catholic Europe* (Jonathan Cape, 1994), p. 257.
2. *How Far Can You Go?* (Penguin, 1982), pp. 120–1.
3. *The Diaries of Evelyn Waugh*, edited by Michael Davie (Weidenfeld and Nicolson, 1976), p. 793.
4. *The Independent*, 19 September 1996.
5. *Evening Standard*, 13 January 1997.
6. *Contemporary British Novelists*, The British Council, 1995.
7. John 12:42–3.
8. *Faithful Fictions. The Catholic Novel in British Literature* (Open University Press, 1991).
9. *Understanding the Present* (Picador, 1992), p. 12.
10. *La Pensée Politique* (No. 2, 1994), translated by Paul Seaton and Daniel Mahoney for *Crisis* (September, 1995).

25

Eros Defended

Pornography, by which I mean the use of words to conjure up images which excite sexual desire in the reader, is an ignoble adjunct to the perversions of voyeurism and masturbation. Where the writer shows some skill – Cleland, say, in *Fanny Hill* – there may be some literary value in the work but essentially pornography is a prostitution of talent, and when effective is a swindle because it stimulates appetites which it cannot satisfy.

There remain many contexts, however, in which explicit references to, or descriptions of, human sexual behaviour are proper and even necessary; and where euphemism or circumlocution makes writing insipid. Sex, after all, is a powerful force at some stage in the lives of most men and women: when linked to love it is often the most dramatic and intractable aspect of our condition. To disguise it, or ignore it, or merely suggest it, as the Victorians were obliged to do, detracts from the veracity of fiction which – precisely because it is both private and explicit – can treat such an intimate aspect of our lives. Painting and drama, which are enjoyed in public, are more circumscribed in this respect.

Certainly scenes of sexual significance – say the lust for Joseph of Potiphar's wife, or Valmont's seductions in *Les Liaisons Dangereuses* – can be written without explicit descriptions of naked bodies, but there are also times when the inclusion of a graphic detail can make a point which would be lost without it. When the prophet Ezekiel chides Israel for lying down with 'those big-membered neighbours, the Egyptians', the adjective tells us something about Israel's lust. Similarly some of the value of Boswell's or

Pepys's diaries comes from the explicit descriptions of their sexual encounters. There is a sense in which *Les Liaisons Dangereuses* by the pious Laclos is more pornographic than the diaries of Boswell and Pepys. It is not the explicitness as such which makes writing pornographic, but the author's intention in writing a scene, and the effect that scene has upon his reader.

Of course the diaries of Boswell and Pepys were not written for publication, and would not have been so explicit had this been so. As a general rule, however, it seems to me better both for literature, and for the society which in some sense it serves, if men and women write as they feel and think, and do not reflect in their fiction a respectable image of themselves while the true picture is hidden in a locked drawer. Self-censorship detracts from the author's sincerity and spontaneity, and deludes his readers about their true condition. Indeed the art which is condemned as unwholesome, decadent or obscene is often the art which most accurately reflects the true state of society. Certainly the books and paintings condemned by the Nazis were those that were harsh but true to the times.

Times change, of course, and particularly in respect to sex the pendulum swings back and forth between modesty and candour. The writers of the Restoration reacted against the Puritanism of the Cromwellian era; the Victorians reacted against the licentiousness of the late-eighteenth century. In the 1960s we reacted against the prudery of the Victorians. Today one senses that the pendulum has started to swing back again. I now find myself more reserved in my own depiction of the sexual exchanges between my characters which may be a symptom of my age, but may also be a reaction against the aftermath of the sexual revolution.

Yet I can remember quite well my determination when I started writing in the 1960s not to shy away from the harsh and often gruesome truths about human sexuality or emulate the evasiveness of earlier writers. I remember reading and re-reading passages in *The Wings of the Dove,* trying to make out what was going on between Merton Densher and Kate Croy, and thinking James had gone to absurd lengths to avoid stating what he should have made clear.

'If you decline to understand me, I wholly decline to understand you. I'll do nothing,' says Densher.

'And if I do understand?' Kate replies.

'I'll do everything.'

'Well, I understand.'

'On your honour?'

'On my honour.'

'You'll come?'

'I'll come.'

Understand what? Do what? Come where? For what? In retrospect I now realise that this was the Edwardian equivalent of 'Your place or mine?' but at the time it exasperated me that James should be so coy.

It is difficult today to remember the pervasive conspiracy to ignore human sexuality which arose in the nineteenth century but persisted until the 1960s. It is only that context which explains the ponderous descriptions of human copulation in *Lady Chatterley's Lover*, or the witty obscenity of *The Tropic of Cancer*. We may now laugh at Lawrence, and dismiss Henry Miller, but it is thanks to their audacity that writers today can be as candid about sex as the Victorian novelists were about money and social position.

It is a pity, of course, that in the 1960s so many cast off their principles with their inhibitions, and doubtless the anthropological explanation of our neo-prudery is an unconscious attempt by society to repair the damage done to marriage and family life by an overdose of eroticism. The harm done by ignorance about sex is replaced by unrealised and unrealistic expectations. It would be a pity, however, if writers, as they take the heat out of the libido, revert at the same time to the genteel pretence that we are all really much nicer than we seem to be. Then the strong current of human sexuality flows underground and may surface in an unpleasant and unexpected way.

26

The Quest for Graham Greene

A review of *The Quest for Graham Greene* by
W.J. West (Weidenfeld and Nicolson), first
published in *The Sunday Times*

LIKE MARCEL PROUST, GRAHAM GREENE is an author
whose life has fascinated the reading public as much as his
work. When living, he epitomised the novelist as existential-
ist hero, the armchair traveller's correspondent in the exotic
spiritual and temporal hot-spots of the world. Now that he is
dead, he has become a rich source for a number of authors.
There have been at least three biographies of Greene as well
as a memoir by his friend Fr Leopoldo Durán. Now we have
W.J. West's *Quest for Graham Greene* promising revelations
missed in the trawl by earlier researchers.

My own fascination with Greene began long before I had
read any of these biographies or even his novels, from
listening to my parents discuss the audacious escapades of
his middle age. Their friendship with Greene dated from
Greene's editorship of *Night and Day* when Greene, in an
inspired act of cross-fertilisation, had recruited my father to
review thrillers for his ill-fated review. Greene became my
sister's godfather, but we never saw him: our only acquaintance with the celebrated novelist was through the
anecdotes told by my parents.

Later, when I started writing, two of my books drew generous endorsements from Greene. In 1975 I went to pay
homage to Greene in Antibes, and four years later, when
living in Nice with my family, I saw him quite frequently with

Yvonne Cloetta and her daughter Martine, who at the time was embroiled in a messy separation with her husband that later became the subject of Greene's *J'Accuse*.

Greene proved himself to be a man of great generosity and irresistible charm. He wore his celebrity lightly and had an almost boyish sense of humour and a love of intrigue – qualities which have won over most of those who have written about him such as Norman Sherry, Anthony Mockler, Fr Durán and now W.J. West.

West's principal 'scoop' came through letters he discovered in Ealing written by Rene Raymond, better known as James Hadley Chase. It is these that reveal details of the complex tax avoidance schemes organised for Greene and other high-earning celebrities such as Chase, George Sanders, Charlie Chaplin and Noel Coward by a certain Tom Roe who was then arrested in Switzerland for circulating forged $100 bills on behalf of the mafia.

It was the prospect of a Board of Trade Enquiry triggered by Roe's arrest which led Greene to 'flee' abroad. He already had a flat in Paris and a house in Capri; now he bought the small flat overlooking the harbour at Antibes which not only reminded him of the visits he had paid to Alexander Korda on his yacht but was also close to Juan les Pins where Yvonne Cloetta lived with her husband.

Another suggestion, which West concedes is conjecture, is that Greene, aged sixteen, had an affair with his psychiatrist's wife, Zoe Richmond. She gave birth to a son soon after he returned to Berkhamstead School. Graham was never told, and only learned about it many years later when Zoe Richmond wrote asking him to take an interest in a book by her son. 'It may have been thought best,' writes West, 'not to tell Greene of the son's birth for the very reason that he might conclude that it was his child.'

West's book is well written, and will be of interest to those not suffering from Greene-fatigue. However, his attitude to his subject is perplexing. West, educated at St Benedict's, Ealing, is presumably a Catholic like Greene, and yet when it comes to Greene, he seems not just to suspend his moral judgement but even perform ethical summersaults to enhance Greene's reputation as a saintly man.

Brendan Behan's description of himself as 'a bad Catholic' implies an awareness of his sins. Greene showed little sign of a comparable remorse, at any rate for his sexual sins. It would seem that the nature of his belief changed after Vatican II. He did not believe in papal infallibility, rejected Pope John Paul II's conservative stance on moral questions and espoused the Liberation Theology of Latin American revolutionaries. 'It meant more to him than any other aspect of contemporary Catholicism,' writes West, 'because it resolved his own personal political and religious quandry.'

It was on this issue that I fell out with Greene in later years: he wrote an angry letter to *The Tablet* attacking an article I had written critical of Liberation Theology, accusing me of siding with the murderers of helpless women (see pp. 117ff.) and children. I in turn sensed a certain inconsistency in this radical stance by a man who had taken such pains to avoid contributing to his country's Welfare State.

I was also disappointed by his Catholicism. He seemed to make an intellectual plaything of his faith. Michael Shelden, Greene's least sympathetic biographer, considered Greene to be a bogus Catholic: 'no major novelist has shown as much ingenuity in abusing the God of Christianity.' Anthony Mockler in his *Graham Greene: Three Lives* was more forgiving: 'though intellectually convinced of the claims of the Catholic Church, he took the actual rules and regulations regarding behaviour no more seriously than he had done the rules of school or college.'

W.J. West is still more indulgent, portraying Greene in his concluding pages as a martyr for his faith. 'Greene was to die in exile, one of those good people . . . Britain chose to force into exile . . . Like the countless Catholic refugees who had died in exile in their turn, fleeing the Reformation, he died in the arms of the Church.' For that, we thank God: but the comparison of Greene to a Catholic exile in an era of persecution seems as absurd as Greene's comparison of Philby to a Jesuit missionary in Elizabethan England. West's conclusion mars an otherwise excellent book.

27

The Riddle of Greene's Catholicism

A review of *The Life of Graham Greene. Volume Three: 1955–1991* by Norman Sherry (Cape), first published in *The Catholic Herald,* 22 October 2004

GRAHAM GREENE WAS THE MOST CELEBRATED and yet the most mysterious Catholic layman of the twentieth century. Like his fellow novelists Georges Bernanos and François Mauriac, his fame and his Catholicism were inextricably linked but, because of the enormous popular success of his novels, his 'reach' was far greater than theirs. The mystery lay in the paradoxical nature of his faith – almost a cult of doubt – which, because it was mostly treated in the context of sexual sin, added to the appeal of his novels and explains the abiding fascination of his private life.

Well before his death Greene himself decided to authorise a biography and offered what has turned out to be something of a poisoned chalice to an academic at Lancaster University, Norman Sherry, whose early works on Conrad had impressed him. We now have the third and final volume of Sherry's work which has been eighteen years in the making, has dominated 'a quarter of a century of my life': it takes Greene's life from 1955 to his death in 1991 and covers Greene's excursion into theatre and the writing of the later novels such as *A Burnt-Out Case, The Comedians* and *The Honorary Consul.* It also charts in great detail the slow cooling of Greene's passion for Catherine Walston, the supposed model for Sarah in *The End of the Affair,* and the long liaison with Yvonne Cloetta whom he first met in Africa while researching *A Burnt-Out Case*.

Sherry is thorough: there is a photograph of him sitting on a mule in Mexico retracing Greene's journey researching the travel book *A Journey Without Maps* and his novel *The Power and the Glory*. At times Sherry seems rather too conscientious in giving such detailed descriptions of some of the duller excursions of the restless writer – his visit to Tahiti, for example, with Michael Meyer. One senses that the narrative is led by the material at Sherry's disposal, and so fails to give an overview of the writer's life.

Those who knew Greene, as I did, will be aware of areas of interest that remain untouched. Greene had a way of taking up and then quarrelling with fellow-writers: there is a description of his quarrel with Anthony Burgess but none of his dispute over Philby with John le Carré. Another flaw is the imbalance between the endless and ultimately tedious minutiae of his relationship with Catherine Walston, and the lack of material on Greene's relationship with his family – in particular his children, Francis and Caroline.

It may well be that Francis and Caroline wished it this way, and that there is little about them in Greene's diaries and correspondence. 'How I dislike children!' Greene wrote after complaining that he had had to wait up for Francis then aged twenty-four. Sherry suggests that Greene's neglect of his children (for which Greene felt some shame) was justified by his genius. 'We are dealing with the imperfect artist – the dedicated artist – whose passion for his subject makes him an unloving father.' And an unloved son. His mother Marion is described by a cousin as 'a most formidable and cold woman'. When she dies in 1959 Greene asks the Jesuit, Fr Philip Caraman, to say a few Masses for her but does not change his plans to sail for Africa and so misses her funeral.

Sherry's suggestion – that artists cannot be judged as other men; that genius is an excuse for sin – begs the question as to whether Greene was a genius. Sherry, having spent a large chunk of his life in the service of the writer, would be unlikely to question Greene's status. He suggests, plausibly and with documentation, that it was largely anti-Catholic prejudice that prevented Greene from winning the Nobel Prize. There is no question but that the combination of Greene's popular and critical success made him seem a great writer though there were doubts even in his hey-day. My mother, whose views on the *mari complaisant* are quoted in this volume, used to say that Greene was 'highbrow for the lowbrow'; and Evelyn Waugh quite rightly ridiculed the theology of *The End of the Affair* and, within the scope of this volume, Greene's play *The Potting Shed*: 'The play is great nonsense theologically and will puzzle people needlessly,' he wrote to his wife.

A further criticism of Greene's work, made as early as the 1950s, was that his women characters were implausible and this is consistent with the profile established by Sherry's third volume of a man who was chronically immature. It was not just that he was unable to settle down to marriage and family life; but that his puerile promiscuity continued well into and beyond middle age. Sherry publishes as an appendix the list of Greene's forty-seven 'favourite prostitutes'. He found in Catherine Walston, the rich American wife of a Labour peer, a woman who shared and even out-did him in sexual depravity. Sherry counts two Catholic priests, one a Jesuit, one a Dominican, among her lovers. Fr Philip Caraman's report of one of them to the higher Church authorities turned Greene against him. 'I am afraid Fr Caraman is a Jesuit whom I dislike very much,' Greene wrote. 'He was a man who tried to intervene in my private life and he knows nothing of my conception of the priesthood except that his own priesthood has been to me very suspect.' Walston's alleged lover, Father Thomas Gilbey OP, Sherry tells us 'was a priestly libertine and debauchee'.

Greene's choice of prostitutes and other men's wives as his sexual partners was partly, no doubt, to preserve that independence – emotional but also financial – that he felt necessary to his art. He was cold, selfish and sexually depraved but perhaps the root sins were idolatry and pride. Nothing was so sacred that it should not be sacrificed for his art. It seems likely – though Sherry does not say so – that he decided that the label 'Catholic novelist' was hampering his ambition; and that *A Burnt-Out Case* which charts the loss of faith of its hero Querry was an attempt to shake it off. It is perhaps significant that Greene, hoping for the Nobel Prize, arranged for the novel to appear first in Stockholm in Swedish translation; so too his play *The Living Room* in 1952.

Was God, then, merely one of Greene's literary devices? His faith, or lack of it, remains an unsolved riddle. Sherry believes that Greene only became a Catholic to be able to marry his wife Vivien, but that his faith took root when he witnessed the persecution of the Church in Mexico. Subsequently, the great critical and popular success of *The Power and the Glory* showed that the mixture of sex, faith and guilt was an effective cocktail for the time. It should be remembered that *The End of the Affair* and *The Heart of the Matter*, like *Brideshead Revisited*, were published in a period of great religious fervour in Britain. As Callum G. Brown notes in *The Death of Christian Britain*, 'The late 1940s and 1950s witnessed the greatest church growth that Britain had experienced since the mid-nineteenth century.' It was therefore perhaps not opportunism but sensitivity to the changing *zeitgeist* that led Graham to posit a loss of faith in *A Burnt-Out Case* and, when he returned to it, adopt the post-Conciliar fashion for Liberation Theology.

Sherry quite rightly criticises Greene for his political posturing: 'it was his tragic flaw; he could never pass up a fight.' Greene happily played the role of 'a useful idiot' for left-wing dictators in South America such as Fidel Castro: 'Greene was given VIP treatment [in Cuba], indeed almost like a head of state. Many left-wing leaders and left-wing dictators in South America found it politically prudent to treat the famous Greene well. He was a useful and worthwhile friend. How could this brilliant mind be so easily taken in?' It is the same with his defence of Philby who, as Sherry points out, 'did have friends he'd worked with killed: he had blood on his hands'. Greene's contention that he would rather live in the Soviet Union than the United States and that the Vatican should learn from the Kremlin were perhaps forgivable as the barbs of an *enfant terrible* and *agent provocateur*; but there was surely a certain hypocrisy in a man who posed as the champion of the poor and oppressed taking such trouble to avoid – and even evade – the British taxes that funded Overseas Aid and the Welfare State.

Time and again when reading this and other biographies of Greene one returns to the riddle of his religious convictions. It seems baffling that a man who called himself a Catholic and loved theology should not only show such disregard for the virtue of chastity but such insouciance in sleeping with other men's wives. Lord Walston was, perhaps – and up to a point – a *mari complaisant:* but Greene's claim that Jacques Cloetta was also *complaisant* was denied by his daughter Martine.

Sherry believes that towards the end of his life Greene began to fear that he might be punished after his death for his sins and that this accounts for his friendship with the Spanish priest, Leopoldo Durán.

> Greene . . . organised his relationship with Durán so that he had his own priest to officiate over his final departure . . . He needed this security blanket because increasingly as Graham grew older he felt the proximity of punishment after death for his sexual transgressions. Perhaps he believed in sin after all. But he never gave up cuckolding Jacques Cloetta.

A window into Greene's soul came in an interview with John Cornwell in *The Tablet* in 1989. Here he suggests a fairly heterodox kind of 'cafeteria Catholicism' – so heterodox, indeed, that in Sherry's views 'it was difficult to believe Greene was a sure and certain Catholic' at the time. One learns more by considering Greene's story 'A Visit to Morin' to which he referred enquirers, among them myself. Morin has no belief in Christianity but believes that this is the consequence of his (sexual) sins. Thus there is a residual *faith* and so the hope that, were he to return to a State of Grace, his belief would return.

What, then, was his condition at the hour of his death? Greene's Spanish friend, Count Creixell, confirmed Sherry's hypothesis that, like an eighteenth-century nobleman, Greene kept Fr Durán on hand to shrive him at the last moment. He told Sherry that Graham pursued his pleasures secretly as a 'voluptuary would and thought that freedom he'd given himself could and probably would lead to punishment everlasting. Secret remorse often overwhelmed him . . . Father Durán was an absolute necessity, his final hope that the good Father could prevent him from being condemned.'

Sherry tells us that Graham sent for Durán who arrived at the Hôpital de la Provence at 11.45 on Tuesday, the day before Graham died. Graham was conscious, recognised his friend, but couldn't easily speak. Durán administered the last sacraments . . . But Sherry concedes that this account differs from that of Fr Durán; and it contrasts with Yvonne's recollections. When she suggested to Graham 'summoning his friend, the Spanish priest Leopoldo Durán,' she later wrote, 'he raised his hand casually and said, "Oh, if you want to . . ." That implied he was indifferent.' Thus the riddle of Greene's Catholicism remains unsolved even after Professor Sherry's quarter-century of research. No doubt the conjecture will continue: may Greene himself Rest in Peace.

SAINTS

28

St Margaret Clitherow

ST MARGARET CLITHEROW, WAS THE WIFE of a butcher in York in the second half of the sixteenth century. She was executed in March 1586 for refusing to plead either guilty or non guilty to the crime of harbouring a priest.

At first sight her very normality makes her a suitable object for our veneration today. The life of a butcher's wife under Queen Elizabeth I was not so very different to the life of a butcher's wife under Queen Elizabeth II. The very banality of her worldly calling emphasises the heroism of her end. She was a woman, not a man, which gives a feminist flavour to her martyrdom; yet she was a wife and mother, not a nun, which makes her example pertinent at a time when the laity is examining its role in the life of the Church. If she had died in her bed it is unlikely that anything about her would be known today. She was, one might say, a common woman to inspire us in the age of the common man.

Yet a closer scrutiny of her life, or more particularly of her death, reveals certain uncomfortable contradictions – and even after her canonisation, St Margaret has her detractors among Catholics. It is said now, as it was said at the time, that she courted martyrdom – indeed that she insisted upon it when she could quite easily have avoided it – and that this showed an uncharitable indifference to the fate of her husband and children. It has even been suggested that there was perhaps some truth in the stories put about at the time of her martyrdom that she had had love affairs with the priests she harboured – and that her final confessor, Father Mush, whose account of her suffering is our only source, was a government double agent who invented the story of her martyrdom for reasons of his own. Also, in this ecumenical age, her obstinate refusal to countenance the Church of England seems anachronistic. 'I will not pray with you,' she said to the Anglican minister who accompanied her to her death, 'and you shall not pray with me; neither will I say Amen to your prayers, nor shall you to mine.'

Before giving a brief account of her life and death let me say something about York which I know well from my childhood in Yorkshire. It is now a flourishing city, second only to London as an attraction for tourists from overseas. Indeed the crowded streets give a good idea of what York must have been like in the later Middle Ages. The area of the city within the city walls, much of which is now a pedestrian precinct, is the same confined space in which the citizens lived at the time. It takes only ten minutes or so to walk from the King's Manor which once formed part of St Mary's Abbey, but by St Margaret's time had been commandeered by the government as the headquarters of the Council of the North, to the Shambles where John Clitherow had his butcher's shop; ten minutes to walk from there to the Castle where recusant Catholics were imprisoned; another ten to the Bridge over the Ouse where there was a secondary prison where St Margaret was held; and another ten back to the Guildhall where she was arraigned before her judges.

Thus even today we can see how compact and crowded the city must have been in St Margaret's day; how confined and yet valuable were the houses and shops; how familiar with one another the citizens must have been; how quickly gossip and disease must have passed from house to house and street to street.

There was, however, one great difference between present-day York and York in the past: York no longer plays a political role in the government of northern England. From the time of the Romans, however, it was of considerable strategic significance as the last major city before the border with Scotland. It was in York that Constantine was proclaimed emperor and so it might be said that it was in York that the seeds were sown of Christianity as a state religion. William the Conqueror had used it as his base for laying waste all the land between the Humber and the Tyne. As long as Scotland was independent and therefore a potential base for the invasion of England, York was the key to the security of the realm, and its role was never more critical than in the early years of Elizabeth I.

At the time there was what today we might call a North-South divide. The dissolution of the monasteries under Henry VIII had been particularly unpopular in the north, and in 1536 – about twenty years before Margaret Clitherow was born – had provoked the rebellion called the Pilgrimage of Grace. It was a rising in defence not just of the monasteries but of the Catholic religion. On the banners of the rebels were painted the image of Christ crucified and the Chalice and Host. The revolt failed, as we know, and its leaders were executed.

After the death of Henry VIII came the short reign of Edward VI when Protestant ideas spread rapidly throughout England; then the even shorter reign of Queen Mary who tried to restore the Catholic religion by reviving the heresy laws of the Middle Ages. In five years around three hundred Protestants were burned at the stake – among them Cranmer, Ridley and Latimer.

It is important, I think, to bear this Catholic intolerance in mind for it clearly justified to some Protestants some kind of revenge when the boot was back on their foot; it made others, not necessarily Protestant, afraid of another Catholic monarch; and others still, and these undoubtedly a majority, tired of the kind of religious enthusiasm which led to executions and *autos-da-fé*.

Queen Elizabeth came to the throne in 1558 when Margaret Clitherow was around five years old. She decided to impose a settlement of religion with a Church which embodied a compromise between Catholic practices and Protestant ideas. There were bishops as there were in the Catholic Church but there was no role whatsoever for the Pope in Rome. Elizabeth became the Supreme Governor and the clergy had to adopt a uniform service based upon the Protestant prayerbook of Edward VI. The settlement was probably acceptable to a majority of her subjects: only two or three hundred of the eight thousand clergy refused to accept it. In general it suited the mood of the English at the time, and has survived as the Church of England to the present day.

Under the Act attending the Anglican service, and taking Anglican communion, was compulsory and those who refused were marked down. Thus a Catholic or, for that matter, a Puritan could be smoked out and would be known. At first the Catholics had only to pay a fine for non-attendance, and perhaps the government might have been content with this extra source of revenue had it not been for the political implications of this dissent.

Even today it is difficult to disentangle the political from the religious in the Elizabethan era – indeed they cannot be disentangled because monarchs made claims over the spiritual lives of their subjects and Popes made claims over the temporal allegiances of their flock. It is unfortunate, for the Catholic apologist, that so many Popes allowed themselves to be swayed in their spiritual judgements by political calculations. The fact remains, however, that St Peter's successor had refused to annul the marriage of Henry VIII to Catherine of Aragon; thus his daughter Elizabeth by Anne Boleyn was illegimate and ineligible to Catholics as Queen of England.

Since in theory it was an age when rulers decided the religion of their subjects, and since the legitimate heirs – either Philip of Spain, the widower of Queen Mary, or Mary Queen of Scots – were both Catholics, one can understand why Pope Pius V excommunicated Queen Elizabeth and declared her deposed: but since the Queen was popular with her subjects – particularly those *nouveaux riches* who had profited from the privatisation of the confiscated monastery lands – it was an edict likely to succeed only in making life uncomfortable for those in England who remained loyal to the Catholic religion. Rather like Communists in western democracies in the heyday of the Third International, Catholics became by definition potential enemy agents: and as that enemy became less vague but more specific – as an Armada was assembled in Spain for the invasion of England – the elimination of this fifth column became of paramount political importance.

Thus the sanctions against Catholics were dramatically increased to the point where not only Catholic priests were liable to be executed for treason but also those who hid them. Enforcing these laws was considered by Elizabeth's Privy Council to be particularly important in the north of England where Catholic sympathies remained strong. In 1569 there had been another uprising led by the northern Earls of Westmoreland and Northumberland which had the marks of a Catholic crusade. This too was suppressed. Its leaders fled to Scotland but were brought back and in 1572, when Margaret Clitherow was around nineteen years old and newly married to John Clitherow, Thomas Percy, the Seventh Earl of Northumberland, was beheaded on a scaffold erected within a hundred yards of the Clitherows' house in the Shambles.

Since such executions were public spectacles in those days it is highly likely that St Margaret would have witnessed this execution, and would have heard the last words of this popular and glamorous young nobleman who died, he said, in 'that Church which, throughout the whole Christian world, is knit and bound together . . . In this same faith I am about to end this unhappy life. But as for this new English Church, I do not acknowledge it.'

Here he was interrupted by a Protestant minister called Palmer. 'You are dying an obstinate Papist,' he said, 'a member not of the Catholic but of the Roman Church.' To which Thomas Percy answered: 'That which you call the Roman Church is the Catholic Church which has been founded on the teaching of the Apostles, Jesus Christ himself being its corner-stone, strengthened by the blood of Martyrs, honoured by the recognition of the holy Fathers; and it continues always the same, being the Church against which, as Christ our Saviour said, the gates of Hell shall not prevail.'

After his death the body of Thomas Percy was buried in the Church of the Holy Cross at the end of the Shambles while his head was stuck on a pole on the top of Micklegate.

Whether or not it was his example which inspired her, we do not know, but it was shortly after this execution that Margaret Clitherow sought instruction in the proscribed Catholic religion. There was in York – and she would have known it – a circle of recusant Catholics around a couple called Vavasour – the husband a doctor and graduate of St John's College, Cambridge who by this time had gone underground – and his wife, clearly a remarkable woman, who ran what has been described as a Catholic maternity home which provided a useful pretext for gatherings of Catholic women.

Again it is not known which priest received Margaret into the Catholic Church. A point that should be made, however, is that she was not a recusant – not the daughter of parents who had stubbornly clung to the old religion – but a convert from the Church of England. Indeed her stepfather, Henry May, who plays a central, sinister but imprecise role in this whole affair, was apparently a zealous Protestant though probably from opportunism rather than conviction. It is possible that Margaret was instructed by a priest called Henry Comberford who like Vavasour was a graduate of St John's, Cambridge. Comberford was at this time imprisoned in York upon some suspicion for complicity in the Earls' rebellion: but since conditions in the prisons were lax he was able to minister to some extent to the Catholics in York. Although Margaret, like all women at the time, had received no education, it is clear from the answers she gave at her trial that she had received a good grounding in many of the theological issues involved in the Reformation.

Margaret's conversion not only convinced her but made her pious. She soon conceived an aversion to the kind of worldly proccupations which went with the life of a wife of a butcher and a prominent citizen of York. There is no doubt that she was punctilious in her duties as a wife and a mother. Her husband was clearly fond of her, and despite her disappointment that she could not bring him to share her beliefs, it is clear from her protestations that her conscience was clear so far as her treatment of him was concerned. It should be remembered, however, that John Clitherow was a widower with two young sons by his first marriage – the eldest of which was eight at the time of his marriage to the eighteen-year-old Margaret. Indeed because of the indiscriminate mortality at the time, the generations were topsy-turvy. Margaret was much nearer in age to her sinister stepfather, Henry May, than she was to her husband and there is evidence that her stepfather tried to seduce her. Perhaps it was to punish her for fending him off that he arranged her marriage to a man who was older, coarser and of a lower social class.

A devil's advocate might say that had Margaret married a younger and a more impressive man she might have been less susceptible to the influence of priests. Certainly, at that time, spiritual direction by a ghostly father was considered necessary for the soul's progress towards sanctity: but what was exceptional in this case was the high calibre of some of Margaret's spiritual directors. Certainly to Margaret, as to the other Catholic women of York, the imprisonment which they suffered on and off during the 1570s for their refusal to conform to the Elizabethan settlement was welcomed rather than dreaded: and the somewhat easy-going regime which the wife of a rich merchant could arrange by bribing the jailors made the prisons – only a few minutes' walk from their homes – into academies for the Catholic religion. There Margaret would keep the company not just of Dorothy Vavasour, but also of other York women with solid Yorkshire names like Janet Geldard, Frances Hall, Isabel Porter, Anne Cook, Margaret Tailor, and with them might hear Mass said by a priest held in the same jail.

In 1580 the Jesuits started their mission to England. Among the priests passing through York in 1581 was Edmund Campion who almost certainly stayed with the Vavasours. In July 1581, he was arrested in Berkshire, then taken to the Tower of London where, under torture, he gave the names of the Catholics who had hidden him in the north. Mrs Vavasour's house was raided, a priest was found, and Mrs Vavasour arrested and imprisoned. Margaret's house therefore became the centre for hiding priests and hearing Mass. It is thought that she had a secret entrance from the attic of her house in the Shambles to a room in the loft of her neighbours who were relations of her husband John.

A number of priests were hidden by Margaret as they passed through York, and a number who stayed elsewhere in the city may have come to her house to say Mass. Among them was Father Mush who became her confessor and later wrote the 'True Report' of her last days. According to Father Mush several of Margaret's confessors were discovered, arrested and executed on the Knavesmire a mile or so outside York on the Leeds road – among them Father William Lacey, Father Richard Kirkman, Father James Thomson, Father William Hart and Father Richard Thirkeld. Their courage and cheerfulness in their suffering were undoubtedly the example which Margaret prayed to have the strength to follow should Almighty God ask her to do so. Martyrdom, in this Elizabethan persecution, was not a calamity which was dreaded but a privilege which many prayed should come their way.

Margaret certainly took elementary precautions to safeguard herself and the priests who stayed in her house. Vestments and chalices were hidden to avoid providing evidence that could be used in court. She did not pretend, however, that she was anything other than a Catholic and in the winter of 1584, without telling her husband, she sent her eldest child to school in France. The boy was only twelve, so it could not be said that he had left to become a priest, but it was quite clear all the same that he had gone to receive a Catholic education which might eventually lead to a seminary. Certainly Margaret's stepfather, Henry May, must have been exasperated because he was a candidate that year for the office of Lord Mayor of York.

As I have said before, his role in the affair is central but shady. He was a close collaborator with the Protestant President of the Council of the North, the Earl of Huntingdon, and perhaps the arrest of Margaret was a quid pro quo for the post of Lord Mayor; but he was also vulnerable to her conviction as a traitor because the year before his wife, Margaret's mother, had died and the inn which May ran on Coney Street passed on her death to Margaret. If Margaret was convicted of treason, this property – including the Lord Mayor's house – would be confiscated by the state. Perhaps May had reached an arrangement with Lord Huntingdon whereby he could buy it back and saw in her prosecution a chance to cheat her of her inheritance. Certainly the desire to frustrate him, and to secure the inheritance for her husband and children, might have been a reason for her refusal to plead.

The first move against Margaret came when the Council of the North called John Clitherow to King's Manor. Margaret seems to have realised that this was to get him out of the way when his house was searched. In due course the sheriffs arrived, searched the house and – after threatening a Flemish boy who was being taught there with the Clitherow children – found a cache of vestments, chalices and Catholic books. The whole household was then arrested and Margaret taken to prison.

The next day she was arraigned before the Assizes held in the Guildhall. Her stepfather was present, wearing his chain of office, together with the entire bench of aldermen in their red robes. Margaret had no counsel: she answered for herself. She was charged before the five judges with harbouring a priest, Father Francis Ingelby. One of the judges, Judge Clench, asked her how she pleaded, to which she answered: 'I know of no offence whereof I should confess myself guilty.'

'Yes, you have harboured and maintained Jesuits and priests, enemies to her Majesty.'

'I never knew nor have harboured any such persons, or maintained those which are not the Queen's friends. God forbid I should.'

There then followed a prolonged exchange during which the judges tried to get Margaret to plead and Margaret persistently refused, telling her judges that she would not be tried by a jury but only by God and their own consciences. Katherine Longley, the biographer of Margaret, believes that she did not know what punishment was due by law for those who refused to plead but this seems to me unlikely. From the skill of her answers it would seem that she knew exactly what she was doing. She knew that unless she apostatised she had little chance of avoiding the gibbet because in November of the previous year a layman, Marmaduke Bowes, had been hanged on the Knavesmire for harbouring a priest.

Her reason for taking this course of action may have been either, as I have suggested, to secure her inheritance for her family or to save her neighbours, whose attic she had used to hide priests or, most likely, to save a jury from the dilemma that her case would have presented to them. As a matter of policy the jurors would have been chosen from among her friends, neighbours and relatives – possibly with a number of Catholic sympathisers among them – so that the Council of the North could spread the odium for its persecution as widely as possible among the citizenry of York. A juror would face the choice of condemning Margaret, and so incurring the sin of being complicit in her martyrdom, or acquitting her, and face the wrath of the Council.

It was therefore not only noble but also right of Margaret to insist upon putting the blame for her death where it belonged – upon the government of the Queen. When the sentence was read the following day it undoubtedly shocked her, as the words shock us to this day. 'If you will not put yourself to the country,' said Judge Clench, 'this must be your judgement. You must return from whence you came, and there, in the lowest part of the prison, be stripped naked, laid down, your back upon the ground and as much weight laid upon you as you are able to bear, and so to continue three days without meat or drink, except a little barley bread and puddle water, and the third day be pressed to death, your hands and feet tied to posts, and a sharp stone under your back.'

What shocked her, I suspect, was not the sentence itself but the thought that she was to be stripped naked to suffer it because the thought of this immodesty seems to have proccupied her in the days which preceded her execution. The sentence itself, as she had intended, placed the blame for her death firmly where it belonged – on those who enforced the law. 'If this judgement be according to your own conscience,' she told the judge, 'I pray God send you better judgement before him. I thank God heartily for this.'

Judge Clench, like Pontius Pilate, was clearly unhappy about the whole business. 'Nay, I do it according to law, and tell you this must be your judgement, unless you put yourself to be tried by the country. Consider of it, you have husband and children to care for: cast not yourself away.' To which Margaret replied: 'I would to God my husband and children might suffer with me for so good a cause.'

Clench tried one last time. 'How say you, Margaret Clitherow? Are you content to put yourself to the trial of the country? Although we have given sentence against you according to the law, yet will we show mercy, if you will do anything yourself.'

'God be thanked, all that he shall send me shall be welcome; I am not worthy of so good a death as this is. I have deserved death for mine offences to God, but not for anything that I am accused of.'

Clench continued to try to find a way out of his dilemma. When a rumour was put about that she was pregnant, he insisted that the execution be postponed. 'Mr Hurlestone,' he said to another judge who wanted the execution to proceed, 'God defend that she should die, if she be with child, although she hath offended, yet hath not the child in her womb. I will not for a thousand pounds, therefore, give my consent until she be further tried.' Savage though they were in Elizabethan times, they were more sensitive than we are to the right to life of the unborn child.

Clench then departed and in the week during which Margaret's execution was delayed she was subject to various kinds of coercion and persuasion to apostatise. Perhaps the most interesting was the visit of Giles Wiggington, a Puritan preacher, who had interceded for her during her trial. He now tried to persuade her to recant. 'Cast not yourself away,' he said. 'Lose not both body and soul. Possibly you think you shall have martyrdom, but you are foully deceived, for it cometh but one way. Not death but the cause maketh a martyr. In the time of Queen Mary were many put to death, and now also in this Queen's time, for two several opinions; both these cannot be martyrs. Therefore, good Mistress Clitherow, take pity on yourself . . .'

Margaret parried his arguments with a certain wit, and avoided all the pitfalls set for her by the Divine. He tried to trick her into the admission that she would be saved by what she suffered, but it was not her martyrdom that would save her, she said, but 'Through Christ Jesus his bitter passion

and death'. She also made excellent answers against his
jibes about superstition, and insisted upon the seven
sacraments against Wiggington who said there were only
two, 'Baptism and the Supper of our Lord'. 'As for all the
other, they be but ceremonies, good, holy things, but yet not
sacraments.'

Wiggington clearly wished to save her, and was sent by the
Council to persuade her to apostatise, but she had been
sufficiently well instructed by her spiritual directors to deal
with the arguments he presented. She only showed herself
sensitive to the charge which is made to this day that she
had deliberately provoked her own execution. 'I die not
desperately,' she said, 'nor will willingly procure my own
death.' Nor would she allow others to think that she was
reckless of her obligations as a wife and a mother. 'As for my
husband,' she said, 'know you that I love him next unto God
in this world, and I have care over my children as a mother
ought to care: I trust I have done my duty to them to bring
them up in the fear of God, and so I trust now that I am dis-
charged of them. And for this cause I am willing to offer
them freely to God that sent them to me, rather than I will
yield one jot from my faith.'

It is this detachment from familial ties which shocks the
modern mind, yet Jesus himself said that we must be prepared to sacrifice them to follow him and it was doubtless
this that Margaret had in mind. The supernatural does
sometimes seem unnatural – and never more so when the
natural good of parental affection comes into conflict with
the supernatural good of giving evidence of one's faith. It
was a sign not just of Margaret's great faith, but also of her
trust in God, that she was willing to rely upon him to see
that her children would not suffer as a result of what she was
to endure.

Her only anxiety, as I have said, was the thought that she
was to die naked. It seems that she was led to understand
that she might be allowed to wear a shift of some kind, and
her last days were spent making one with tapes tied to the
arms. There was undoubtedly some symbolism in the making of this skimpy wedding garment: it was common to see
martyrdom as marriage with Christ.

She spent the night before execution in prayer. 'At about eight o'clock,' wrote Father Mush, 'the sheriffs came to her, and she being ready expecting them . . . carrying on her arm the new habit of linen with inkle strings . . . went cheerfully to her marriage, as she called it, dealing her alms in the street which was so full of people that she could scarce pass them. She went barefoot and barelegged, her gown loose about her . . .

'The place of execution was the Tollbooth, six or seven yards distant from the prison . . . The martyr, coming to the place, kneeled her down and prayed to herself. The tormentors bade her pray with them, and they would pray with her. She refused. They then asked her to pray for the Queen. She said she would, but prayed first for the Catholic Church, then for the Pope, then the Cardinals and other fathers that have charge of our souls, then for all Christian princes and especially for Elizabeth, Queen of England, that God turn her to the Catholic Faith, and that after this mortal life she may receive the blessed joys of heaven. For I wish as much good,' she said, 'to her Majesty's soul as to mine own.'

One of the sheriffs now burst into tears and could not proceed but the other, Fawcett, said: 'Mrs Clitherow, you must remember and confess that you die for treason.'

'No, no, Master Sheriff,' Margaret replied. 'I die for the love of my Lord Jesus.'

Then Fawcett told her to take off her clothes, 'for you must die naked as judgement was given and pronounced against you.'

Margaret, and the women around her, begged him to let her wear the smock she had made but the Sheriff refused. 'The women then took off her clothes and put upon her the habit of linen. Then, very quickly, she laid down about the ground, her face covered with a handkerchief, and secret parts with the habit, all the rest of her body being naked. The door was a laid upon her. Her hands,' Father Mush reported, 'she joined towards her face but the Sheriff said: "Nay, you must have your hands bound." The martyr put forth her hands over the door still joined in the attitude of prayer. The two sergeants parted them, and with the inkle strings which she had prepared for that purpose bound them to two posts so that her body and her arms made a perfect cross. They willed her again to ask for the Queen's forgiveness and to pray for her. The martyr said that she *had* prayed for her. They also willed her to ask her husband's forgiveness to which she replied: "If ever I have offended him, but for my conscience, I ask him forgiveness." After this they laid weight upon her which when she first felt she said, "Jesu, Jesu, Jesu have mercy on me!" which were the last words she was heard to speak. She was in dying one quarter of an hour. A sharp stone, as much as a man's fist, was put under her back; upon her was laid to the quantity of seven or eight hundredweight at the least, which breaking her ribs caused them to burst forth of the skin. This was nine in the morning, and she continued in the press until three in the afternoon.'

It is difficult for us, I think, when reading about St Margaret's dreadful yet exemplary end to relate it in any way to the present day. She has been compared for the cruelty of her execution and the cheerfulness with which she suffered it with the saints thrown to the lions under the Roman Empire, and there is a danger, I think, of relegating St Margaret to myth.

There is also a danger that the very horror of her martyrdom distracts us from the cause – that we ascribe her fate to the savagery of the times when Catholics, after all, killed Protestants in an equally cruel fashion. Indeed Queen Elizabeth's compromise religion, when compared to the rigour of the Spanish Inquisition, seems to our modern mind to have been eminently sensible – and the Church of England survives to this day as the Christianity of common sense. Reading the transcript of Margaret's trial, one is even tempted to pity Judge Clench and see in Margaret's fanaticism the last gasp of mediaevalism which has little pertinence to the present day.

I think this is wrong. Certainly her persecutors were acting from mixed motives, and while some were fanatic Puritans who loathed popish superstition and mocked our martyrs on the gallows, others were impelled not by religious fanaticism but by political necessity. They believed quite sincerely, and with some justice, that Papists were by definition the agents of foreign powers hatching plots to oust Queen Elizabeth and bring a Catholic to the throne.

What is salutary about St Margaret was that as a woman she could not have played any political role, and that this must have been clear to everyone in York. She could not dabble in politics and so died conspicuously for her faith alone.

But what was that faith? In our own Ecumenical age it may seem a little absurd that she insisted unto death that the Church of Rome was the Church founded by Christ while the Church of England was not. All those around her, after all, were baptised Christians – some of them, like Wiggington, virtuous and sincere. Why was it so important to Elizabethan Catholics to keep the link with Rome alive?

The first answer, it seems to me, and one of great relevance to us in England today, was the question of the *unity* of the Church. It is a paradox that now, when the Catholic Church in England is more secure and more influential than at any period since the Reformation, it should at times seem to see itself as one Christian sect among the many which go to make up the Church of Christ; and that it somehow has a holy obligation to compromise its beliefs and practices to ease a merger with other denominations.

What was clear to the Catholics during the Reformation – even when they were reduced to a handful of fugitives – was that fidelity to the papacy is integral to the unity of the Church, and that it was therefore for this unity that they died. The Earl of Northumberland, you will remember, made this point when he said that he died in 'that Church which, throughout the whole Christian world, is knit and bound together . . . But as for this new English Church, I do not acknowledge it.'

Archbishop Heath had said the same kind of thing in 1559. 'By the relinquishing and forsaking of the See of Rome, we must forsake and flee the unity of the Christian Church, and, by leaping out of St Peter's ship, hazard ourselves to be overwhelmed and drowned in the waters of schism, sects and divisions.' St Margaret too, according to

Father Mush, was active among her friends and neighbours, 'if they were schismatics, to reduce them again to the Catholic unity; if they were heretics . . . to have them init-iated in the true faith.' Thus, far from seeing her death as an embarrassment in this ecumenical age, we should regard her as a martyr in the cause of the true unity of the Church.

The second cause for which she died was the Mass and the two elements which the Protestants denied: (1) that it was Christ's sacrifice for the sins of the quick and the dead, and (2) that the consecrated bread was the flesh of Christ. The need for priests was the need for the sacraments – not just the Eucharist, but the other six. Margaret, when she could, confessed once a week, went to Mass every day and 'her most delight was to kneel where she might continually behold the Blessed Sacrament.'

What contemplating her life should surely teach us is that we should be wary of modern Giles Wiggingtons who with guile rather than terror would persuade us that the papacy is an obstacle to the unity of the Church and that the Mass and the Eucharist are less important than baptism; and that while rejoicing in the present climate of religious tolerance which means that no one, Catholic or Protestant, need die for their faith, we should nonetheless cherish those Catholic beliefs for which St Margaret gave her life.

29

Ignatius of Loyola

A review of *Ignatius of Loyola. The Psychology of a Saint* by W.W. Meissner SJ MD (Yale University Press)

It is difficult to think of a man or woman whose personality has left as distinctive a mark on human history as Ignatius of Loyola. The Society of Jesus which he formed in his own image and likeness largely created the culture of the Counter-Reformation. In such far-apart cities as Goa, Lvov, Madrid, Munich or Asuncion, the baroque churches, seminaries, schools and universities remain as evidence of the enormous influence wielded by the Jesuits. Even in our own time, the catastrophic wars of liberation in Central America were often inspired by Jesuits, and the mistrust of Catholicism still to be found in countries like England, Denmark or Russia can be traced back to a reaction against the fanaticism of Ignatius.

W.W. Meissner is a Jesuit but he is also a doctor and a psychoanalyst, now Professor of Psychoanalysis at Boston College. In his earlier work, *Psychoanalysis and Religious Experience,* he attempted to synthesise his two fields of knowledge, and in this new 'psychobiography' he applies his theories to the founder of his order. It is a courageous thing to do since it risks offending those in both camps. Catholics will not like the idea that Ignatius's visions came from his subconscious: Freudians will not accept that there is a *deus ex machina.* Yet once one has got over an initial resistance to some of his Freudian assumptions and psychoanalytic jargon, Meissner's hypothesis becomes increasingly plausible, and increasingly significant for our understanding of the spiritual life.

Ignatius was born in 1491, the youngest child of a Basque nobleman, Beltran of Loyola. His mother died soon after, and the baby Inigo (as he was then called) was suckled by a wet nurse, the young wife of the local blacksmith. His father was frequently absent on military campaigns, but the young Inigo was formed in the mould of his family's tradition, 'instilled with the pride of the Loyolas which called them to be leaders, heroes, extraordinary men'. 'The life of the Loyolas,' Meissner tells us, 'was a rich amalgam of deep religious tradition, sincere piety, burning passion and lust, fierce pride, and an attitude of aristocracy and nobility.'

When the French besieged Pamplona, Inigo, a young commander, refused to surrender. 'His refusal to capitulate,' Meissner comments, 'even in the face of overwhelming odds, seems foolhardy, if not suicidal . . .' In the ensuing battle, a cannon ball fractured his thigh. Inigo's military career came to an end and he returned to Loyola to recuperate under the care of his beautiful sister-in-law, Magdalena.

With nothing to read but pious works, Inigo's dreams of glory changed from the worldly to the spiritual, and when he recovered he set off on a pilgrimage to the Holy Land. At the monastery of Montserrat, he gave his clothes to a beggar and left his sword at the shrine of the Madonna. Wearing the sackcloth costume of a pilgrim, he moved down to a cave at Manresa where, after months of 'fasts, sleepless nights, vigils, penitential practices like flagellations, and inflicting pain . . . on the body as the seat and source of physical desire and pleasure', he developed his celebrated Spiritual Exercises and the sense of mission which eventually led to the founding of the Society of Jesus.

Meissner's account of Inigo's life is well told – an achievement in itself, since most of the sources are cloyingly hagiographic. But simply to follow the story, skipping Meissner's analysis, would be to avoid the challenge of this work. Clearly, to the Freudian, much can be made of the death of Ignatius's mother, followed by his abrupt removal to the castle from the wet nurse in the blacksmith's cottage. Was not his insensate courage at Pamplona, Meissner asks, possibly 'an identification with the state of death itself, reflecting an unconscious wish to achieve reunion with the lost parent'? And was not his vision of Our Lady with the child Jesus 'the reflection of Inigo's idealised image of his own mother as well as that of Magdalena, toward whom his unconscious libidinal impulses had been stirred'?

And what are we to make of his absent father? 'The father, after all, represents to his children the model or image of masculinity, by way of identification for sons, by way of adaptation to masculinity for daughters. If the father is inadequate or weak or distant, the identification of his sons must suffer.' Thus, Inigo, 'the brash young courtier is permeated with signs of phallic narcissism, in response either to 'a sense of shame derived from an underlying identification with a weak father figure' (in Inigo's case, weak because absent) or perhaps to 'the unconscious shame derived from the fear of castration by an aggressive and hyper masculine father' which he hides behind an 'arrogant, assertive, aggressively competitive, often hypermasculine and self-glorifying facade'?

Ignatius's vanity appears to be proved by his undergoing an extremely painful operation simply to remove a lump on his leg: and it was only the terrible, self-inflicted mortifications in the cave at Manresa that changed his worldly 'ego ideal' into a total commitment to the will of God. The courage and fanaticism of the Basque soldier was turned upon the enemy within, and the flesh so prone to sin. Even later in his life, 'witnesses recalled his fasting, the hairshirt he wore at all times, the metal chain with sharp points with which he girded himself, the lacerations and festering wounds on his shoulders from the self-inflicted scourgings'.

This militancy and fanaticism extended to the intellectual discipline required of those who joined his order. 'To be right in everything, we ought always to hold that the white which I see is black if the Hierarchical Church so decides it'. Unlike some other contemporary biographers from the Society of Jesus, Meissner does not play down the commitment of Ignatius and the first Jesuits to blind obedience to the Pope. 'To a certain degree, freedom was threatening in the mind of Ignatius and he sought to regulate the risks of his own inner freedom by obsessive devices, constant self-examination and accusation, self-denial and repression of inordinate desires.'

To the modern reader, it becomes increasingly clear that Ignatius was a psychotic. Meissner does not shy away from such a conclusion. 'In my opinion, Inigo's severe penances were a form of masochistic perversion in that they reflected the degree of intrapsychic conflict he endured with regard to his instinctual life.' In the same way, sadistic impulses lay behind the disciplines which he imposed upon his followers: 'a current of sublimated sexuality – heterosexual in the case of his female adherents, homosexual for his male followers' of a sadomasochistic sort was the dynamic behind the success of the Society of Jesus. Meissner goes further, suggesting that 'a major contributing factor in the phenomenology of his illness was a form of limbic epilepsy or complex partial seizures.'

At first sight, this picture of Ignatius as a sexually perverted epileptic seems to confirm the most extreme anti-Jesuit propaganda. But having taken us to the edge of the abyss in an apparently reductionist portrait of Ignatius, Meissner steps back to consider the implications of what he has done. 'If Ignatius was in some sense psychotic, what does this imply in the wider arena of human history and human religious experience?'

First of all, the general reader must realise that words like sadism, masochism, narcissism, which we have been horrified to see Meissner apply to a saint, have technical, non-pejorative meanings for the psychoanalyst which remove their sting. 'In its fundamental meaning,' he writes, 'narcissism is an expression of libidinal drives'; and the libido, as Freud himself said, 'is an expression taken from the theory of the emotions of those instincts which have to do with all that may be comprised under the word "love".'

So too, Ignatius's masochism 'is not simply the masochism of the neurotic or the moral masochist; it is masochism suffused with love and placed in the service of a highly narcissistically invested ego ideal, an ideal that is itself imbued with the highest spiritual aims.' Thus the diversion of instinctive drives from their primary goal into heroic virtue does not detract from the value of that virtue. Meissner has no doubt, for example, that Ignatius's zeal for the reform of prostitutes in Rome came from his suppressed sexuality. 'This observation is in no sense intended to disparage these admirable and saintly endeavours, but even the noblest human purposes are never free of more basically human and instinctual drive-derivatives.'

One might say, more simply, that 'the Lord works in mysterious ways his wonders to perform'. From a worldly point of view, Ignatius's piety may have been a sublimation, even a perversion, of his sexual drive; but, from a divine perspective, it is perhaps perverse to expend one's sexual energies solely on sex.

The Witch's Brew

and other poems

SUNNYSIDE
PRIMARY SCHOOL

Wes Magee

Illustrations by Marc Vyvyan-Jones

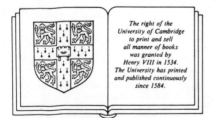

The right of the
University of Cambridge
to print and sell
all manner of books
was granted by
Henry VIII in 1534.
The University has printed
and published continuously
since 1584.

CAMBRIDGE UNIVERSITY PRESS
Cambridge
New York   New Rochelle
Melbourne   Sydney

for Janet

Published by the Press Syndicate of the University of Cambridge
The Pitt Building, Trumpington Street, Cambridge CB2 1RP
32 East 57th Street, New York, NY 10022, USA
10 Stamford Road, Oakleigh, Melbourne 3166, Australia

First published 1989

Printed in Great Britain at the University Press, Cambridge

British Library cataloguing in publication data

Magee, Wes
 The Witch's Brew and other poems.
 I. Title
 821'.914

Library of Congress cataloging-in-publication data

Magee, Wes, 1939–
    The Witch's Brew, and other poems/Wes Magee.
 1. Children's poetry, English. [1. English poetry.]   I. Title.
 PR6063. A328W58 1988
 821'.914–dc19   88–14983

ISBN 0 521 36119 2 hard covers
ISBN 0 521 36941 X paperback

Contents

The classroom circle of friends

and I like Anne
Van likes me
Dee likes Van
Titch likes Dee
Del likes Titch
Mitch likes Del
Ray likes Mitch
Lai likes Ray
George likes Lai
Thai likes George
Faye likes Thai
Seth likes Faye
Chris likes Seth
Beth likes Chris
Ken likes Beth
Phil likes Ken

start here

I like Anne
Anne likes Wayne
Wayne likes Raj
Raj likes Shane
Shane likes Paul
Paul likes Pam
Pam likes Shaz
Shaz likes Sam
Sam likes Parv
Parv likes Jo
Jo likes Mick
Mick likes Mo
Mo likes Val
Val likes Jill
Jill likes Trish
Trish likes Phil

The best thing

Today's
my day.
There are cards,
presents,
and the sun's shining.
I'm 7
and tonight
we'll go skating
for my birthday
    treat.

The best thing,
though,
is in class.
Everyone sings
'Happy Birthday'
as I walk out
and dip into
teacher's jar
for my birthday
    sweet.

Down by the school gate

There goes the bell
it's half past three
and down by the school gate
you will see . . .

. . . ten mums talk talk talking
nine babies squawk squawking
eight toddlers all squabbling
seven grans on bikes wobbling

six dogs bark bark barking
five cars stopping, parking
four child-minders running
three bus-drivers sunning

two teenagers dating
one lollipop man waiting . . .

The school is out,
it's half past three
and the first to the school gate
. . . is me!

ME!

our school band

(a clapping song)

our school band
our school band
best band heard
in all the land
start at teacher's
sharp command
   in
     our
     school
     band

our school band
our school band
tambourines
piano (grand)
homemade shakers
filled with sand
   in
     our
     school
     band

our school band
our school band
listen to the
tunes expand
music we all
understand
   in
     our
     school
     band

our school band
our school band
drummers getting
out of hand
lesson ends
and we all stand
     that's
     our
     school

     band!

What is the Sun?

the Sun is an orange dinghy
   sailing across a calm sea

it is a gold coin
   dropped down a drain in Heaven

the Sun is a yellow beach ball
   kicked high into the summer sky

it is a red thumb-print
   on a sheet of pale blue paper

the Sun is a milk bottle's gold top
   floating in a puddle

Summer sun

Yes,
the sun shines
  bright
in the summer,
and the breeze
  is soft
    as a sigh.

Yes,
the days are
  long
in the summer,
and the sun
  is King
    of the sky.

The S-S-S-Seashore

Sharma and Shona and Sancho
heard the swish of the surf,
sniffed the sweet scent of seaweed,
and stared at shrimps
shifting in still pools.

Sancho and Sharma and Shona
spied children swimming and sunbathing.
They saw a starfish
stuck on a sandcastle
as they searched for shells on the shore.

Shona and Sancho and Sharma
got stuck in squelchy,
sloshy, sinking sands
as seagulls squawked and screeched
in the sun-struck sky.

What do you collect?

What do *you* collect?
Coins, dolls from other lands?
Or jokes
    that no one understands?

What do *you* collect?
Stamps, gem-stones, model cars?
Or wrappers
    ripped from chocolate bars?

What do *you* collect?
Skulls, posters, badges, bells?
Or walking sticks,
    or seaside shells?

What do *you* collect?
Leaves, photographs of cats?
Or horror masks,
    or party hats?

What do *you* collect?
Books, fossils, records, rocks?
Or comics
    in a cardboard box?

Skippers

Here comes Abigail
her turn now
  skip
  skip
  double jump
and moo like a cow.

Here comes Eleanor
she's too slow
  skip
  skip
  touch your toes
and flap like a crow.

Here comes Jarindeth
leap in quick
  skip
  skip
  round-a-bout
Ugh! She's being sick!

Here comes Katherine
high kick and twist
  skip
  skip
  close your eyes
tell us who you kissed!

Here comes Natalie
she's doesn't care
  skip
  skip
lift your skirt
oooh! leg's all bare!

Here comes Nasima
all on her own
  skip
  skip
rock 'n' roll
and give the dog a bone.

Here comes Marianne
looks so sweet
  skip
  skip
  hold your nose
she's got smelly feet!

Here comes Teacher-Sir
big fat man
  skip
  skip
  what's his name?
DESPERATE DAN!!

Here comes Winifred
let's give a shout
  skip
  skip
  clap your hands
and all fall out!

Here comes the skipping line
quick, jump in
  skip
  skip
  scream it now
WE ALL WIN!!

A skipping alphabet

Hey!   bee
sea   dee
    eee
    eff
    gee
aitch   eye
jay   kay
    ell
    emm
    enn
    oh!
    pee
queue   are
ess   tea
    you
    vee

double–you
ex
why?
ZED
and

OUT

Climb the mountain

Climb
the
climb
the
mountain
high,
touch
the
clouds
and
see
the
sky.
Feel
the
wind
against
you
blow,
see
the fields
far
far
below.

The digging song

In your hands you hold the spade,
Feel its well-worn wood,
Now you drive it in the earth,
Drive it deep and good.

> Dig dig digging dirt,
>> Dirt inside your vest.
> Dig dig digging dirt.
>> Digging dirt is best.

Here are worms that twist and loop
Tight as knots in string,
Here are spiders, ants and bugs
Running in a ring.

> Dig dig digging dirt,
>> Dirt inside your vest.
> Dig dig digging dirt,
>> Digging dirt is best.

Soon your hands are red and raw,
Blisters on the way,
But your spade just wants to dig
All day all day all day.

> Dig dig digging dirt,
>> Dirt inside your vest.
> Dig dig digging dirt,
>> Digging dirt is best.

What is a million?

The blades of grass growing
   on your back lawn.
The people you've met
   since the day you were born.

The age of a fossil
   you found by the sea.
The years it would take you
   to reach Octran Three.

The water drops needed
   to fill the fish pool.
The words you have read
   since you started school.

Four pirates

1. Pebble-Eye Jones

Captain Jones of the 'Golden Locket'
lost an eye while off Cape Crockett,
stuffed a pebble in the socket.

Liked his prisoners to walk the plank
and giggled as they fell . . . and sank.
Grew fat and rich – a walking bank.

2. Peg-Leg

Each day old Peg sat on the quay
and stretched out straight his wooden knee,
told tales of monsters of the sea.

The cabin boys turned pale and stark
when told how, swimming after dark,
Peg lost his leg to a hungry shark.

3. Pinkbeard

This pirate had no beard at all,
pink chin smooth as a marble hall
and voice clear as a robin's call.

This pirate strange with big brown eyes
and flowing hair and sudden sighs.
The truth? A woman . . . in disguise.

4. Captain Death

He bossed a ship of forty guns.
He called his crew 'bloodthirsty sons';
they fought and swore like savage Huns.

Grim Captain Death strode decks of teak.
He sank a treasure ship each week,
and when he calls . . . *you'll* hear him speak.

Moonrakers

Moonrakers are mad.
    They think the Moon is made of cheese
    so gobble it while on their knees.
    (That's why the Moon will not grow trees.)

Moonrakers are crazy.
    They like to swim in all that dust
    Then sneeze and sneeze until they bust.
    (That's why the Moon is thick with rust.)

Moonrakers are daft.
    They hop between the Moon's two poles
    Then burrow deep like loony moles.
    (That's why the Moon is full of holes.)

Moonrakers are crackers.
    They never need to drink or cry;
    They keep their central heating high.
    (That's why the Moon is, oh, so dry.)

        Moonrakers are nuts;
            they have heads,
            but no guts.
        Moonrakers are goons
            who use shovels
            for spoons.
        Moonrakers are clots
            and are covered
            in spots.

The mystery space beasts

They live on a planet
not far from the Sun.
Some fly through the air
while others just run.

Some have big heads
which are hairless as tin
while others have hair
which sprouts from their skin.

They dig food from dirt,
and gobble dead meat;
the young squeal like pigs
if you tickle their feet.

They slurp, burp, and grunt;
their manners are bad.
Their eyes become waterfalls
when they feel sad.

They come in most colours,
some yellow, some white.
Some dye their hair pink
and do look a sight.

These creatures vary
from tiny to tall,
and in salty water
they've been known to crawl.

Well, who are these space beasts?
Can't you guess who?
The answer is easy:
it's you, you, and YOU!

The Blob

And . . . what is it like?

Oh, it's scary and fatbumped
and spike-eared and groany.
It's hairy and face-splumped
and bolshy and bony.

And . . . where does it live?

Oh, in comets and spaceships
and pulsars and blackholes.
In craters and sheepdips
and caverns and northpoles.

And . . . what does it eat?

Oh, roast rocks and fishlegs
and X-rays and mooncrust.
Then steelmeat and sun-eggs
and lava and spacedust.

And . . . who are its enemies?

Oh, Zonkers and Moonquakes
and Sunquarks and Bigbags.
Dumb Duncers and Milkshakes
and Smogsters and Zigzags.

And . . . and . . . what does it wear?

Not a thing.
It's *bare!*

21

Are you ready?

It's
September
the
sixth,
the
day
before
school,
we
go
back
tomorrow
and
I
feel
like
a
fool.
I
can't
find
my
bag,
my
ruler,
my
pen.
I
can
hardly
recall

if
I'm
Andy
or
Ken!
I'm
all
of
a
dither,
tomorrow's
a
haze,
the
school
starts
in
hours
and
I'm
in
a
daze.

The school year

September starts a fresh school year,
new pupils feel a twinge of fear.
Our Harvest Festival's displayed;
our thanks to farmers duly made.

October's damp; the leaves fall down.
We make a book called 'Our Home Town'.
Big pictures pinned on wall and door;
there's thick mud on the cloakroom floor.

November brings us Bonfire Night
with blazing Guy and fireworks bright.
The Christmas plays – rehearsals start.
Who'll sing songs? Who'll speak a part?

December's cold; there's frost and snow.
To 'Peter Pan' in town we go.
We decorate the school, have treats;
at parties there are prizes, sweets.

January's iced; pond frozen hard.
The snowmen freeze in our school yard,
but sliding and snowballing's banned.
This classroom's coldest in the land!

February's slushed with hail and sleet.
Make Valentines . . . for someone sweet.
Pancakes tossed and caught and eaten.
Snowdrops tell you winter's beaten.

March is wild; gales from the hills.
Our classroom bulbs . . . are daffodils!
A Pet Show's held . . . no dogs or cats.
For Easter we paint eggs, make hats.

April's fresh; spring's in the air,
slow buds unfurling everywhere.
Our topic title – 'Beast and Bird'.
The year's first cuckoo can be heard.

May comes cool, but trees still drip.
We leave for our field-study trip
and visit castles, climb steep hills
and get soaked through and all catch chills.

June's so warm; the summer's here.
Our Sports Day banners wave; we cheer.
That loud crack is the starter's gun.
Our parents watch us jump and run.

July! Phew, hot! The days are long.
We give a concert . . . dance and song.
For Open Night our work's on show.
At Leavers' Disco faces glow.

August . . . time for holidays,
whole weeks to simply lounge and laze.
On beach, in caravan, at home
you're free to come and go, to roam.

The school year's gone, our teachers smile.
Forget the book work . . . for a while.
But soon September's here, and then
we all troop back to school again.

The visitors keep walking in

The visitors,
here they come,
smiling, frowning,
looking glum.
Bald or tall
or fat or thin
the visitors
keep
walking
in.

An Education Man in grey
drove all the way from County Hall.
He talked non-stop for half a day
and sent our teachers up the wall.

Some students looking scared to death
took drama lessons with small groups.
They made us dance, and hold our breath,
and jump through glass and fiery hoops.

The visitors,
here they come,
smiling, frowning,
looking glum.
Bald or tall
or fat or thin
the visitors
keep
walking
in.

A very old Magician bloke
last Christmas gave a show for us.
He broke his wand, forgot a joke,
and you should just have *heard* him cuss.

A Schools' Inspector – awfully posh –
got all the teachers in a flap.
When shown our books he muttered, 'Gosh!'
and called the Head, 'my dear, old chap.'

The visitors,
here they come,
smiling, frowning,
looking glum.
Bald or tall
or fat or thin
the visitors
keep
walking
in.

A famous author spent an hour
teaching us to write a line.
We messed around. He said, 'You shower!'
and called Jeff Stubbs a 'little swine!'

Supply teacher, Miss Oblong-Burt,
came in today and taught us craft.
She spilled pink paint and ruined her skirt
and horribly we laughed and laughed.

The visitors,
here they come,
smiling, frowning,
looking glum.
Bald or tall
or fat or thin
the visitors
keep
walking
in.

The Head from next door's Infants' School
toured all our classrooms, never smiled.
She scowled, she winced, she looked right cruel.
To Mark she croaked, 'revolt-ing child!'

An angry parent, Annette's dad,
stormed into school and thumped the door.
He told the Head, 'I think you're mad!'
and tried to knock him to the floor.

The visitors,
here they come,
smiling, frowning,
looking glum.
Bald or tall
or fat or thin
the visitors
keep
walking
in.

Visitors!
Welcome . . . everyone!
We all
feel better

when

you've

gone.

St. Horrid's
School

An A–Z of items found on the school roof by the caretaker

Apple core (brown)
'Better English' book
    (spotted with ink)
Crisps (unopened bag)
Dead bird (a starling
    . . . I think)

Earwig (inside a matchbox)
Felt pens in a case
    (thirty!)
Golf ball
Handkerchief
    (dirty!)

Ink cartridge (full)
Jaguar
    (model car)
Key (rusty)
Lunch box
    (labelled Paul Starr)

Marble (a bluey)
Nose
    (false one: red)
Orange (all shrivelled)
Pencil (chewed at one end:
    no lead)

Queen's crown (from 2J's play)
Ruler
    (broken: old design)
Sock (shocking pink)
Tennis ball
    (mine!)

Underpants (Y-fronts)
Valentine Card
    (to 'Farida Good')
Wellington boot
Xylophone block
    (wood)

Yellow scarf (Norwich City)
Zombie (a rubber horror
    . . . not pretty!)

All
  brought
   down
    from
     the
      school
       roof
        by
         the
          caretaker . . .

Twenty six items
from A to Z.
'Now, write a story,
3 pages at least,
mentioning
every item,'
my
teacher
said.

Countdown to the school bell

TEN . . .   seconds to go.
NINE . . .   we're off home in a mo.
EIGHT . . .   pencils packed in their case.
SEVEN . . .   bookmark secure in its place.
SIX . . .   'Chairs up! No noise!'
FIVE . . .   smiling girls, laughing boys.
FOUR . . .   'Great care as you cross the road.'
THREE . . .   bag on shoulder. What a load!
TWO . . .   last book stowed away.
ONE . . .   it's the end of the day.

ZERO!

Here we go!
Here we go!
HERE WE GO!!

Puddle and Peel

Puddle and Peel
were positively polite
and pleasant
to parents,
policemen
and penguins.

Puddle and Peel
kept parrots, pigs,
ptarmigans,
pelicans
and polecats
as pets.

Puddle and Peel
picked peaches,
podded peas,
and peeled
potatoes
for pennies.

Puddle and Peel
packed their
pink pants
in panniers
and pedalled away
to Paris.

Witch Nastee Spella's arrival at the Hallowe'en party in Hangman's Wood

The clock struck
  One.
Will Witch Nastee Spella soon arrive?

The clock struck
  Two.
Will we all leave this wood . . . alive?

The clock struck
  Three.
Here she comes! Her broomstick's smoking!

The clock struck
  Four.
She's as fat as butter, no joking.

The clock struck
  Five.
Her skin . . . a ghastly shade of green.

The clock struck
  Six.
Those piggy eyes so sly and mean.

The clock struck
  Seven.
Her cloak in tatters, hair like weed.

The clock struck
  Eight.
Her warty chin huge as a swede.

The clock struck
    Nine.
In her pockets squirm nests of rats.

The clock struck
    Ten.
Gliding beside her . . . six red-eyed bats.

The clock struck
    Eleven.
'She's landing now!' yelled Wizard Good.

The clock struck
    Midnight.
As Nastee crashed into Hangman's Wood!

The witch's brew

Hubble bubble at the double
Cooking pot stir up some trouble.

Into my pot
there now must go
leg of lamb
and green frog's toe,

old men's socks
and dirty jeans,
a rotten egg
and cold baked beans.

Hubble bubble at the double
Cooking pot stir up some trouble.

One dead fly
and a wild wasp's sting,
the eye of a sheep
and the heart of a King;

a stolen jewel
and mouldy salt,
and for good flavour
a jar of malt.

Hubble bubble at the double
Cooking pot stir up some trouble.

Wing of bird
and head of mouse,
screams and howls
from that haunted house.

And don't forget
the jug of blood
or the sardine tin
or the clod of mud.

Hubble bubble at the double
Cooking pot stir up
SOME
TROUBLE!

Our cats

Our cats stay out all night
. . . moonlighting.
You should hear them spitting and
fighting.

At breakfast-time they come in
. . . purring,
and curl on chairs, no hint of
stirring.

Then when it's dark they're off
. . . exploring
while thunder growls and gales are
roaring.

When we're tucked up in bed
. . . fast-sleeping
they're out there in the darkness,
creeping.

The tortoise

Boxed for winter,
Placed in the shed,
Our tortoise sleeps;
You'd think him dead.

There he will stay
Locked in his shell.
He does not stir
At shout or yell.

When spring arrives
We lift him out
And watch him wave
His legs about.

Our old tortoise
Will never know
December's frost
Or winter's snow.

A week of winter weather

On Monday icy rains poured down
and flooded drains all over town.

Tuesday's gales bashed elm and ash:
dead branches came down with a crash.

On Wednesday bursts of hail and sleet.
No one walked along our street.

Thursday stood out clear and calm
but the sun was paler than my arm.

Friday's frost that bit your ears
was cold enough to freeze your tears.

Saturday's sky was ghostly grey:
we smashed ice on the lake today.

Christmas Eve was Sunday . . . and
snow fell and fell across the land.

Calling, calling

The sky is grey
And flakes are falling.
  I hear the snowmen
    Calling, calling.

Outside it's wild.
Dad's car is st-st-stalling.
  Next door my friends are
    Calling, calling.

Sliding, sledging
And, oh, snowballing!
  The winter winds are
    Calling, calling.

Questions on Christmas Eve

But *how* can his reindeer fly without wings?
Jets on their hooves? That's plain cheating!
And *how* can he climb down the chimney pot
    When we've got central heating?

You say it's all magic and I shouldn't ask
About Santa on Christmas Eve.
But I'm confused by the stories I've heard;
    I don't know what to believe.

I said that I'd sit up in bed all night long
To see if he really would call.
But I fell fast asleep, woke up after dawn
    As something banged in the hall.

I saw my sock crammed with apples and sweets;
There were parcels piled high near the door.
Jingle bells tinkled far off in the dark;
    One snowflake shone on the floor.

It's Christmas time!

Carols drift across the night

holly gleams by candlelight

Roaring fire; a spooky tale

Ice and snow and wind and hail

Santa seen in High Street store

television . . . more and *more*

mince pies, turkey, glass of wine

Acting your own pantomime

Socks hung up. It's Christmas time!

Christmas Day walk

Down to the end
of our housing estate,
across fields
to Hanging Man's Wood
where skeleton trees
stand black and bare
and the chilled air
freezes your blood.

In Wellington boots
we crunch through the snow,
watch a magpie
flutter and squawk.
A fluffed-up thrush
trembles on a thin twig
and the sky is grey
as wet chalk.

At the edge of the wood
we stand stone-still
as moth snowflakes
start to whirl down.
There are no cars on the roads,
not a sound
as Christmas Day
blankets the town.

Counting sheep

They said,
'If you can't get to sleep
try counting sheep.'
I tried.
It didn't work.

They said,
'Still awake? Count rabbits, dogs,
or jumping frogs.'
I tried.
It didn't work.

They said,
'It's very late. Count rats
or vampire bats!'
I tried.
It didn't work.

They said,
'Stop counting stupid sheep!
Eyes closed! Don't peep!'
I tried,

and fell asleep.

Noises in the middle of the night

The wind
whistled and howled.
A dustbin lid clattered.
Downstairs,
parents nattered.

A dog barked
as it prowled.
Flash! BOOM!
Thunder growled.
Rain at the pane pattered.

At midnight
those sounds
woke me in fright.

But now
all seems
quiet and still

so

(yawn, yawn)

goodnight.